Girl, Get Your Credit Straight!

Also by Glinda Bridgforth

Girl, Make Your Money Grow!

Girl, Get Your Money Straight!

The Basic Money Management Workbook

Girl, Get Your Credit Straight!

A Sister's Guide to Ditching
Your Debt, Mending Your Credit,
and Building a Strong
Financial Future

Glinda Bridgforth

BROADWAY BOOKS
New York

PUBLISHED BY BROADWAY BOOKS

Copyright © 2007 by Glinda Bridgforth

All Rights Reserved

A hardcover edition of this book was originally published in 2007 by Broadway Books.

Published in the United States by Broadway Books, an imprint of The Doubleday Broadway Publishing Group, a division of Random House, Inc., New York.
www.broadwaybooks.com

BROADWAY BOOKS and its logo, a letter B bisected on the diagonal, are trademarks of Random House, Inc.

Content from the FICO Web site is copyright © Fair Isaac Corporation. Used with permission. Fair Isaac, myFICO, the Fair Isaac logos, and the Fair Isaac product and service names are trademarks or registered trademarks of Fair Isaac Corporation.
Recommended Guidelines for a Balanced Budget pie chart copyright © 2005 Consumer Credit Counseling Service of San Francisco. Used with permission.

Library of Congress Cataloging-in-Publication Data

Bridgforth, Glinda, 1952–
   Girl, get your credit straight! : a sister's guide to ditching your debt, mending your credit, and building a strong financial future / Glinda Bridgforth.
      p. cm.
   1. African American women—Finance, Personal. 2. Women—United States—Finance, Personal. 3. Credit—United States. 4. Debt—United States. 5. Money—United States. I. Title.
HG179.B72753 2007
332.024'02082—d   3 9082 09373 4898

                                                                    2006019240

ISBN 978-0-7679-2674-4

PRINTED IN THE UNITED STATES OF AMERICA

10 9 8 7 6 5 4 3 2 1

First Paperback Edition

To my husband and childhood sweetheart, Edward.
What a precious gift you are this second time around.
Thank you for your endless love and the powerful
insight that brought us back together again.

Contents

Acknowledgments

My philosophy in life is to put one foot in front of the other and move in the right direction. Who, other than God, would have guessed that my personal and professional journey could lead me down such an awesome path! I am a woman who is blessed and highly favored. So I wholeheartedly say, "Thank you, God. I will continue to trust in you."

There are many people I would like to thank who have knowingly and unknowingly contributed to the completion of this book in obvious and not so obvious ways:

My wonderful parents: Walter and Opal Bridgforth. Thanks for giving me your blessing to move to California in 1977. That was the best move I ever made because it allowed me to grow up and become an independent woman. Returning to Detroit in 2000 to spend more quality time with you was my second best move ever. Thanks for so many new, precious memories and for helping me come full circle.

My incredible siblings and family: Ann and Joe for putting me on the prayer list at church; Barbara and Robert for showing me what perseverance is all about; Doris and Darrell for Saulsberry Resort and Spa; Yvonne and Van for the perfect mantra; Walter for being the best brother a girl could ask for; Anita for encouraging me to celebrate my accomplishments; and Paula for stepping up even more when my schedule got insanely busy. To my nieces and nephews whose growth makes me realize how quickly time is passing. I am proud of your many achievements: Sharon and Sonja, Yvette, Victor and Justin; Stephanie, Walter (welcome to the family), and Tracey; Kimberly, Elgin, Kaelyn, and EJ; and finally, Walter and Eddie.

My fabulous new family: Sandra and James Gantt; Martin Robinson, Jr.; LaShonda, Greg, Jonathan and Jalen Jackson; Leon Curtis; Lanard and Tanya Ingram; Glenn and Danette Culver; and Bob and Jo Seppla. Your acceptance, love, and timely words of encouragement mean more to me than you will ever know. Most importantly, thank you for loving and supporting Ed for so many years.

My remarkable Memphis family: Ruth Ellen Lester, Orell Bridgforth, Glenda Bridgforth, Lavan Kenney, Glennie Clark, Henry Ellen Taylor, Sabrina Gulledge, Annie Pearl Smith, Elaine Jackson, Denise Kenney, Janice Partee, Virginia Sanders, Deanna Roam, Rita Hines, Tina Birchett, Claudis Bridgforth (by way of Detroit), Gertrude and Eddie Bridgeforth. Thanks for being so warm, welcoming, and showing the real meaning of Southern hospitality. It is possible we may one day soon be neighbors!

My awesome sisterfriends: I get lifted each time our busy schedules allow us time to talk. Thank you Jackie Kennedy for being my best friend these last fifty-four years; Karen James for your objective insights that keep me centered and balanced; Charmaine McClarie for amazing wisdom and for offering to fly across the country in my hour of need; Venti Valdez for being my amazing photographer and for having a computer guru for a husband (thanks, Dino); Phyllis Bowie for sharing that emotional bruises do heal; Brenda Wade, Ph.D., for teaching me that treasure maps do work; Jwahir Gold, Vivian Vanderwerd, and my other Southwest Detroit sisters for hangin' tough with me; and the entire wedding party not previously mentioned who had almost as much fun as me and Ed: Brenda J. Allen, Theodus Hall, Tim and Verna McDaniel, Connie Ellis Brown, Andrew Hopkins, Gene and Angela Louque, Rhonda and Stephen Moore.

Oprah Winfrey—the phenomenal woman personified—and her staff (especially Katy Davis, Candi Carter, and Tina Yee). Thank you for the opportunity of a lifetime. Participating as a financial coach in "America's Debt Diet" was an incredibly rewarding experience reaching millions of viewers who tuned in and followed the steps. It has also made me stretch and grow in ways I never imagined. Thank you for the priceless gift. And heartfelt thanks to Jean Chatzky and David Bach for your support during our Debt Diet adventure. I am honored to call you my colleagues and my new friends. To Carol Hunter, Joycelyn Thompson, Lanta Evans-Motte, Gail Perry-Mason, and Dr. Ara Thomas-Brown: Thank you not only for your ideas and input during the yearlong process, but also for your affirmation and assistance.

My amazingly talented team: Thank you Nikki Carter, Kate Berardo, and Michele Berger—your distinctive skills helped me bring Bridgforth Financial Management Group to a new level; Pamela Johnson and Darlene House for getting this project up and running; Kristin Loberg for seeing me to the finish line with amazing skill, talent, and much-needed encouragement not only related to writing, but also to my personal well-being. I've never had so much fun! You each came into my life at the divine right time and I consider you a true godsend.

My fantastic publisher, editor, and agent: Thank you Broadway Books for believing in me and the GIRL brand for a third book! Thanks Ann Campbell for continuing to astonish me with your abilities. You make my work infinitely better! And Bonnie Solow for great representation, but more importantly for the perfect advice at the perfect time.

Other marvelous people who made a difference: Thanks John "Mason in the Morning" for the weekly radio gig; Donyale Adams-Winters for giving me peace of mind by helping Dad and therefore helping Mom; DeWayne Hayes and Cynthia Hathaway for inviting us to have fun in the midst of an intense schedule; Sisters United Network for your prayers and emails (sorry I couldn't get back to you, but I read them all!); television viewers for taking time to send lovely comments via telephone and e-mail (sorry I couldn't get back to you and I *tried* to read them all!); booksellers and events organizers for helping me empower sisters across the country; *Essence* for continuing to reference *Straight* and *Grow* in the magazine month after month; and finally my past, present, and future clients. Helping you helps me help others. Thanks for your willingness to reach out for support and for your ongoing confidence in my abilities.

My spiritual teacher: Thank you Pastor Joel Osteen for explaining the practical applications of God's Word and encouraging us to live favor-minded with abundant joy.

Last but not least I thank my loving husband, my best friend, Edward L. Hodges, Jr. I am always filled with warm thoughts of you. Thank you for helping me recognize what is important in a partner and mate—being a truly good man and a praying man. Establishing our morning ritual of spiritual reading and prayer sets a positive tone for each day and strengthens our relationship with each other and with God. Thank you for understanding my work and sometimes hectic schedule. You are a great sounding board for ideas and an avid proofreader. I should have you check everything before it goes out! And thank you for the humor you bring to our lives daily. Yes, my family thinks you're kinda crazy—but in a really good way. I love you much.

The Straight Story

Let's be honest. Peering into the lives of the rich and famous—by way of glossy magazines and glitzy celebrity-obsessed TV shows—makes us envious of their lifestyle, clothes, bling, and the mansions they live in. We feel pushed to buy into designer culture and to measure up. We want to feel like members of the exclusive club and not outsiders looking in. Granted, we aren't famous and don't have the outrageous financial resources that celebrities do. But on our own level, it means reaching for the restaurant bill even when a little voice inside says, "Oh well, just because of this I'm going to be short again this month." Or, "I have to spend a lot on this gift so I don't look cheap." Or maybe you're just a sister who spends $500 on clothes and $300 on shoes, while making only $7.85 an hour. This is all possible, of course, largely through the use of credit.

There are plenty of people today whose spending is out of control. In 2004, writer Yolanda Young had an article published in *USA Today* that immediately began circulating on the Internet to brothers and sisters. One year later, it was still being forwarded, because I received my fifth copy of it—this time coming from a friend in California. The article indicated that even in today's hard economic times, we African-Americans haven't curbed our spending. It went on to report that "in many poor neighborhoods, one is likely to notice satellite dishes and expensive new cars . . . Blacks spend a significant amount of their income on depreciable products. In 2002, the year the economy nose-dived, we spent $22.9 billion on clothes, $3.2 billion on electronics and $11.6 billion on furniture to put into homes that, in many cases, were rented."

Clearly, debt and credit have become major issues for just about everyone today, regardless of your race or background. And they play an enormous role in the shape our lives take—whether good or bad—as our lives go forward. So how can we begin to understand what credit means and begin to make it work for us? Let's start by going back to the beginning; I'll tell you how I came to appreciate the power of credit, and how I committed myself to helping others to do the same.

My Story

If you've read either of my previous books, then you're already familiar with my story. I'm not someone who's always had her stuff together and likes to preach what I've been practicing all my life. To the contrary, I'm someone who had to fall into an abyss before I could acknowledge my mistakes, let go of old, destructive beliefs and behaviors, and rebuild myself professionally, personally, and *financially* with a future in mind. I see versions of myself in many of my clients, and I can easily recall the emotional, spiritual, and financial debt that I faced during an extremely difficult period in my life nearly twenty years ago as though it were yesterday.

Back then, my debt was so bad that three financial professionals, including two attorneys, advised that I file for bankruptcy. I was also in debt emotionally, still struggling with the fallout from a failed marriage. I was professionally in debt, having said good-bye to the banking industry so I could pursue something greater yet sensing that I'd lost my identity because I was no longer a bank manager. And I was spiritually in debt, feeling so ashamed and embarrassed about the state of my life that I could barely keep in contact with friends and family. I simply wanted to crawl into a cave and be left alone. It was quite ironic that I had managed a $90 million unit in a major California bank with twenty-two employees under my supervision, yet I couldn't account for my own financial well-being. I had ascended through the ranks of a thorny corporate ladder as a black woman but let my personal life descend down a slippery slope. The year 1988 will always be marked in my mind as the year I experienced the "Three B's": Breakdown, Breakout, and Breakthrough. It was a surprising outcome, given the expectations I'd set for myself long before then.

I grew up in a blue-collar family in Detroit, the fourth of six children. My parents worked extremely hard—Dad worked at least two jobs at a time and Mom toiled long hours as CEO of the family. Sometimes she did occasional domestic work in the homes of middle-class white folks, but maintaining our home and nurturing us was more than a full-time job. As a kid, however, I had no concept of real wealth and was well into adulthood before I realized that my family was not middle class. My parents' strong work ethic kept our household up and running; even though they struggled to meet their obligations, we were always well cared for and they always maintained good credit. My dad knew that creating excessive debt was never an option for him. As he told me recently, "It was not hard to get credit, just hard to pay it back." If only I, too, had learned and understood that message before reaching adulthood.

When I was eight years old, I made the decision to always be in control of my money and my life. I decided this as I watched my parents, and in particular, my mother, go through hard times and endure the stress of living in a world still rife with racial segregation and discrimination. I knew my mother felt trapped; with six children and one overworked breadwinner, my mom's urge to leave home for a time-out or escape on a brief vacation could never be satisfied. I understood her economic dependence on my father, and I was determined not to place myself in a similar situation. I never wanted to be without my own resources or without a place to go for support. At least, that was my plan. Little did I know that even as a well-paid, independent, professional woman, I'd fall into other financial traps.

By the time I met my first husband, whom I'll call Jeffrey, I was a bank officer with a good income and good credit, my own apartment and a car, but I was still living paycheck to paycheck. Jeffrey had had prior careers in professional sports and sales, and by the time we married, he'd become an entrepreneur. Like many couples, we didn't discuss money, financial history, or spending patterns before making a commitment. Nevertheless, I was looking forward to greater financial stability and having a partner in the journey to wealth.

From the beginning, Jeffrey and I always had clear goals—to be financially successful and enjoy a lavish lifestyle. Long story short: These dreams were squelched by a series of poor decisions and a constant, risky pattern of banking on future income. Jeffrey had little to no credit, and as an entrepreneur, his income was inconsistent. I wasn't an ideal saver either, and together we lived in what I call "virtual prosperity" to maintain an image of wealth and success that was far different from reality. We lived on credit, avoided price tags, and got caught up in a vicious cycle— the more we made, the more we wanted and the more we spent. To make matters worse, our emotional connection to each other grew as empty as our bank accounts.

Eventually, our lavish lifestyle caught up to us to the tune of $50,000 in unsecured debt (i.e., money we owed to people and companies with no collateral attached) through credit cards, lines of credit, and personal loans. It sunk my credit rating straight down. The debt began to haunt me so much that it affected my job and ability to think clearly with my own clients at the bank. But trying to take charge of the problem merely opened the proverbial Pandora's box: As I attempted to regain our financial footing and pay off the debt, I became so stressed and fearful that I found I was struggling to do my job to the point where I needed to take a break. But how could I? I was dependent on that income, living paycheck to paycheck! Unwilling to leave my job, I continued to let the anxiety gather negative energy and strength. I tended to everyone else—my husband's happiness, my employees and job responsibilities at the bank, our creditors' demands, requests from in-laws, and even our dog's needs. Meanwhile, I was eroding on the inside. Anger, shame, and resentment morphed into depression. Something had to change.

As it happened, a lot needed to change before my life could be right again. And a lot has continued to change since then. I resigned from the bank, got divorced, put forth a plan to pay off the $50,000 debt that I was left with, started a business, wrote two books, and returned to my roots in Detroit after having lived in the Bay Area for twenty-four years. A few years ago, I reconnected with a childhood sweetheart—my first boyfriend and the first boy I ever kissed. Three months after that we were engaged, and three months after *that,* we were married. Our whirlwind romance and marriage is possibly a book for the future, but suffice it to say that during our courtship there were many, many, many hours of conversation about our finances. A major difference between this marriage and the first one was not just Ed's willingness to discuss money, but the fact that he initiated it! Before we got married we talked about our incomes, debts, spending patterns, savings habits, *and* we reviewed each other's credit report. Mine was good, and thankfully his was even better!

But meeting Ed and finding my "happily ever after" doesn't mean I can sugarcoat the journey I took. My road back to financial prowess didn't happen overnight, and I didn't do it alone. It was long, soul-searching, and arduous at times. I sought the guidance of many professionals, including financial counselors and psychologists who helped me reformulate my perspective on my failures, learn from my mistakes, and reprogram my behavior when it came to money. In other words, it was a team effort. I had a lot of work to do. I had to relinquish a toxic ego and establish a new one. I had to shift my self-righteous mind-set over to a modest, self-effacing one that didn't care so much about job titles, materialism, and what other people thought about me. I'll be pointing out many times in this book that you're not alone in your journey and that together we can begin to pull you up from whatever bottom you currently stand on. It doesn't matter how far you think you've fallen. The same rope that helped me can help you so long as you hold on and have faith in yourself.

In this book, I'll continue to use my story as well as other sisters' stories to share examples of how we can sabotage our own financial stability in various ways. Through therapy I've learned a lot about subconscious beliefs and unconscious decisions that translate to repeated disappointments and failures in real life, which can persist in all our actions like a lingering cough. You can't be emotionally happy while financially bankrupt. And it's equally rare to be financially happy while emotionally bankrupt. The two often go hand in hand, which is why I firmly believe that a holistic approach to cash flow and debt management that integrates emotional and spiritual elements with practical techniques is the best financial healing—and the only lasting form of treatment.

When I founded Bridgforth Financial Management Group in 1990, I knew that unlike most other financial coaches, I could offer something special to my clients on account of my own personal experience. I could finally take all that I had learned not only as a bank manager, where I got my foundation for the financial-management methods I teach now, but also as a victim myself of money's cruel lessons when it's poorly managed. If you've never examined the emotional and cultural issues at the root of your spending patterns, this may be the real reason why you can't seem to heal your bank account. I'm going to help you do just that in this book.

I feel blessed to have the opportunity to teach other sisters the how-tos of financial healing, as well as inspire them to keep thinking positively. Remember, if I can do it, so can you.

Why Another GIRL Book?

This book is the third in a series of GIRL books on financial empowerment for African-American women. My first book, *Girl, Get Your Money Straight!*, challenges black women to get their finances in order and to think deeply about why they allowed themselves to get into financial trouble in the first place. In addition, it covered the nuts and bolts of money management and taught readers to consider the factors in their personal and spiritual lives, and those of their families, that caused them to hurt themselves financially. The second book, *Girl, Make Your Money Grow!*, was written with two goals in mind. It helps those ready to move on to the next level with their new-found fiscal expertise and personal self-knowledge, and it also meets the needs of women who have some ideas about the financial markets but are timid about pulling the trigger and actually making investments. If you haven't read these two books, I encourage you to check them out. But you don't necessarily need them as a foundation for reading this one. At times, however, I may refer to my previous books and suggest that you review certain topics that bolster the material here but that are beyond the scope of this book.

Like my previous works, *Girl, Get Your Credit Straight!* challenges you, the reader, to look deeply into what's pulling your financial strings regarding credit and debt management. It focuses on the behaviors and emotional states that come into play when money problems arise—particularly those that lead to debt, bankruptcy, and other conditions that prevent black women from being able to afford the American Dream. While my first book did address issues of debt and credit, the information here is much more focused and detailed, and if you are really struggling with debt you will benefit from this more intensive plan of action. Still, this book will be useful to anyone seeking superior financial health, including blue-collar workers, entry-level workers, professionals, managers, and business owners—and even stay-at-home moms.

Why a Book on Credit?

In the mid-1990s, my business really began to take off. My practice was no longer confined to the walls of an office and occasional speaking events. I suddenly found myself touring, giving keynote speeches and seminars, and helping individuals and families from all corners of the country cope with their debt and credit issues. Throughout my travels, it became abundantly clear that the vast majority of people's money problems revolve—

literally—around their credit status. In fact, anytime I did a radio talk show or gave a seminar, 90 percent of the questions I received were about credit. It also surprised me to learn how little people really knew about their credit—what it means, how it works, and what the difference is between good and bad debt. This is an age when the word "credit" has never been more popular in our everyday lives—we encounter it dozens of times a day in advertising alone. Even the term "credit score" has become a topic of conversation at dinner parties, but few people can define what that means.

It was obvious that my third book had to cover this topic, including all the other topics that are related to credit but that few people consider. Did you know, for example, that the price you pay for car insurance can be based (partially) on your credit score? Or that paying off large balances in full every month with low credit limits can work *against* your credit score? These are some of the things you're going to learn about in this book. I'm going to share with you the information that savvy financial advisors know, including what the banks, financial institutions, creditors, and credit-card companies *don't* want you to know.

The ideas and recommendations I offer in the chapters that follow are extensive and unlike any of the programs I outlined in my previous books. The subject of credit is closely intertwined with every other element of money management and financial planning. Much like how well we sleep, our credit status ultimately and quite inadvertently affects how we think, make decisions, act in the present, and plan for the future. Maintaining good credit is a vital sign of health—both emotionally and financially.

The real-life examples and self-revealing exercises you'll find in this book are holistic in nature. They are designed to help you become credit savvy, expand your thinking, and demand a better life. I'm going to help you identify your behavior patterns and attitudes toward money that hold you back and hinder your financial future. With new and powerful strategies for change, this is the only credit guide that offers sisters opportunities for spiritual, emotional, and financial healing along with a detailed road map for cleaning up credit, one step at a time.

How to Use This Book

The lessons I learned as I reassessed, restructured, and regained financial stability in my life are still with me today. Now in my fifties, I can again enjoy the benefits of an excellent credit report and credit score. But it's not something I take for granted. A brief lapse in financial focus can easily destroy years of hard work. Rebuilding good credit is a slow process, but it's well worth it. In the pages that follow, I'll give you the plan of action you need to get out of debt, increase your credit score, and prepare yourself to finance the dreams of your choice. Not everyone is blessed to receive a large chunk of money, like inheritance or lottery winnings, that can be used to pay off debt. Most of us have to do it the old-fashioned way—$10 or $20 at a time. And for many sisters, that's the most self-fulfilling, satisfying, and rewarding way to do it anyhow.

As you begin, keep this in mind: No one is born with a higher credit score than the next person. Credit scores reflect the choices we make—not the jobs and connections we have, the clothes we wear, or even the lifestyles we live. You have as much potential to achieve excellent credit and your financial dreams as anyone else.

This book is divided into three parts, each of which should be read in sequence. Part One ("Digging the Debt Ditch: Life in the Financial Hole") explores the why, what, and how of credit. *Why* we mismanage credit—the core emotional, cultural, and psychological issues at the root of our problem. *What* societal measuring sticks are used to evaluate us—credit reports and credit scores. And *how* we get into debt—the abuse of various credit products.

Part Two ("Climbing Out of the Hole: Practical Tools and Debt-Reducing Strategies") breaks down step-by-step what to do with the money you already have to pay down debt and establish a spending plan, specific strategies you can use to increase your credit score, and the most difficult issues couples face in pursuit of financial harmony.

Part Three ("On Level Ground: Forward-Thinking Strategies to Prevent Debt, Preserve Credit, and Keep Your Spirit in Check") covers all the ways in which you can ultimately set yourself up for never falling into a financial abyss again. Part Three inspires you to consider ideas for increasing your income or making a career change, and setting long-term financial goals. It also shows you how to protect yourself from the perils that can wipe you out financially so you're better prepared the next time something bad happens that can usher in new debt and derail your good credit. Finally, the last chapter shares my hints for using healing rituals to get through any struggle in life, whether it's financial or not. By keeping your spirit in check throughout your journey, you can achieve all that you've ever dreamed.

If you've never thought about your legacy until now, I'll challenge you to do so in this book. Just when you thought your money problems were enough to fill your life with worry and constant restructuring, think again: If you implement the ideas and action plans I offer in this book starting today, you will find yourself on the road to wealth much sooner than you ever thought possible. You'll be in the green rather than the red in no time. And you'll start to wonder how you can exponentially multiply that success to the point that you've got more than enough money to leave behind to future generations. That, sister, is a very exciting place to be in.

This book isn't just a nuts-and-bolts guide to fixing your debt and credit problems. As I said earlier, financial health is about much more than dollars and cents. It must include emotional and spiritual connections within ourselves, within the frameworks of our communities, and with the world at large. This is why the journey you are about to take will mend more than your credit and bank account. It will open up the universe so you can realize your greatest potential, achieve solace in your soul, and capture the honest, authentic sense of self that God intended you to have.

Getting Started

If you're a sister who read and embraced the concepts in *Straight* and *Grow,* then you likely have started a GIRL journal and know the importance of documenting feelings as you go through the program. If this is the first GIRL book you've read, it's important to be organized as you chart the progress you make in getting your credit straight. So there are a few tools you'll need as we proceed. Now, don't go to much expense! Just purchase a three-ring binder, a package of writing paper, a three-hole punch, monthly dividers (January through December), and enough regular dividers to cover a section for your thoughts and feelings, spending plans, and one section for each of your creditors.

Keep in mind that it won't be necessarily easy going through this program. Many of you are already overwhelmed with the responsibilities of your daily lives. Jeanne Sahadi, a columnist with Money.com, calls this period in our lives The Yoga Years—"where you find yourself stretched in ways you never imagined existed. Everyone and everything's pulling on you—from bosses and subordinates, to spouses and kids, to pets and parents." But it's true that there is no gain without pain. The next steps will definitely require some willingness on your part. However, improvement is possible without depriving yourself too much. Just commit to taking baby steps in a positive direction. Be patient with yourself and expect to win, not fail. In fact, remove "failure" from your vocabulary! Know that it has been done before by many of the sisters you'll meet in this book, so why not you, too? Enjoy your journey on this GIRL road to empowerment.

Here's one final secret: Getting your credit straight doesn't mean you have to be entirely debt-free. Surprised? Now you can all do a collective exhale. It's great if you have living debt-free as the objective. Anyone who has carried debt—whether for a season or a lifetime—has felt burdened by it and has wondered, "How am I ever going to pay this mess off? How will I ever improve my credit score and be creditworthy again?" **But your**

Tools for Straightening Up!

Three-ring binder

Writing paper

Hole punch

Monthly dividers (January through December)

General dividers labeled for thoughts/feelings, spending plans, and one for each creditor

goal is *progress*, not perfection. Your aim is to get your financial house in order, not to put so much pressure on yourself that you end up feeling worse, rather than better. Be patient with yourself and strive to see your finances through eyes of faith. Because this is a holistic program, the "whole" of your being can benefit if you are serious about having a shift in your life—mind, body, and spirit. Reconnect with faith in having an abundant life after the "disconnect" from hope that comes from carrying a heavy debt burden. Begin to believe in yourself again and anticipate God's goodness and favor in your life.

Part One

Digging the Debt Ditch: Life in the Financial Hole

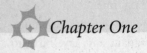

Why We Debt: The Emotional and Cultural Factors at the Root of Your Debt Balance

It doesn't take a genius to understand that looks can sometimes be deceiving. A case in point is a sharp young sister named Deena. The classy, professional-looking twenty-five-year-old sat confidently in the office chair wearing a Donna Karan suit, Prada shoes, and carrying a $400 Zero Halliburton briefcase. She had just sailed through her first interview at a major Chicago-area bank. Mrs. Clark, the woman who would be her new boss, was clearly impressed with her. She indicated that there was every reason to believe she would soon be scheduling a second interview. For Deena, this news was a welcome relief.

"I'd done a lot of other jobs, like selling cosmetics and working as a waitress," Deena recalled, "but becoming a teller and working with money as a stepping-stone to an executive banking career just seems like the perfect fit for me." And it was coming right on time.

Years earlier, Deena had been through some rough times. As a nineteen-year-old college student, she became pregnant and gave birth to Tiffany. Although motherhood came as a surprise, she was determined to continue her education and expand her opportunities. Still, it was a struggle to care for herself and her bright-eyed daughter. Deena often found herself overwhelmed with the responsibilities of being a single mom and a part-time student. To make ends meet, she sometimes charged groceries and diapers—not to mention the occasional designer clothes and shoes. When she complained to her parents that her credit-card balance had risen to more than $2,000, her father suggested that she file for bankruptcy, as he had done years earlier.

"It's only $2,000," she told him, feeling silly about going to all that trouble for such a small amount of money. Yet between her father's confidence in the idea and an incessant TV commercial that advocated bankruptcy and promised "$99 sets you free!," Deena gave in. Filing for bankruptcy would get everybody off her back and get rid of the debt so she could focus on taking care of her child and continue to pursue her dream of obtaining a college degree.

Five years later, when she was twenty-four, everything in Deena's life seemed to be coming together. She was engaged to Clifton, a PhD candidate, and they were raising her daughter, Tiffany, as well as a new son, Marcus. But Deena's debts started to climb again. Her credit-card balance was up to $1,000 and she owed $500 on her cell phone. As a student, Clifton wasn't bringing in much money. And Deena, with a part-time job of her own, was just helping them get by. Their fights over money got heated, and after another year they decided to split up. Deena was left scrambling again.

"Clifton always cried broke because of his soaring educational expenses, so only Tiffany's father provided any kind of steady child support," Deena recalled. "I ended up having to move back home with my parents. It was cheaper to live there, but I still didn't have enough money and I was still determined to finish those last few credits for my degree."

Then threatening letters started to arrive in the mail and bill collectors began harassing her on the phone. In the midst of this chaos, Deena still spent money trying to keep up appearances, in large part because she was self-conscious about being a never-married mother of two. She continued to dress impeccably as her children donned Baby Phat, Sean Jean, and FUBU. Deena made sure her clothing and her image were a priority. Now, with her second interview at the bank pending, Deena could finally imagine a day—not far in the future—when she could put the struggles behind her.

A few days later, Deena sat in her car in front of her daughter's school, enjoying the sunshine and waiting for the final bell to ring. Her cell phone rang instead. It was Mrs. Clark, the woman at the bank who'd interviewed her. Deena broke into a smile.

"I'm afraid I have a bit of bad news," Mrs. Clark said. Deena braced herself. "It's your financial history. We always run a credit report, and there are a few things that, well . . . I'm afraid we won't be able to move forward. I hope you understand."

Deena thought about her past bankruptcy and the new bills that had just gone into collection. "Of course, I understand," Deena assured her, trying to sound pleasant, even though she burned with embarrassment and disappointment.

When she hung up the phone, the typically cool-as-a-cucumber Deena fell apart. Then she looked up and saw her daughter skipping toward the car. Once again, she composed herself and accepted the fact that she was back at square one. "Here I'm supposed to be this role model for my daughter," she said to herself, "but the reality is, I'm an unemployed mother of two living at home with her parents." A week later, Deena came across my book *Girl, Get Your Money Straight!* By doing a little digging, she found my telephone number, called me, and said, "Glinda, I'm ready to clean up my credit. I need help."

Committed to Credit

For better or for worse, we Americans are married to our credit cards. It's simply the American way to make purchases. We do everything with them, and it doesn't take unanticipated medical bills or a job loss to entice us to abuse credit. Our list of charges may include picking up that slinky dress for the New Year's Eve party, getting our teeth cleaned, or paying for a round of drinks during happy hour at our favorite rendezvous spot. Overspending for luxury items, vacations, entertainment, eating out more, and buying unnecessary goods quickly racks up the bill.

Having credit, the ability to get something now and pay for it later, is a good thing. It makes life so much easier and more convenient. If we had to fork over all the money at once to buy a house or car, we might be living in tents and riding bicycles. If we had to carry around wads of cash to cover regular living expenses like groceries and gas for our cars, we'd all be targets for thieves. What if we flew to another city, checked into a hotel and rented a car, and had to drop several hundred dollars up front? How many of us would have the money to do it? How many of us would feel comfortable traveling with that kind of cash, even if we had it?

Yes, credit is a wonderful thing, but as with a box of Godiva chocolates, you can overdo it. As a former weekly guest financial expert on a popular call-in radio show in Detroit, I heard from countless people who had run up sky-high bills and then had trouble repaying them. Even the most polished and successful-looking women are often in debt up to the highlighted tips of their hair. And just like Deena, they eventually come to realize that in today's financial world, your credit is your credibility. People are constantly scrutinizing your credit history, assessing your character, and, at the same time, determining whether they want to deal with you or not.

So if we know logically that debt is bad, that we shouldn't spend beyond our means and run up credit-card bills, why on earth do we do it? The answer lies in a complicated web of societal and personal factors that conspire to get us to spend, spend, spend—without a plan for how we will ever pay it back.

Seduced by Advertising

Advertising today is savvy and manipulative. Advertisers know how to get you to buy, and even how to get you thinking that debt isn't all that bad. At this writing, the commercials put out by Visa include many hidden messages. Think about what the following voice-over really means: "Enjoy life's opportunities. Life . . . it takes risk and joy; life takes spontaneity; it also takes a little help. That's where we come in, to give you the freedom to experience life the way you want to. So go on, live life, and remember that no matter what it takes, life takes Visa."

Sounds great, doesn't it? But if you think your credit card gives you the freedom to experience life and buy whatever you want, you're right . . . and wrong. For every purchase we make that we can't pay, we take away from our future freedom in how we can choose to live.

But it's not just television advertising that is to blame. Each year, billions of credit-card solicitations go out to people with letters that appear to offer unique personalized opportunities and rewards. They make you feel special—a *chosen* one—so it's harder to resist the invitation. Moreover, the government pushes us to spend money because it adds to the economy and protects jobs. Whenever a recession looms or the indicators of the economy point to a slowdown, the government persuades us to renew the economy by spending our hard-earned money. No one will talk about saving or cutting back or even the consequences of excessive spending on an individual level. Why? Because the government is less concerned about individuals than it is about the masses and the power that the masses have as a whole on the economy.

Nearly two-thirds of the GNP (gross national product), an indicator of the state of the economy, is a result of consumer spending. So if we're not spending money on goods and services—including goods and services we don't need to live, like weekly manicures, designer heels, and fancy bottled water—that GNP goes down and you'll hear the media talking about a weak or slow economy. During the holiday season, the media like to cover how much people are spending in retail stores and how much profit those stores are making as an ultimate end-of-year indicator of just how well America is doing. But, once New Year's is over and those credit-card bills start arriving, people get the "holiday hangover" and worry about how they will pay for those bills. The second wave of worry comes around April 15, when Mr. Taxman wants to get paid. If you're due a return, you're a happy sister. But if you owe money, it can be a very stressful time period. That's when the Internal Revenue Service endorses credit cards as a "convenient" way to pay your taxes (albeit with a "convenience fee"!). Everywhere we turn, we are encouraged to use credit. And our reliance on it continues to increase at a staggering rate— as we buy everything from lattes and leather purses to vacations and Volvos.

Societal Changes in How We Treat Money

If you're asking yourself, How did this happen to me?, keep in mind that one of the reasons for our debt problems is simple economics: Americans have been experiencing higher costs of living and falling median family incomes. Housing costs, child care, and health insurance have all had double-digit growth while incomes have stagnated or dropped. Even a *booming* economy can share some of the blame. In fact, the economic boom of the 1990s was driven largely by consumer spending as people tended to spend more on goods and services and save less.

In addition, the way we treat money has changed in recent decades, and unfortunately, these changes set the consumer up for trouble. One shift that has occurred is in how we as a society actually view money, and the second is in how the lending industry gives money to us, including credit. Combined, these two forces add up to a distorted sense of our own wealth, encouraging the mentality that every purchase we make can eventually be paid for with future income.

A lot has changed since our grandparents' and great-grandparents' generation. Families who experienced the Depression were thrifty savers, but decades later we've become big spenders. Part of the reason baby boomers have had the luxury of spending a lot (and fueling the resulting economic boom) is that they inherited money from their parents and grandparents who had saved and invested so well. But today less and less is getting passed on to future generations as families spend more and save less. No one has a Depression mentality anymore; in fact, we have the opposite. Marketers encourage us to spend both what money we have and what money we *don't* have. And the money we don't have typically comes from credit cards, which are easily abused for the sake of living beyond one's means and keeping up with the Joneses. And when all those lifestyle purchases add up to a lot of money, it becomes increasingly hard to visualize paying off that debt without winning the lottery or hitting it big in Hollywood.

Twenty and thirty years ago, credit was rationed based on your ability to pay it back, your reputation, and even your character to some degree. Now it's seemingly based on your *inability* to pay it back, because that's how creditors ultimately make money off you: via high interest rates and late charges. The industry discovered that the most profitable consumers were the least responsible ones, including college students, people who'd declared bankruptcy, housewives with little experience and no education on money management, and those who were consuming beyond their means. That's when creditors began targeting people who would pay anything—any fee or any interest rate—because they needed more credit.

Other changes have also factored into society's debt and credit equation. One is the lack of regulation. Since the early 1970s, usury laws—that is, laws that specify the maximum legal interest rate at which loans can be made—have virtually been eliminated, so credit-card companies can basically charge whatever interest rate they want. Second, technology has made transactions quicker than the blink of an eye. Back when Visa was just getting started in the late 1960s and early 1970s, credit-card processing took a long time. Not anymore it doesn't. You can buy a high-ticket item in less time than it takes to extract and count the dollars from your wallet.

Finally, our philosophy toward credit has shifted. It used to be that bankers objected to credit cards out of sheer ethics; they didn't like extending credit to individuals who they knew couldn't pay it back. That was considered immoral—like giving consumers the gun with which to shoot themselves. So in some respects bankers also assumed the role of being regulators. Well, we all know that that's not the case anymore. Now bankers and lenders throw money at us under the guise that it's practically free . . . for the time being. They try to distract us from focusing on the payback while we're in the highly emotional flurry of feeling good about spending and buying. Which is why so many of us are now deep underwater.

The financial industry doesn't only prey on those who've already messed up their credit or have fallen into debt. It also goes after those on the verge—those who have some home equity, who have been responsible, and who have saved a little. When such people accept high-interest loans and go from living within their means to living beyond them, they can quickly find themselves going from solid middle class down to poverty levels, taking their creditworthiness and sense of well-being with them.

If this all sounds depressing, it is. But here's the good news: You can fight back and reclaim good credit no matter how far you might have fallen. The flip side to all this information is that *because of* how our world now operates, you hold power that many sisters before you did not. Women in general aren't financially dependent on their husbands anymore. We can make our own money, pay our own bills, and buy our own

Misery Has Company

The average household has more than seven credit cards, and in 2005 the average balance carried among those cards totaled $9,300, according to the nonprofit Consumer Credit Counseling Service in Dallas. CardWeb.com, a Maryland firm that tracks the payment-card industry, reports that revolving consumer credit debt continued to hover at the $800 billion level in early 2006. CardWeb also reports that about 1 in 5 households have "maxed out" or otherwise spent up to their credit limit. And at the end of the month, about 60 percent of cardholders don't pay off their balances in full. To make matters worse, according to Consumer Action, a nonprofit organization that surveys credit-card issuers, if you send your payment in late one time, nearly 70 percent of credit-card issuers will hike your interest rate to more than 29 percent! Even if you pay on time and have good credit, having too much debt can put you behind the eight ball, and leading lenders will likely decline to extend you further credit until you bring your debt load down.

Realizing that you're not alone in debt is comforting. But you're also not alone in the journey that you're going to take to get out of debt and become financially whole. I encourage you to use the power of prayer and daily affirmations to get through the rough parts, especially at the start when you face your debt and credit report. Keep a positive outlook and eventually you'll see the payoff in your bank account and feel it in your spirit.

houses. In fact, in 2005, single women snapped up one of every five homes sold. That's nearly 1.5 million—more than twice as many as single men bought, according to the National Association of Realtors. No matter what the advertisers or credit-card companies would have you believe, you are in charge. I'm going to show you how to change your money mentality and take the power back, one step at a time.

Some people, after wrestling with the heavy debt for as long as they can, file for bankruptcy. Personal bankruptcy filings totaled a little more than 2 million in 2005, according to the Administration Office of the U.S. Courts. At the time, that number was the highest total ever, up from 1.56 million in 2004. While bankruptcy filings fell in 2006 due to the new change in bankruptcy law, experts predict record numbers again in the near future as interest rates rise and people find it increasingly difficult to make their mortgage payments.

Although bankruptcy can pull you out of the fire by getting your creditors off your back by either eliminating or restructuring the amount you owe, it leaves a negative mark on your credit report that stays there for up to ten years. What's more, bankruptcy isn't what it used to be prior to the Reform Act that took effect in late 2005 (more on this later). It's now a lot more difficult to simply shed all of your debt through a routine Chapter 7 filing in which most consumer debt (i.e., credit cards) can be wiped away relatively easily.

African-American Women and Debt

In addition to the factors described above, I have found that women—especially those in the African-American community—tend to share similar issues that result in serious money drains. After years of working with hundreds of sisters and speaking to thousands more on the road, I believe there are four common mistakes we make when it comes to our money:

1. **We expect financial security from the wrong source.** Many women believe having a job and earning an income will be the

ticket to a secure future. But anyone who works for someone else is vulnerable and at the mercy of her employer. We live in an "at will" job world where you can walk away from a job just as easily as your employer can say good-bye to you. No job is so secure that you are guaranteed lifetime employment. Moreover, JOB often stands for "just over broke," and unless you get something else going—for instance, entrepreneurship and/or investments—you'll likely continue a paycheck-to-paycheck lifestyle even as your salary goes up. (In Chapter 7, you'll get a guided tour through 101 ideas that can become your next career, funding your good credit forever.)

Another misguided source of financial security for some women comes from the hope of marriage or relationships. If your husband or partner doesn't have his financial head on straight, he can be the source of the problem, or a hindrance that holds you back. The expectation that Mr. Right will come along and correct our financial "wrongs" is a big risk to take. About 52 percent of marriages end in divorce, 22 percent of women never marry, and 75 percent of women become widowed. To put this into greater perspective, get this: **The average age of widowhood is a young fifty-seven years old,** and the overall life expectancy for women is seventy-eight years. Are you prepared to live fifteen to twenty years beyond retirement at your current lifestyle without having to work at Wal-Mart or McDonald's? This reality is probably why the National Women's 2005 Retirement Survey indicates that 8 percent of women between the ages of thirty and fifty-five worry about living at or below the poverty level and 53 percent of women of color worry about losing their financial security. The cost of live-in elder care and housekeeping assistance may be prohibitive for some families, and those who make the necessary compromises to help care for their elderly members often resort to stretching their budgets maximally and taking on more expenses than they can realistically carry.

Finally, though we may be counting on Social Security to provide for us as we get older, its status has been uncertain for quite some time. It remains to be seen what will be available for us when we retire. Perhaps it will be a small supplement to those with pension benefits. More and more companies, like United Airlines and National Steel, are going bankrupt and scaling back or even eliminating pension plans—an unconscionable shame after many of their workers have put in thirty years at the same company.

2. **We fail to communicate with our spouse or partner.** Sharing the intimate details of our money problems with our spouses can be tough. Even in the best of marriages and partnerships, a breakdown in communication can occur along financial lines. But such a breakdown can be crippling to one's inner peace and outer relationship with a loved one. Do you and your partner share similar values when it comes to money? Do you fight over money? Is it a source of continual conflict that never ends no matter how much money you do—or don't— have? Love and money always intertwine at some point in a relationship, even though it's not usually on the first date. We don't typically fall in love because of money, but we often fall out of love because of it.

   In Chapter 6, I'll dive into this topic in more detail and give you the tools you and your partner need to develop a smart, healthy relationship with money that will help you get your credit straight and foster a strong, long-lasting partnership. You can't get out of debt alone if you're in a committed relationship. If you're legally married and/or legally share accounts in the form of a mortgage, credit card, or other loan or line of credit, you are as much responsible for any debt and poor credit as your partner—even if you weren't the one who was financially irresponsible. It may not take teamwork to create debt and plummet credit in a relationship, but it takes teamwork to reduce debt and rebuild credit when you're in a relationship. This is why I've devoted an entire chapter to helping you navigate your journey in clearing up your credit with your partner.

3. **We take care of other people.** Amazingly, 62 percent of African-American women say they have no money after paying bills, and most cite financial responsibility for adult children and grand-children as the reason. While a three-year-old certainly relies on his parents to provide food and other necessities, too often we continue to support our children as they get older—no matter the cost. Many children today have a false sense of entitlement; they act as though the world owes them something. But our chil-dren need to learn that they can earn money—not just request it be given to them. You can teach young children valuable lessons by not always putting money in their hands when they ask for it. If you start taking this approach when they are young, they will learn to be responsible early on and won't grow up to become fi-nancially dependent adults. Too often, able-bodied grown chil-dren are constantly needing a few dollars in between paychecks or a financial bailout from time to time. Don't do yourself or them an injustice by becoming a crutch. It's not necessary or even appropriate for you to say yes every time just to buy their love and affection. So learn to say no and stop trying to please everybody at your financial expense. If you take care of yourself first, and make your own financial security and stability the pri-ority, you'll be in a greater position to take care of others when they need it most.

4. **We overspend, plain and simple.** This mistake encompasses a lot of issues, many of which we'll explore more deeply later on in the chapter. It's tough to learn the difference between a need and a want. We need shoes but want Manolos, or we need food but want filet mignon. These days, I'm more of a minimalist in terms of my decorating tastes, but as you already learned, once upon a time I was lavish and materialistic. I still keep a few me-mentos from those days just to remind me of how addicted I used to be to credit cards: The Waterford crystal brandy decanter and four brandy snifters that I leave on my kitchen counter are reminders of how, regardless of cost, "things" used to be more

important to me than financial peace of mind. That Waterford crystal cost me about $450—and I barely even drink alcohol!

According to James Clingman, author of *Blackonomics,* blacks tend to have displaced values. He says, "On a larger scale, we earn $750 billion annually, but 95 percent of it is spent outside of our community. Our self-esteem is found in things. There is little delayed gratification." We tend to let the addictive tendencies of spending dominate our lives, just as drinking dominates the life of an alcoholic. And ultimately there is no financial legacy left for our children.

I remember doing a seminar for a group of about fifty black women. I began by asking the question "By show of hands, how many of you are expecting a large inheritance?" After about ten seconds of nervous laughter from the group as sisters turned and looked at each other, only one hand in the group shot up into the air. It happened to be that of a four-year-old girl sitting in the front row with her mother! I have no idea what possessed her to raise her hand when no one else in the room did, but it still amazes me because I doubt she even knew what an inheritance was! But truth be told, why shouldn't she expect an inheritance? We African-Americans earn billions annually. What are we doing with our money?

It's really not rocket science. According to Alfred Edmonds, editor in chief of *Black Enterprise,* when interviewed on *America's Black Forum,* "Get out of the notion that we have nothing to work with. We have less than others, but we have something." It's not that we're not making money. But for most of us, there's a finite amount of money that comes in, and there's an infinite amount that *could* go out. These figures need to be balanced and prioritized. We must move beyond the concept of budgeting, which feels limiting and restrictive, to the concept of being proactive in planning and tracking our finances—lessons you'll soon learn when I have you create your own spending plan with debt in mind.

One significant mistake we make that perpetuates our

overspending in general is that we tend to avoid reevaluating our financial status on a routine basis to take into consideration new forces that should call for less spending. For example, the loss of one income while continuing to spend as though there are two incomes is a common way we sabotage ourselves. Lynnette Khalfani, author of *Zero Debt: The Ultimate Guide to Financial Freedom,* says that often people with heavy debt loads have fallen victim to "The Five Dreaded D's"—divorce, downsizing, death, disability, or disease.

Any one of these situations can happen unexpectedly and significantly reduce your monthly revenues in addition to bringing emotional drama. Divorce can cause a big financial avalanche, especially for women. Statistics have routinely proven that after divorce women suffer a decrease of about 27 percent in their standard of living. Not only does the divorce itself cost thousands of dollars, but women are left having to adjust to a lifestyle that's far from what they enjoyed for many years. Downsizing isn't so easy after we've become accustomed to a certain standard of living. It's human nature to wish ourselves back to a better standard of living through irresponsible spending. Becoming ill or disabled often leads to decreased or even no income for a period of time, during which we don't make the necessary adjustments to our spending to accommodate that pinch in the income stream.

A lot of these D's are intertwined, as one can instigate another and then another. Enveloping all these D's is money, which becomes a form of medication that can ultimately spiral out of control and result in another D that can be exceptionally crippling: depression.

The History of Credit

Before going into greater detail about *why* we make the above-mentioned mistakes over and over again, and how hidden emotional factors come into play, let me start by defining credit. What is it? Simply put, it's an agreement you make to get something now and pay for it later. Credit is a method of exchanging goods and services in lieu of money. Or using someone else's money with the promise to return it at some point in the future. It is the ability to borrow.

So what is debt? Debt is what's created from a credit transaction where you are obligated to pay it back. It's what you owe. Your lender is your creditor, and you become a debtor. There is good debt as well as bad debt; debt attached to appreciating or long-term assets, like a home or education, is considered "good" debt, but debt that results from the purchase of depreciating or quickly used-up assets, like a new stereo, a wardrobe, or a trip to Europe, is considered "bad" debt. Financing good debt with credit is often a smart move when done responsibly, whereas financing bad debt with credit is often a risky move. As we'll see, the difference between these two types of debt becomes a factor in your credit score, most notably as "types of accounts." A credit-card account with MasterCard doesn't hold the same weight as a mortgage account with a bank. Your debt, however, whether it's relatively good or bad, must be considered in light of your well-being, because all debt can be categorized as bad if it infringes on your sense of self-worth and prevents you from realizing your dreams in life.

While the concept of credit dates back to Assyria, Babylon, and Egypt 3,000 years ago when it was first used, credit that is paid back over a period of time—called installment credit—began in the United States with the Pilgrims. Even in the 1700s, merchants could not survive without extending credit. Store or book credit was extremely common. Credit sales back then were not structured as installment sales—meaning equal payments were paid back to the lender each month for a specific period of time. Instead, debtors would pay back as they could. In the case of farmers, their debt was usually repaid after harvesting crops each year. The good news/bad news is that this early acceptance of installment debt began integrating borrowing into every facet of our lives. We no longer purchased only those items necessary for our survival; our mind-set changed to "If we want it and don't have the cash, we can borrow to get it."

Even so, there were always those who understood the lure of debt and avoided it. When Georgia Montgomery moved from Florida to Michigan during the 1940s' "Great Migration" period, she brought substantial savings with her. That meant Georgia and her family could afford to purchase things Alabama natives never needed before—including winter boots and coats. When housing became available, Georgia and her plant foreman husband, Dennis, were able to afford a house with space enough for a beauty shop. "I wasn't wasting my money or having big times out on the town," Georgia recalled. "I was always more into saving money than Dennis, but he saw how our friends struggled to make it who didn't have any, and they had to take out loans or extend their credit options, putting them in debt." Being financially savvy put Georgia's family miles ahead of many of their contemporaries who moved up north to work in factories and earn more money. This vibrant sister—at 107 years young—still enjoys living on her own and cooking for visitors, including immediate, adopted, and extended family members.

By the way, today's form of "plastic money" didn't arrive until the twentieth century. In 1950, Diners Club and American Express launched their charge cards in the United States, and in 1951, Diners Club issued the first credit card to 200 customers, who could use it at twenty-seven restaurants in New York. But it wasn't until the establishment of standards for the magnetic strip in 1970 that the credit card became part of the Information Age. Now it's largely to blame for the Debting Age.

Credit in the Black Community

For generations, blacks have been discriminated against and denied credit by lending institutions nationwide. Racial bias toward minorities is demonstrated through redlining—the refusal to grant mortgage loans to certain residential areas—as well as predatory lending practices—such as charging exorbitant interest rates and fees.

In black neighborhoods of major cities, African-American families frequently relied on what many viewed as the kindness of neighborhood merchants to survive challenging times. Growing up in Detroit on the near eastside, Dr. John L. Kline, former Harlem Globetrotter and author of *Never Lose,* experienced shopping at corner stores where merchants kept ledgers recording customer expenses while letting them continue to obtain goods they didn't have the money to pay for at the time. Ironically, these merchants were often viewed as allies, although their goods frequently had price markups and they added interest to bills. Some families had large account balances they would probably never pay off. This cycle ended for many of the families when stores throughout Detroit were destroyed during the riots of 1967.

"Thinking about this brings back memories of my loving aunt Ree, who bought things to help others without regard for her financial standing," recalled Kline. "She was concerned about the happiness of her family then and there, not the future . . . she always paid her bills, but she never gave a thought to the 65 percent interest that would be incurred."

Today, many people believe that creditors force us into dire financial straits because of these kinds of practices. When we find ourselves burdened with debt, the common lament is that we are victims of lenders, payday-loan outfits, credit-card companies, banks, and financing scams. Granted, they share the responsibility by extending credit to those ill prepared to manage it, but to blame our current debt problems on the credit cards themselves would be a mistake. The truth is that overspending is a frequent cause and is many times a result of a desire for things that compensate for issues in other parts of our lives.

Why We Overextend Ourselves: We Got Issues

All of our problems around credit abuse don't come from outside forces. Often they come from within. Recall the four common mistakes sisters routinely make that I outlined earlier, which result in serious debt and credit problems. Why do we make these mistakes when we inwardly know they can sabotage us? Well, the outside forces can trigger unhealthy responses that are further exacerbated by our own warped internal processing. This internal processing ultimately brutalizes our egos until we feel the need to act out with money that we don't have—especially in our African-American culture.

Our insecurities grew out of being stolen from our homeland of Africa, forced into the violation of slavery and life under humiliating Jim Crow laws. Sadly, discrimination continues to be reinforced by subtler forms of racism. These negative day-to-day experiences contribute to high levels of self-criticism and self-doubt and further diminish our self-esteem. When asked if this kind of self-doubt plays a significant role in her patients' behaviors with money, Dr. Ara Thomas-Brown, a marriage and family therapist in the Washington, D.C., area, says, "Definitely. The first thing I look at is self-esteem. Why are they doing it? What are they feeling?"

Dr. Ara goes on to explain how these issues are passed from generation to generation. Children inherit low self-esteem from their parents. If parents don't get the support they need to boost their own self-esteem issues and thus change their behavior for the sake of their children, they won't be able to make their kids feel good about themselves. So any negative behavior toward money practiced by the parents simply will be replicated, or copied, by their children. It's called the Cognitive Behavior Theory. We inherit how to act and think from our parents, whether they are good role models or not. The message we channel from our parents start very early in life, instilling us with either a strong sense of self-worth and confidence, or a weak sense of self-worth. It's nearly impossible to gain self-respect and healthy self-esteem when you have parents who lack their own sense of self-worth and ability to see themselves as valuable. Dr. Ara says, "The early experience with our parents often puts a message in our heads, like a recording: 'You're not good enough.' "

Ever hear of retail therapy? That's when we feel sad, lonely, bored, or depressed and decide to go shopping to lift our spirits. And all too often, this involves spending money that we don't have. It's emotional and impulsive. Almost every client I've worked with has at least one of three common threads as a primary component of their money woes—low self-esteem, deprivation—either financial or emotional—and fear. And retail therapy is often the easiest way to squelch these feelings—at least for the moment.

A favorite anecdote of mine from *Girl, Get Your Money Straight!* is the story of a sister who drove up to her financial counseling session with me in a shiny black Mercedes with her hair coiffed and makeup meticulous. Girlfriend was dressed in designer attire from head to toe. She went on to describe her house with its spiral staircase and crystal chandeliers. It was obvious she was proud of her material possessions. Interestingly, when the conversation turned to the state of her finances, she confessed having filed for bankruptcy twice. Then she went on to say, "I may be broke, but I look good!" Even though there was enormous drama in her life because of her spending habits, the desire to appear successful to the outside world outweighed the chaos created by this destructive pattern. She found her self-esteem in objects and luxury items instead of from inside herself. But you can't spend your way to higher self-esteem, just as you can't borrow your way out of debt. Worst of all, most of what we spend our money on doesn't contribute to our net worth in any way. Michelle Singletary, author of *Spend Well, Live Rich: How to Get What You Want with the Money You Have,* has one of the best lines I've ever heard to describe the problem in a most practical way. She says, "If it's on your ass, it's not an asset."

The Three Main Culprits in Overspending—The Real Reasons Why We Make Mistakes

Ask yourself if any of the following three scenarios sound familiar:

SCENARIO #1: On the job you notice a distinct difference in how you are treated in comparison to your white counterparts. Your boss, a classic type-A personality, is brash and condescending to you. He cares only about what you have done lately that makes him look good within the company. You never receive any compliments or words of encouragement from him, while you watch others get them. Your self-talk says, "I'm not good enough and I'm not doing enough. I don't feel good about myself, so I'll buy this new Escada suit to make me feel better." So you spend $900 on the suit and you feel good momentarily. But the reality is it doesn't matter how many outfits you buy, they will never fix the ongoing problem you have at work with your boss. The purchase of the suit temporarily soothes the emotional wounds caused by your interactions with him, but the $900 suits won't stop and you'll be driven deeper into debt until you address the roots of your spending.

This scenario illustrates how self-esteem issues come into play. When you see something in the store window and immediately decide to march in and make an impulse buy, have you ever stopped yourself at the cash register and gauged your self-esteem at that moment or on that day? Often that question is just as important as knowing how much money you have in your wallet. Even if you have the resources to spend, it doesn't make sense to do it if it's based on a purely emotional reason. Case in point: One time, I was interviewed by a major network television anchor for a magazine article. As I described the concept of how self-esteem plays a role in our spending habits, he responded, "Gee, that's fascinating, because when my self-esteem is low, I just buy another house!" Now, we aren't all able to do that, of course. Some of us buy clothes, cosmetics, or jewelry. And some of us buy houses!

The point is, it's all relative. Young people typically have a greater tendency to fall into debt not only because their incomes are lower than those of older adults with more experience, but also because they're more likely to have less confidence in themselves as they try to determine what they want to do with their lives. While it's not always true, self-esteem and confidence often come with age and life experience. We grow stronger the more we understand our place in our world and our purpose for being here. As we move farther away from the influence of our parents and *their* potentially flawed money habits, we move farther away from ways of thinking about money that we've been conditioned to practice—and have a greater chance to turn over a new financial leaf.

SCENARIO #2: Money has been tight in your household for years, and you and your husband can't discuss money without getting into a vicious argument that leaves you feeling frustrated and empty inside. You don't think he gives you enough money, and it reminds you of those days when you asked your dad for money and he said no. You can't stand not being able to buy the things you want, even though he complains that you spend too much money. You feel trapped in your everyday grind, confined to a world where you'll never have enough money or things. One day, you say to yourself, "I've done without so long that I've got to get away on vacation." So you book a seven-day cruise to the Caribbean for $2,000. The reality is that it doesn't matter how many Caribbean cruises you take, they will never fix the fact that you have not been able to get to a place of financial comfort or the lack of communication in your marriage. In fact, the arguing is likely symptomatic of deeper relationship issues that go beyond money. Getting control of your spending isn't only going to be about forgoing cruises from now on and getting control of your money situation so that you can enjoy nice things now and then—if you want to make lasting changes, you'll also need to invest in couples counseling to help identify the problems in your relationship and fill the emotional holes between you.

This scenario shows how feelings of deprivation can stimulate overspending habits. Areas of lack and scarcity—whether fiscal, intrapersonal, or spiritual—can cause holes or voids in our lives and we may consciously or subconsciously try to compensate for this condition through money. Sometimes those voids are deeply rooted in childhood, and as adults we may buy things to fill those holes created by what we were missing as a kid. Adding to the void can be even deeper issues from feelings of abandonment, neglect, or even emotional abuse. Buying "stuff," taking trips, and staying busy distract our attention from experiencing our feelings and, more important, resolving our issues. If we're in a relationship where we feel deprived of love and affection, we may try to win back our partner's love and attention through frivolous spending.

One of my clients grew up in an impoverished environment. Throughout her childhood, she only received one pair of shoes per year. Now, as an adult, this sister has more than a hundred pairs of shoes in her closet. But no matter how many pairs of shoes she buys today, it will never compensate for what she was deprived of as a child—and this kind of unchecked spending may prevent her from having a sound financial future as well. For this reason, it's important for us to check ourselves on a regular basis and examine the motives behind each purchase we make. Very few of us were taught as kids how to handle money and credit. Sometimes we were indulged, but some of us may have been deprived and, quite automatically, developed an unquenchable thirst for material pleasures and possessions.

SCENARIO #3: You have children who are fashion conscious from watching *106 & Park* on BET and a multitude of music videos. They consistently ask for material things to keep up with their hip-hop idols, and they lash out and say hurtful things, comparing you unfavorably to other parents, whenever you try to draw the line. After all, the other kids at school always sport designer outfits and have the latest toy or gadget. Of course, you want them to have advantages that you didn't have as a child. And your self-talk says, "I'll probably never get completely out of debt, so how much difference does it make if I miss a loan payment here or there because money is short? My kids and their happiness comes first." It doesn't matter how much you juggle your bills, you'll never be able to turn your finances around if you can't say "no" to your children, either, because you fear the loss of their love or fear that you're a bad parent if you don't provide for them the way you wished your parents had provided for you.

Fear is the third common thread that I see with clients who experience challenges managing their money: Fear that there's not enough money, there's never enough money, there'll never be enough money, so I may as well spend what I have since it will likely evaporate if I don't. Fear of losing the respect of peers or loved ones if you don't keep up appearances or provide for them the way they want. Or there is a fear of taking control of your finances, which can at first seem overwhelming and unfamiliar. There is a fear of not being smart enough or doing it wrong. A fear of losing money. But as they say, knowledge is power. In my experience, knowledge is the antidote to fear. The more you know about your money and what your options are, any fear that may influence you to make poor financial choices diminishes.

Breaking the Cycle

Low self-esteem, feelings of deprivation, and fear are the three main underlying triggers for overspending that eventually land you in debt. You don't have to experience just one of these culprits, either. It's entirely possible to have low self-esteem while feeling deprived and fearful. In fact, these feelings are often intertwined, each one feeding on the other and culminating in poor spending habits. The debt that follows then incites more negative feelings, particularly ones of shame, anxiety, and failure—which in turn drive us to spend more. It ultimately makes for an ugly, vicious cycle. Breaking that cycle begins with a structured plan that entails paying down the debt, creating a realistic spending plan, and learning how to manage the emotional and sometimes physical triggers of unhealthy spending habits. I know this because I've been through it all and have taken countless other sisters through the same process, regardless of what issue plagues them the most or how deeply in debt they are.

Recall my story in the introduction. By the time Jeffrey and I divorced I felt like I was lying at the bottom of the ocean, paralyzed under the pressure and weight of my debt, professional dissatisfaction, and personal failure in my marriage. This was my rock bottom, but it was also the place I needed to reach in order to then launch myself back up to sea level and onto solid ground. For me, the breakthroughs didn't start to come until I was shocked by my life's circumstances. Prior to this awakening, I had been terribly self-righteous. I thought I knew all the answers. But in truth, I had been "addicted" to Jeffrey, and the extended periods of emotional distance between us fueled a craving inside me to find any morsel of love, affection, and support from him. So I spent lots of money, hoping to gain his approval. During the latter parts of our marriage when he showed only occasional interest in or sensitivity toward me—or our problems—his attention could provide just enough of a fix to make me feel good for a little while. The resulting high separated me from the reality of our wrecked lives. But when the high wore off, things would be no better than before.

My emotional issues with Jeffrey, which then translated into money issues, were also secretly linked to my upbringing. I had subconsciously believed that if I were the main breadwinner (like Dad), my partner would be dependent on me (like Mom) and would thus never leave. So as you can tell, I had fear issues tunneling through me, too—the fear of being left alone. My fear of losing Jeffrey further fueled more spending. But the truth was that Jeffrey had already abandoned me emotionally if not physically, and I realized I deserved to have more than that from my relationship. I deserved to be in a relationship that didn't perpetuate this vicious cycle and that could heal the wounds I'd been carving into myself for years in an unhealthy environment.

Debt and Credit Is Blind to Age, Income, Political Party, and Marital Status

Just as money is an equalizer, so is debt. Debt affects all of us—rich or poor, black or white, gay or straight, liberal or conservative. One myth about debt and poor credit that I want to get straight from the start is the idea that you have to have a low income or have dependents to fall into a financial trap. Not true. Generally speaking, the greater your assets become, including income, the greater your liabilities (and potential debt!) can become, too. So a high salary doesn't ensure you against debt and credit problems. It's all relative. Likewise, you can be a single sister with two kids and no husband and be just as much in debt as a sister with no kids and a husband with a decent income. To illustrate this point, let me show you two different families and their debt issues.

Single Sister Sydney

Sydney is a forty-five-year-old, unmarried sister who has the potential to be extremely wealthy. She has no children or obligations, like child care or college tuition. Her money is her own. As recommended in *Girl, Make Your Money Grow!*, Sydney created five streams of income. She has a full-time position, a part-time job, two home-based businesses, and rental income from a duplex she inherited from her mother. The problem is that Sydney has a spending addiction. No matter how much money she makes, she continues to spend beyond her means. If she sees someone in a sharp suit, her mind-set is "I have to have it, too!" If she needs a new outfit for a wedding, her boyfriend has to have one, too, and she buys him a $300 to $400 suit. Other times she'll spend $600 on eyewear when she knows she should say to herself, "I have a $250 budget, so what can I get?" Instead she says, "These look nice," and makes a purchase costing almost three times what was planned. Sometimes she triumphs over these impulses. Once, while shopping with friends, her eyes caught sight of a nice jacket, but she assessed the situation rationally and walked out the store saying, "It doesn't make sense to buy another jacket."

As a result of this behavior, Sydney has been through a series of loans: a $40,000 debt consolidation here, a $50,000 debt consolidation there. The latest is a $20,000 equity line of credit on top of her $297,000 first mortgage. By the way, the house had only a $100,000 mortgage when Sydney inherited it three and a half years ago. So in addition to her near-$90,000 annual income, she has spent $217,000 worth of her home's equity.

After years of denial, Sydney now admits that paying off debt and living within a budget was not a priority in her life—even when she knew she needed to watch her spending and made a budget, she never followed it. Sydney believes her main issue is that she has no clear goals and isn't inspired to make any changes to her financial habits. That's why she spends all of her cash on short-lived gratifications and then accumulates debt time after time by using credit cards. Buying things is a lot simpler than doing the work necessary to identify her financial demons and abolish them. But when I showed her the actual numbers—that she'd burned through nearly $387,000 in three and a half years between her home equity and income—she was shocked into finally taking the challenge to make those changes. Seeing the depth of her debt gave her that inspiration.

Married Sister Sabrina

It's easy to say, "Well, Sydney is a single woman without family responsibility, so it's easy for her to be irresponsible with her money." But I see similar patterns with those who have children. Take Sabrina and Darnell, who are married with two girls. Darnell works two jobs for a total of

$109,000. Sabrina has twenty-three years in the food services industry and earns $73,000 annually. Even with a household income of $182,000, they live check-to-check with frequent late payments. Sabrina and Darnell don't open bills as they come in and often bounce checks. Subconsciously, there is resistance to paying bills on time, because even if they write out the bills, sometimes they don't mail them. Financial housekeeping is not a priority. Even so, for several years now they've been uncomfortable with their debt situation.

Sabrina and Darnell pretty much handle the household finances separately. Most household bills are split 50/50, but Darnell pays $2,000 monthly toward the mortgage and Sabrina adds another $500. She never wants to track her money; she already knows she's drowning financially. Child care costs are $1,288 per month, and she believes the only way to eliminate them is if she doesn't work. Her ten-year-old Lexus has constant maintenance problems totaling about $2,000 to $3,000 each year. Ironically, the vehicle is only worth about $6,500. Sabrina's consumer debt is $39,260, with a $906 monthly payment. In addition, she took a $24,000 loan from her 401(k) plan that was used as a partial down payment for the home. Because her finances are separate from Darnell's, she's unsure about his debt situation but believes he's drowning in debt, too. The home-purchase interest rate was a whopping 10.25 percent because of past credit and collection accounts, but they both believe a new refinance could help ease Darnell's feelings of financial despair and hopelessness.

After months of financial counseling, Sabrina admits to being a compulsive spender. For example, she used her American Express card during Christmas to the tune of $3,158, plus an additional amount on her corporate credit card. On top of that, she impulse-spends month after month, unconsciously imitating what she perceives to be her husband's behavior. For example, he purchased a $500 digital camera, and she feels that if he can spend money on something he wants, she should be able to as well. Still, she knows that something is not right—even with these purchases, Darnell is always crying broke. Sabrina does not think it's women or drugs, but possibly gambling on the Internet. There's resentment and bitterness in the marriage.

There are other forces that tempt Sabrina as well. Recently, one of her girlfriends purchased new bedroom furniture. Sabrina had longed for her own new bedroom furniture for a few years and impulsively ordered a bed and frame for $3,677 for herself. Feeling justified in her decision, Sabrina remarked, "I'm going to get something *I* want." Fortunately, we had a financial counseling session scheduled for the day after she made the purchase, and after talking through her motivations, she canceled the order. However, true to the "I've got to do something for me" mind-set, she later bought an exercise program for $400 and new window treatments that cost $750.

"I'm so hungry for money, I can't think straight," Sabrina told me soon thereafter. It was time to take more serious action. We mapped out a plan and started with methods of reducing her and Darnell's outward-moving cash flow so they could pay down their debt quickly. They also had to get serious about their grand total in debt, disclosing to each other the extent of their debt problems if they were going to approach their problems as a team. One of the ways in which they decreased their expenses right away, which you'll learn more about later on, is modifying the mortgage contract with their lender and reducing the interest rate to 7.25 percent fixed for twenty-eight years. Their payment dropped from $2,400 to $1,800 per month.

Sound Familiar?

The examples I've used in this chapter are commonplace among sisters across the country. Maybe you saw yourself in one of these stories. Maybe your story isn't so bad, or perhaps it's even worse. You don't have to be working for minimum wage and supporting a family of five to have debt and credit issues. Lots of sisters with credit and debt troubles are perceived as wealthy on the outside, driving fancy cars and living in an upscale neighborhood with secure jobs and stellar reputations in the community.

The stories of Sydney and Sabrina point to the blind nature of debt and credit that can often mirror our own blindness to the underlying issues we've got that perpetuate the problems. Money problems are not limited to just one type of person; debt lurks everywhere. It can be blind to how much you make, where you live, and what kind of job you have. None of that matters if you can't manage money well.

As you're going to find through the tales I tell in this book, wealth is often an illusion. What we see on the outside is not what's really going on inside. Our society makes it easy to appear rich and stable. As we've mentioned, it's never been easier to borrow money, access credit lines, and falsely believe that money does grow on trees. Even our government falls prey to the notion that you can borrow all you want today and worry about paying it back later—much later. Hence our $8.4 trillion national debt. So in many ways, the world in which we live conspires against our efforts to live within our means and accumulate real wealth.

I ask you, what does "abundance" mean to you? Does it mean a closet full of couture suits and shoes? Or how about the freedom to do what you want when you want because you've got more than enough money in the bank to support your every desire? I'll take a guess and say you'd pick door number two. Money is not something that should conjure feelings of dread or fear in you. After all, it's the means of comfort, education, and freedom. It's what allows you to choose exactly what you want to do in life without meeting resistance and dead ends. What you learn in this book is not just for you, either. It's for your family, your spouse, your kids, and even your kids' kids that may come much later.

By the end of this book, I hope that you will have established your own definition for what abundance means to you, and work every day at fulfilling that definition.

Exercise One: How Do You Feel About Money?

Take an inventory of your emotions wrapped around money. This exercise will show how the parental behaviors that you were taught or absorbed during childhood can actually lead to emulation and/or rebellion in your adult financial patterns. Spending some time with the questions that follow will help you discover the origins of the financial drama in your life and understand how and why you spend what you do.

Answer these six questions in your journal:

- Who managed the money in your home when you were growing up?
- What kind of relationship did you have with that person?
- What did you learn about money from being in that environment?
- What negative—or positive—messages about money did you learn as you grew up?
- How does your childhood experience with money affect your spending and debting behavior today as an adult?
- Do your current money habits mirror someone else in your family—past or present? Do your money habits reflect the absolute opposite of someone who influenced you as a child?

Exercise Two: Have a Conversation with Your Credit and Your Debt

This exercise is familiar if you read *Girl, Get Your Money Straight!*, where I first asked you to "Meet Your Money." Just as important a starting point now is to have a conversation with your credit and your debt. Do each one separately. First write a letter to your credit, which is really a disguise for money. Commence a dialogue with it as if it were a person. Use your journal and write out the back-and-forth, heart-to-heart discussion.

Start by expressing your feelings about your credit. What are you afraid to look at? Why are you afraid to look at it? What's negative about your credit? What's positive about it? What observations can you make about patterns you've noticed throughout the years? How does your credit enhance your life? How does it limit you? Continue this conversation until you feel you've said everything you can say about your credit. Then let credit say what it needs to about you. And don't try to control the dialog. Allow your stream of consciousness to explore any thoughts that come to mind. Here's an example:

Dear Credit: I just love how you pay for things whenever I need it, no questions asked. You come to me at the drop of a hat, and usually in the nick of time, too. You make life seem easy, free, and affordable for anyone no matter the income size. But you do have hidden costs that you don't like to talk about until you send that monthly statement that reminds me that you're *not* free and that nothing is free in life. That's when you scare me. You are powerful, and you are sneaky! You've ruined me in a lot of ways. I can't get a good car loan, and my attempts to refinance my house have been crushed by my poor credit report.

Dear Sasha: I sense that you have a love-hate relationship with me. You like that I can pay for things quickly and conveniently, but you don't like being responsible for that payment at a later date. You don't like how your choices show up on the report I create for you—based on your actions. I want you to know that I don't aim to make your life miserable or debt-ridden. I want to make your life easier and give you the freedom to buy now and pay later under the assumption that you can, in fact, pay later. You make the choice to use or abuse me. I never hold a gun to your head and say "Spend!" The voice inside your head that says BUY is coming from deep within you. It's coming from your own issues related to feeling deprived and ill-confident. Don't blame me or use me as an excuse to cover up other stuff or issues that are really bugging you. You know what I'm talking about.

Dear Credit: I don't know what you're talking about.

Dear Sasha: Do I have to lay it all out? Your weight. Your relationship with your sister and mom. Your insecurities at work and the stress related to climbing the corporate ladder in white America. Your miscommunication with your fiancé. Need I go on? Stop using me to solve your issues around these things. You can't use credit to buy love and happiness.

Dear Credit: Gee, I never thought of it like that. This hurts! I really don't like you all that much right now. But thanks for the advice. I see your point. I'm going to try to improve my relationship with you. I'll learn to appreciate you for all the good and positive things you bring to life. I'll stop taking you for granted. If I can do those things for you, Credit, I can do them for myself.

Now go back and do the same process for your debt. Write out your dialogue with Mr. Debt. Include both positive and negative aspects about debt that come to mind. Focus on how your debt makes you feel. In a later chapter, we'll go through the difference between good and bad debt, but for now just do this exercise given what you currently know and how debt makes you feel. Here's an example:

Dear Debt: Boy, do I wish they warned us about you in school. For the most part, I see you as wicked and evil. You can make life really miserable and worrisome. You add up too quickly and don't go away easily. Other than the numbers I see on paper, I can't see you . . . and I'd really like to throw stones at you, see if I can just chip away at you until you are gone forever.

Dear Sasha: Girl, I wish you weren't so negative about me. I'm not the Devil. To the contrary, I help people establish good credit and pay for things like homes and cars. Sometimes you have to rely on me if you're ever going to get educated and pay for larger assets. Besides, if you didn't accept me along your journey in life, your credit score would go down and you'd find it hard to use my copartner—credit—to finance those purchases to begin with.

Dear Debt: How can I possibly look at you as being a good thing when I'm in the hole and powerless? You've destroyed any chance I have of achieving true wealth!

Dear Sasha: No I haven't. I am merely a consequence of your own decisions. And much to my dismay, I don't hold the power—you do. You create me, whether for good reasons or bad—and you have the power to take me away. I know a lot of people say I tend to show up unannounced and stampede through people's lives when they least expect it, but if you could see it my way, you'd understand that you hold the remote control to my actions. You get to say what kind of debt you're going to take on, when, how much, and for how long. I'm just along for the ride.

Dear Debt: Okay, I think I'm beginning to see it your way. I guess I have to change my attitude about you and see you as an object I can, in fact, control. I have to learn how to create you when I need you for good things, such as continuing my education and starting a business, and to erase you quickly when I've created you for bad things, such as to fund my vacation and Christmas spending spree. It's like you have multiple personalities!

Dear Sasha: If you want to look at it that way, go ahead. But keep in mind that *your* personality in this game is the most influential factor in what side of me you're going to see—good or bad. If you don't change your own behavior patterns and attitude about money first, you'll only see my bad side. And you'll never get the opportunity to appreciate my good side. Got it?

Dear Debt: Yeah, I think I do. Thanks. Let me focus on my spending habits and reasons for them, and hopefully I'll begin to see only the good in you. Wow. This is powerful stuff!

When you are done, congratulate yourself for being honest, as you have taken the first step to facing your finances and clearing up your credit. Feel free to take a short break before you begin Exercise Three.

Exercise Three: Digesting and Translating Your Conversations

1. Condense your conversation with credit and debt into a list of the top three concerns or issues that prevent you from successfully managing your money. Example: (1) I work in a very sophisticated office where everyone dresses more nicely than me; (2) I hate looking at my credit-card balances, because it makes me anxious; and (3) I can't handle getting and opening my mail, because there's always a past-due bill or collection notice in the pile.

2. Now, what are your top three financial goals for the next twelve months? Where do you want to be this time next year? Example: (1) I will pay off two credit cards; (2) I will start a savings account and contribute to it every month; and (3) I will study where my money goes on a monthly basis and find a way to reduce my expenses by 10 to 20 percent.

Now that you've completed the first few exercises, relax and exhale for a few minutes. Congratulate yourself for being courageous enough to take action. It's a big step on your journey to financial peace of mind. And you're moving in the right direction.

Let's press on!

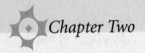

Chapter Two

Your Credit Report and Score: What They Mean and How They Work

It's so perfect and painless the way it's depicted on the TV commercial: A family eyes their shabby living and dining room, they head to the furniture store, and one credit-card swipe later, their home is fabulously furnished. Then they throw a lavish housewarming party to show off their digs, which look camera-ready for a high-end home-furnishings catalog. Presumably they make a lot of money, pay their bills on time, and never have a second thought about charging hundreds—even thousands—of dollars on their credit cards. I see these success stories on TV all the time. And I enjoy watching people grow and prosper. But more often I work with people like Deena, Sydney, Sabrina, and Darnell—those people whose stories you just read about in Chapter 1—who whip out their

credit cards just as fast to satisfy a desire that has significantly more troubling financial consequences.

Many of us are closer to the people I outlined in the previous chapter than we are to the fictional family in the TV commercial. Sisters, like
many American consumers, often have problems because we can't dis-
cern a "want" from a "need." We overextend ourselves with debt, leaving
no wiggle room in our spending plans for unanticipated expenses, emergencies—or heaven forbid, a loss of job income. Our tight finances lead
to late and sometimes missed payments, IRS debt, and medical bills. Our
credit history gets blemished and our credit score—the three-digit number that represents our creditworthiness to lenders—suffers. And there
are greater, more emotional sacrifices that result from these behaviors.
Our relationships can begin to deteriorate because of financial stress and
tension. We miss family reunions. We live in fear of a parent's illness or
demise knowing we can't afford the cost of an airline ticket home. In
addition, we endure excruciating anxiety that the state of our finances
will be exposed and the world will know just how inadequate we are.

No matter how much income we make, credit-card debt can be a challenge to deal with. On one end of the financial spectrum is Brittany—a
twenty-nine-year-old divorced mother of two girls whose income and
child support equal $45,000 annually. In 2002, she filed bankruptcy and
got rid of about $50,000 in debt. Three years later, she has accumulated
about $14,000 in new debt by purchasing a computer, clothes, and a fur
jacket. The debt also includes a slew of unpaid utility bills, day-care
expenses, and bounced checks.

Not having the right knowledge isn't the problem. Brittany knows
what to do. Taking action is the problem. She readily admits to having
poor money-management skills and a lack of discipline. The price she's
paid for this behavior is a depleted retirement account from taking hardship withdrawals from her 401(k), and disappointing her kids year after
year because they can't afford to take a vacation together. Like Deena,
Brittany also missed a job opportunity because of her dismal credit
report and low credit score. She was devastated and felt even worse about
herself after the rejection.

At the other end of the financial spectrum are Markayla and her husband of fourteen years. They have a six-figure income. But they also have six-figure consumer-credit debt—and that's without the mortgage. Sure, they make plenty of money. They say their current financial crisis is based on an *expected* windfall of cash that never arrived. But in truth, they've done this before—ran up credit cards and lines of credit, then struggled to find ways to eliminate the horrendous burden. This time, the anticipation of a large influx of cash from a lawsuit settlement resulted in some poor decisions; they rented out their house and purchased a home three times bigger to accommodate their growing family of six. Of course, with a new, much larger house came the need to fill it with new furniture. That, on top of meals out, travel, clothes, entertainment, and attorney fees, blasted them far outside of their monthly means. When their monthly consumer-debt payments reached $2,810 ($2,000 of which was going to interest), Markayla contacted me.

As an objective third person, it was obvious to me they needed someone to help them explore and evaluate their options. Markayla and her husband couldn't agree on a solution to the problem. She wanted to refinance their home again, while he wanted to sell the income property and pay off the debt.

But emotional issues prevented Markayla from seriously considering a property sale. First of all, her children had been conceived and raised in that house; it had tremendous sentimental value to her. Second, she had always envisioned that property providing college educations for her children. The market value had appreciated significantly over the years and, being in a very desirable area, the appreciation was likely to continue.

Unfortunately, after we investigated all of the options available, Markayla had to admit that the best solution to their debt crises was to sell one of their properties. Even if they could qualify for a second mortgage based on a sufficient credit score, their cash flow couldn't support the massive debt. The $105,000 consumer debt and $2,810 monthly payment had to be eliminated in order for their monthly outgo to again match the monthly income. The loss of an appreciating asset was a high cost for Markayla and her husband to pay for digging such a deep financial ditch.

What has been the trade-off for you? What hardship has your family endured in exchange for immediate gratification and the excessive debt it creates? Which of the following situations have you experienced? Review each statement below and circle the ones that apply to you now or have applied to your financial circumstances in the recent past:

1. Can't go to a family reunion or class reunion because you are lacking funds.

2. Can't go to a funeral across the country because you lack funds.

3. Can't travel to a business event or opportunity.

4. Fear of never reaching prosperity because you are living in poverty.

5. Encouraging others to have faith in their future prosperity when you are losing your own faith.

6. Can't get hair or nails done without sacrificing another bill.

7. Can't start a business because of debts.

8. Can't invest in growing your business because of debts.

9. Can't get rid of your debts.

10. Can't change or leave your job because of debts.

11. Can't financially help your children or your parents.

12. Embarrassed to ask for or accept help from your children or your parents.

13. Forced to live in your car for a period of time.

14. Drove your car without car insurance or current registration.

15. Were homeless and had to stay with family or friends.

16. Had a good job or management position, yet had to rent a room from someone because you couldn't afford your own apartment.

17. Lived in a great house, but had no furniture and little food to eat.

18. Lived in a great house, but scrimped to keep toilet paper available.

19. Had sleepless nights, crying spells, and depression that you hid from your family and friends.

20. Children forced to wear secondhand clothing.

21. Had no gifts for Christmas or birthdays.

22. Had credit card declined in front of a guest when paying for a $25 meal.

23. Made excuses to friends who wanted to come visit because you had no money available to entertain them.

24. Had to decide between using gas in your car to visit an ill family member or commute to work the following week.

25. Feared lunch tab with friends would be divided equally instead of according to actual cost spent per person.

If any of these situations apply to you, it's time to take a stand. It's time to plant your feet firmly on the ground, take a deep breath, and prepare to deal with the demons that prevent you from getting your credit straight. Remember: We're focusing on progress, not perfection, and we're taking baby steps on this journey until we're ready for a faster pace. Let's begin with some Credit 101.

Credit Bureaus

The financial history of Brittany, Markayla, you, and nearly every adult in the United States—more than 190 million people—is being maintained and stored on individual computer files. These files are maintained by independent credit bureaus that gather information from banks and other lenders on our financial behavior and credit usage. They also mill through court records looking for lawsuits, judgments, and bankruptcy filings. Searches are done of county records for liens (legal claims) against property. After gathering and tracking your credit information, they sell it to banks, finance companies, mortgage lenders, employers, landlords, insurance companies, and credit-card companies, who then use it to determine whether they want to risk doing business with you. Do you have a say in this tracking? Not really.

No matter how private a person you are, someone is monitoring how you spend money and use credit whether you like it or not. You never authorized this tracking, but it's a fact of life. And so is your credit score—that three-digit number that reflects your credit-risk level at any given time, based on your credit history up to that moment. It is a snapshot of risk at a particular time based on your history of credit management. Usually, the higher the number the less risk for the lender, who uses it as an indicator of your creditworthiness. Your credit score is calculated each time your credit report is pulled—at that very moment—based on a complex formula. So your score will change as soon as you change just one thing in your "credit picture."

This industry is unique and, in many ways, quite mysterious. Unlike other industries, like retail and restaurants, that contain thousands of competing businesses, the consumer-credit-rating industry boils down to three credit bureaus: Equifax, Experian, and TransUnion. And also unlike other industries that cater to your needs, the credit bureaus don't operate as if you're the customer. Many people make the mistake of assuming that the credit bureaus exist to serve individual consumers—you. But that's not necessarily true. As I mentioned, credit bureaus make their money selling information *about you* to other institutions. They do make money off you, but not in a traditional business-consumer sense. They offer some consumer services, including copies of your credit report and score, but that's not the center of their business.

These bureaus are competitors with one another and the information they collect on you may not be exactly the same. Just because a lender reports your credit information to one bureau does not necessarily mean the same info automatically filters to all three bureaus. A lender may report your credit information to one, two, or all of the bureaus. That said, you'll often find that your records among all three bureaus do contain similar information. But when beginning to explore your credit, you'll want to know what's in each of your files in case a discrepancy exists.

Understanding Your Credit Rights

The Fair Credit Reporting Act (FCRA) is a federal law enacted originally in 1970 that restricts who has access to your sensitive credit information

Contact Info on the Big Three

Equifax
P.O. Box 740241
Atlanta, GA 30374-0241
800-685-1111
www.equifax.com

Experian
P.O. Box 2002
Allen, TX 75013
888-397-3742
www.experian.com

Trans Union
P.O. Box 1000
Chester, PA 19022
800-916-8800
www.transunion.com

and how that information can be used. The act has been amended twice since then to keep up with our ever-changing credit industry and fast-paced world of information. The act aims to ensure some balance, rules, and accountability within the credit rating system. It's not a simple piece of legislation, but rather complex with many provisions that are designed to protect you as a consumer. (For a complete copy of the FCRA, visit the Federal Trade Commission's Web site at www.ftc.gov.)

The following are some of the FCRA's most important features:

- *Disclosure of credit report to you upon request.* The credit bureaus cannot hoard your credit report and deny you access to it. They must hand it over at your request, assuming you provide proper identification. (They can charge you a small fee.)

- *Limited access to your information.* The credit-reporting agencies cannot hand your credit report over to anybody asking for it. They can only give it to someone who has a legitimate reason and purpose for viewing it, such as to evaluate your application for a loan, credit, service, employment, and certain business and legal uses. And in many cases, they must get your permission to do so.

- *Consent required before providing your information to an employer.* You must consent in writing to the credit bureaus before they provide your information to an employer or potential employer. (While in the throes of finding a new job, we can easily give this consent without thinking about what's actually on our report, which is what happened to Deena.)

- *Investigations of disputed information.* If you report any inaccurate information in your file, the credit bureaus must promptly investigate. If the investigation fails to resolve the dispute, you may add a statement to your file explaining the matter.

- *Correction or deletion of inaccurate information.* Any information that is confirmed to be inaccurate or can no longer be valid must be corrected or deleted from your credit file. The credit-reporting agencies are not, however, required to remove *accurate* data unless it is outdated or cannot be verified.

- *Deletions of outdated information.* Any negative information must be removed from your file if it's more than seven years old (or ten years for bankruptcies).

- *Removal of your name from marketing lists upon request.* You have a right to ask ("opt-out") that the credit bureaus not share your information with marketers who send unsolicited offers. All you have to do is call 888–567–8688.

- *Identity theft and active-duty alerts.* If you've been a victim of identity theft, you can place a "fraud alert" on your file in an attempt to limit or stop further damage. Military personnel on active duty can also place alerts on their files to help prevent identity theft.

Obtaining Your Credit Report

Thanks to new legislation, you are entitled to one free credit report from each credit bureau during any twelve-month period. The reports can be ordered online from www.AnnualCreditReport.com and viewed immediately. Or they can be ordered by phone at 877–322–8228 or by mail from Annual Credit Report Request Service, P.O. Box 105281, Atlanta, GA 30348–5281. Orders by phone or mail could take up to fifteen days to be received.

You have the option of ordering all three reports at one time or staggering the orders—for example, one every four months. I suggest starting out by ordering all three reports at once to compare the differences in scores given the same financial circumstances. That way you get a complete picture and can start taking action right away. During

Beware of Freebies

Beware of offers for a "free credit report" that are not affiliated with the three main credit bureaus or the Central Source, which is the company created by the credit bureaus for purposes of administering federally mandated free credit reports once a year to consumers through Annual-CreditReport.com. Lots of scams hide in some of those free credit report offers, so you're better off getting your report directly from Equifax, Experian, and TransUnion, or by accessing those same reports through AnnualCreditReport.com.

the following year, you can stagger the requests, pulling one free report from one bureau every four months to ensure accuracy and monitor any potential identity theft. I usually check my credit report twice a year using the three major credit bureaus. Whichever way you want to do it, just make note of when you plan to check it so you don't forget.

The actual credit score, however, is not free. You can get the report for free, but the score comes extra. It's not a huge cost to bear, however, and it's definitely worth paying the extra $6 or $7 to establish a benchmark for your credit standing as you begin the process of getting your credit straight.

Credit reports have become less complicated to read and more user-friendly throughout the years. In addition to your personal information, such as name, address, phone, Social Security number, and employer, the report lists your past and present credit accounts, a record of your on-time and late payments, accounts charged off or referred to collection agencies, negative entries from the last seven years, bankruptcies from the last ten years, and public records, including tax liens and judgments. Explanations are included to help you understand positive and negative information in the report, and ideas are suggested as to how you can improve it, if necessary.

Fixing Errors

As indicated previously, you have the right to dispute any errors on your credit report. Common examples of mistakes people find on their reports include

- personal identifying information that's misspelled, long outdated, belongs to someone else, or is otherwise incorrect (i.e., your name, address, employer's info)

- someone else's information who has a similar name or Social Security number

- credit accounts that you've closed but that are still listed as open

- accounts that are not yours and you have no idea how they got there (possibly identity theft)

- incorrectly recorded balances or money owed

- failure to show a payment or other credit to your account

You can file your dispute by telephone, in writing, or online with the specific credit bureau. They have thirty days to respond to your claim or remove information that cannot be verified. It's smart to create a paper trail by sending a separate letter to each agency where a mistake is found. Be sure to explain the situation in detail and include a copy of the credit report with the faulty information highlighted. Any error that you find must be investigated by the credit-reporting agency with the creditor who supplied the data.

If disputing by telephone, be sure to have the report in front of you.

File Your Dispute Online

All three credit bureaus operate fully functional and comprehensive Web sites where you can download information and even file a dispute online. In fact, you might find it easier to handle all of your disputes online as long as you're good with keeping a record of your actions. Print out pages that prove you've filed a dispute. Set aside a section in your GIRL journal for "credit disputes" where you log your entire dispute experience.

Most important, don't forget to document the "who, what, when, where, and why" when you call: *who* you spoke to, *what* you spoke about (what's being disputed), *when* you spoke to them (date and time), *where* you called (telephone number), and *why* the item is in error. Some disputes can be taken by telephone; some you will need to do in writing. Or you can cover all of your bases by reporting disputes over the telephone and then following up in writing. Once you have written about a possible error, a creditor cannot give out information to other creditors or credit bureaus that would hurt your credit reputation until the matter is resolved. And, until your complaint is answered, the creditor also may not take any action to collect the disputed amount.

I won't lie and say that disputing items on your credit report is easy and can be accomplished overnight. It often takes a certain level of persistence and determination. Keep in mind that you're not the credit bureaus' only customer, and the lines between how the credit bureaus want to help you versus their VIP customers (businesses related to the credit industry) are fuzzy. There's little incentive for the credit bureaus to remove false and negative information from your report. Why? Because they want to keep their main customers—the creditors and lenders—happy. Your creditors and lenders are the credit bureaus' bread and butter. The more negative information on your credit report, the more interest lenders and creditors can charge you, and the more they'll slap you with fees or penalties you can't have waived when you don't play by their rules. Here's the shocker: According to David Szwak, a consumer attorney who spends most of his time suing credit bureaus over errors, more than 90 percent of credit reports have errors on them. So if anything, that's your cue to check your report!

Sometimes, as in the case of a late payment that you feel is in error, you can call the creditor directly. They can verify the date and amount of payment received and you can follow up with proof by sending in a photocopy (not the original) of the necessary documentation to that creditor. But that's the kicker: When attempting to remedy errors on your credit report, you must be able to provide proof of your claim. If I had a nickel for every time I've spoken to someone who disputed information but had no idea where the paperwork was to support the claim . . . well, let's just say I'd have quite a few dollars. This is another all-important reason to get yourself organized and have a system for keeping financial records. You must then follow the trail and make sure the creditor sends the correction to all the credit bureaus reporting the error, as well as verification to you. If you decide to contact the creditor directly in writing, you can choose to send letters to the customer-service department or to the assigned collection agency.

For billing errors, you may find it helpful to start by contacting your creditor first and clearing up the problem, then follow up to make sure the creditor reports the correction to all the bureaus showing the error. Billing errors include any charge:

- for something you didn't buy or for a purchase made by someone not authorized to use your account.

- for something that is not properly identified on your bill or is for an amount different from the actual purchase price or was entered on a date different from the purchase date.

- for something that you did not accept on delivery or that was not delivered according to agreement.

Under the Fair Debt Collection Practices Act, you have a right to obtain validation and verification of debts that are attributable to you. If you dispute a debt, within five business days of contacting the collector you will receive a copy of your validation rights, which outline what your rights are with regard to a debt you don't think is yours. (You can be notified of your validation rights verbally or in a written statement—usually in the form of a statement on a collection letter sent to you.) If, within thirty days of receiving notice of your validation rights, you send a written request to the collection agency for verification of the debt, the debt collector must stop all collection activity until it has mailed proof of the debt to you. This proof should at least consist of (1) the original amount of the debt and any attached fees, (2) when the debt was incurred, (3) the name and contact information of the original creditor, (4) a statement that the debt has not been paid and that the original creditor provided

Your Rights as a Debtor

In addition to understanding your credit rights, it's worth noting your rights as a debtor, especially as you prepare for negotiating with your lenders and creditors in the next chapter. You may have already experienced the frustration of dealing with a harassing creditor or collector and not known how to handle the conversation in the best way. Because it's far too easy for debt collectors to use abusive, deceptive, and unfair debt-collection practices, our government has enacted the Fair Debt Collection Practices Act (FDCPA) as an amendment to the Consumer Credit Protection Act. It applies to personal, family, and household debts, including money you owe for the purchase of a car, for medical care, or for credit-card accounts. Another act in the same vein as the FDCPA is the Fair Credit Collection Practices Act (FCCPA), which also sets some rules to protect you from harassing, abusive treatment. And it doesn't matter how massive your debt is. You are still protected under the law. Here's what you should know:

* Debt collectors may contact you only between 8 A.M. and 9 P.M.
* Debt collectors may not contact you at work if they know your employer disapproves.
* Debt collectors may not harass, oppress, or abuse you.
* Debt collectors may not lie when collecting debts, such as falsely implying that you have committed a crime.
* Debt collectors must identify themselves to you on the phone.
* Debt collectors must stop contacting you if you ask them to in writing.

None of these rights implies that your debts can be forgiven. If you request that a collector stop contacting you, that doesn't erase your debt or stop the collector from suing you. But if any debt collector disobeys any of your rights listed above, remind him of your rights and inform him that if he ignores your rights, you may press charges.

In the next chapter, as I guide you through the process of downsizing your debts, I'll give you a script to use if and when you encounter a harassing collector.

goods or services in consideration of the debt. Different kinds of debts, however, entail different kinds of proof. If the collector cannot verify the debt, it should be removed. If you have to go to court over the dispute, the collector will have to prove the debt is yours in court.

Verification and Validation

These two words are often used interchangeably. Technically, they may be synonymous, but in the credit-disputing world they can get confusing because they take on slightly different meanings. When you request written proof from a creditor or collector that a certain bill is yours, you are asking for *validation,* which then gets *verified* by the credit bureaus. That thirty-day time period during which you can challenge the validity of a debt in writing by demanding proof is also known as "debt validation." In short, you want to have both validation and verification of any debt you dispute. Requesting the credit bureaus' *method of verification* is important. Here's why:

Let's say that after you file your dispute with the credit bureaus, you get a notice from them that says the information you disputed has been verified as accurate. What if you still don't agree? What if you want solid proof in writing of the original record that caused the problem? You can request the method of verification, which is your right under the Fair Credit Reporting Act, section 611 (a) (7). Under this law, the credit bureaus must give you this information within fifteen days of your request. It's possible that the credit bureaus never contacted the original creditor, and instead relied on a third-party database to verify your record. They also may not admit to this tactic, in which case you have to request the original creditor's phone number and do some homework. Call the original creditor and ask for the records. If the original creditor says he doesn't have them and can't help you because your records went to a third-party collection agency, get the name and number of that person with whom you're speaking. (If the original creditor does have the record, request a copy under the Fair and Accurate Credit Transactions Act.)

If you are able to obtain your records, review them for accuracy. If

Sample Dispute Letter to a Credit Bureau

[Your Name and Address]
[date]

[Name of Credit Bureau]
[Mailing Address of Credit Bureau]
[City, State, Zip]

Attention: Consumer Relations

This letter officially informs you that my credit report shows several errors in it that must be corrected. These errors *are not* legitimate negative marks on my report from any wrongdoing on my part. They are as follows:

Item #1: I dispute ABC Bank account #12345. I have never been late on this account.

Item #2: I dispute Acme Financial Services account #1234. This account was not a charge-off; please delete.

Item #3: I dispute the balance due on Visa account #5123-4567-89; it should read $4,460—not $44,460.

Item #4: I do not have an account with XYZ Store. I don't even know what this company is, or how this balance got on my records.

Item #5: I dispute the information about my being employed by General Store Inc. I've never worked for this company.

Please investigate the above items. I know my rights under the Fair Credit Reporting Act, and I request that you immediately delete any unverifiable, inaccurate, or outdated information from my credit report.

Also, please send me an update regarding this investigation, including details on your exact method of verification. I'd like the names and all contact information for all the people you contact in relation to my dispute. If there is a change in my credit history as a result, please send an updated report to anyone who received my report within the last two years for employment purposes, or within the last year for any other purpose.

The following is complete information on me:

Name: _____

Social Security #: _____

Date of birth: _____

Contact numbers: _____

Address: _____

City: _____ State: _____ Zip Code: _____

I expect an updated copy of my report and a note about deleted items within 30 days.

Thank you for your immediate attention to this matter.

Sincerely,

Signature: _____

they are not sufficient proof of your dispute, call the credit bureaus again and notify them that the original creditor has inconclusive records. Open up a new dispute with the bureaus and file the name and number of the person whom you contacted at the original creditor. If the credit bureaus refuse to pursue your claim, threaten to sue for willful noncompliance under the Fair Credit Reporting Act, section 616. If you cannot get them to open a new dispute claim, send a certified letter with the information and include an intent-to-sue letter. In all likelihood, the credit bureaus will open a new claim, and they then have thirty days to investigate it. If you have written proof that the original creditor cannot verify and validate your negative record, send that proof on to the credit bureaus. You can also include another intent-to-sue letter if they do not remove the error.

If you do not agree with the ultimate resolution to the situation, you can always request to add a hundred-word statement to your credit report to explain your side of the story. If your dispute is serious and you believe you have a legitimate case against the credit bureaus and/or a creditor, you may want to discuss your situation with an attorney and

**Sample 100-Word Personal Statement
Added to Credit Report**

Attention: All Creditors and Lenders

As indicated by the negative mark RE: ABC Computer, I dispute an outstanding balance due of $3,250.26. ABC Computer claims to have
shipped two laptop computers to me, when I only bought one. I refuse
to pay for goods not received, and never ordered two computers. They
charged my credit card (MasterCard account number #123456789)
without my authorization. I've filed a formal dispute with all three
credit bureaus, as well as the Federal Trade Commission. I've also
reported ABC Computer to the Better Business Bureau. I hope to get
this resolved ASAP.

consider legal action. You should exhaust all of your own efforts first,
though, before seeking legal help, which can be costly.

You also have the option of contacting the Federal Trade Commission, which is the federal agency that manages consumer credit matters and aims to protect your rights as a consumer. The FTC's mission
is to prevent fraudulent, deceptive, and unfair business practices in the
marketplace and to provide information to help consumers identify,
stop, and avoid scams. This includes the Internet, telemarketing, and
identity theft. Fraud-related complaints become part of the Consumer
Sentinel, a secure online database available to hundreds of civil and
criminal law-enforcement agencies in the United States and abroad.

The Federal Trade Commission keeps an enormous volume of resources
on its Web site (*www.ftc.gov*) that can provide you with valuable information about credit, credit repair, and your rights as a consumer. To file
a complaint or to get free information on consumer issues, visit
www.ftc.gov or call its consumer response center at 1-877-FTC-HELP
(1-877-382-4357).

Fraud and Identity Theft

Today more than ever, we need to be vigilant about monitoring our credit reports, because identity theft can happen to anyone. Roughly 40 percent of all consumer fraud in the United States relates to identity theft. According to Privacy Guard, a credit-monitoring service, approximately 10 million Americans have been victims of identity theft. The scary thing is that millions of people are not checking their credit, so it could be many, many more! It's become the fastest-growing crime and it can happen in a variety of ways. From the common lost wallet, checkbook, or credit card to stolen mail, information can be taken from purchases we make in person, by telephone, or on the Internet.

What's troubling for sisters with poor credit and debt is that they are often the targets *because of* their poor credit and debt. Why? Thieves think you won't notice fraudulent activity on your accounts if you haven't been good with keeping track of your finances.

At this writing, Privacy Guard indicates, "The total cost of identity theft is approaching $50 billion a year, with the average victim losing $4,800." That alone could take up to 240 hours of making calls and writing letters to repair the damage!

I'll go into greater detail about identity theft in Chapter 8, but you need to know that identity theft is cause for immediate action. If, when you do retrieve your credit reports from the bureaus, you have any indication that fraudulent activity has happened in your name, you must do the following: (1) Contact the fraud department of any of the three major credit bureaus to place a fraud alert. The other two bureaus will be notified automatically. (2) Close the accounts that have been tampered with and file a police report. (3) Get a copy of the police report and submit it to creditors or anyone who may require proof that a crime has been committed involving your identity. (4) File a complaint with the Federal Trade Commission. And (5) Notify the Social Security Administration at (800) 269–0271 or www.ssa.gov/oig/hotline.

You won't know if you've got a problem with identity theft unless you get your credit report and scrutinize it well. In an exercise at the end of this chapter, you're going to order your report, read it carefully, identify any errors, and analyze the information carefully to make sure it all accurately relates to you. I'll list tips for avoiding ID theft in Chapter 8.

Credit Scores

When it comes to the policies of lending institutions in America, a lot has changed. Thirty years ago, in the early days of my banking career, we used what was called the "Five C's of Credit" as strong considerations when making loan decisions. The Five C's are: capacity (ability to repay), capital (bank account balances, assets), conditions (state of the national economy), collateral (an asset pledged against the loan), and character (lender's assessment of borrower's prior success in repaying loans).

Obviously, these criteria are much more subjective than credit scores today. They reflect the good old days when you had personal relationships with your local bank employees and you'd visit your banker as you would your local baker and deli counter. Lenders and creditors would know you and would base their decisions on whether or not to extend credit to you based on their knowledge of your character and circumstances. Nowadays, the nature of commerce is a lot more impersonal. The Internet means we can perform a multitude of transactions without anyone else's help except for the click of a mouse and a computer.

The idea that there's one number that signifies how well you manage money, especially borrowed money in the form of credit, and thus determines your application for credit, is very new. And there's no human interaction—no local banker who knows you're a great person to vouch for you. Credit scores are like the SAT scores for adults; they can make or break your ability to take advantage of different opportunities. Just as SAT scores facilitate the passage of high school students into college and beyond, credit scores facilitate your ability to purchase large assets like a house. Granted, scores are not the only factors that lenders consider, but they are by far the largest factor in the decisionmaking process when you apply for a loan or line of credit. So you have to pay attention to them. Think of your credit score as an index of risk to lenders and creditors. It tells the bank how likely you are to pay on time. If your score is too low, they won't approve you. Or, if it's mediocre, they may approve you but gouge you for a higher interest rate.

Based on data in your credit file, an analysis is done of your information using a complex mathematical formula to determine your credit score. These scores are known by various names. The most commonly used credit-scoring system, the FICO score, was developed by Fair Isaac Corp., a company that was founded in 1956. For decades, consumers tried to get information about the mysterious scoring system. By the end of the 1970s, most other major lenders used some kind of credit-scoring formula to approve or decline applications. It wasn't until the early 2000s that the secrecy of credit scores was revealed after E-Loan, an Internet lender, began letting people check their credit scores for free online. This defied Fair Isaac, who wanted those tallies—and the secret formulas behind their calculations—to remain behind closed doors. E-Loan's move, however, put pressure on Fair Isaac to give them up and start explaining to people how they calculated them.

Consumer advocates demanded information, and lawmakers drafted legislation. At that point, Fair Isaac decided to disclose the twenty-two factors affecting a credit score. The company did not, however, hand over the exact method by which they calculate those scores. What it gave us was the ingredients and the rough measurements to the pie, but not the exact baking instructions needed to know how it all comes together.

Today, Fair Isaac still won't go much further than dishing its twenty-two main ingredients, even when *Consumer Reports* (CR) asked the company to walk them through the math explaining how it tallies the numbers. In the August 2005 issue of the magazine, the column titled "CR Investigates" states that a 2005 survey by the Consumer Federation of America, an advocacy group, and Fair Isaac Corp. found that 49 percent of consumers do not understand that scores measure credit risk. CR goes on to say, "What is more troubling is that the proprietary formula behind this all-important number is largely a mystery and the data on which it's based are often inaccurate. Twenty-five percent of credit reports, which list your credit and borrowing activities, had errors serious enough to cause consumers to be turned down for a loan or job, according to a 2004 survey by the U.S. Public Interest Research Group." (And recall that the number of credit reports that contain any errors—whether significant or minor—has been estimated at more than 90 percent.)

Nevertheless, more than 70 percent of the nation's creditors use the FICO system to make financial decisions about consumers. When you go to Fair Isaac's Web site at www.MyFico.com, you can obtain credit reports and credit scores from each of the three credit bureaus. The credit scores, however, will be FICO scores and based on the FICO range of 300 to 850. When you go directly to a particular credit bureau's Web site, you'll encounter a new system of scoring.

It's not surprising that the Big Three credit bureaus wanted to get in on the action by selling their own credit scores based on their own secret formula. In March 2006, they finally launched, after much ado, the so-called VantageScore. (Prior to that, they each marketed their own FICO-like score with its own range of numbers.) Working together, the credit bureaus purport that this new VantageScore—while computed by each bureau separately—is based on the same formula. Remember, however, that not every bureau may contain the exact same information on you, so your VantageScore at Equifax might differ slightly from that of Trans-Union. Complicating this new scoring system is the fact that it doesn't match how FICO scales its numbers. While FICO scores range from 300 to 850, VantageScores go from a low of 501 to a high of 990. How did they arrive at this system? Well, they think it's easier to understand because it works like grades in a classroom. Anything from 900 to 990 is an A, which is excellent, anything from 800 to 899 is a B, which is pretty good, and so on.

Which score should worry you the most? Until the VantageScore system gains momentum in the credit-reporting industry and lenders begin to use that system over the FICO score, it's best to consider your FICO score as the most serious one of the bunch. At this writing, 75 percent of mortgage decisions are based on an actual FICO score. Lenders are used to the FICO system; it's tried and true, as far as they're concerned. Equifax is the only credit bureau that sells FICO scores (that might change, however) in addition to its new VantageScore. So to get all of your numbers collected in one basket, you'll have to order your FICO from either Equifax or MyFico.com, and also order your VantageScores

Focus on Your FICO Score

When you go to MyFico.com, you'll see that financial coach Suze Orman has teamed up with Fair Isaac to provide credit-score "packages" that help you obtain and understand your three FICO scores and credit report. You don't need the more comprehensive packages—you simply order your individual FICO scores (you'll have three, each one based on the information from each of the three credit bureaus) and the accompanying credit reports from Equifax, Experian, and TransUnion, for $15.95 each as of this writing. You can get all of this information from the MyFico.com site. To view your scores as tabulated by the credit bureaus, the VantageScores, you'll have to order those directly from the bureaus. Keep the costs of obtaining your scores down, however. You don't need to get all six at once. Focus on your FICO scores to start.

from each of the three bureaus. Put that FICO score on top of the others if you do decide to request all types.

I'll be honest with you. Trying to predict how your credit scores will be impacted based on changes made to your report is fascinating, frustrating, and nearly impossible at the same time. A friend of mine had a high credit score already but was determined to push it up even higher—to 800+. He acted like a possessed man—ordering reports, analyzing, disputing information, and reordering credit scores to see the changes. He was excited and enthusiastic, and he called me many times to share the upward and downward movement of the score as if it were a stock trading on the New York exchange. At one point, his TransUnion report seemed to take a hit when he personally deleted old accounts. That's what his file online showed, but when the hard copy of his report arrived in the mail, the same accounts indicated that the score had actually gone up—not down. So you see, you can never know exactly what will happen, but certain strategies are likely to make your score go up and certain strategies could make it go down. We'll be examining what those strategies are in a moment.

For some of us, it can be extremely intimidating to see all that information on our report for the first time. Even today, I get a little anxious before viewing my report. It takes me back to those school days when you got a big test back or your actual report card. From an intellectual standpoint, I know my credit report has been good for many years. I diligently work at keeping my credit straight. But emotionally, I experience anxiety in those seconds before my "test score" results pop up on the computer screen. In those few cliffhanger seconds, I fear something negative might have happened unbeknownst to me. I hope that by the end of this book you'll come to view this knowledge as empowering—when you know what's there, you can begin taking action to get your credit back on track.

Decoding the FICO Formula

While it's nearly impossible to explain the nitty-gritty, cloak-and-dagger details of how FICO tallies up your credit history into this all-important number, Fair Isaac does offer a few hints. And because FICO remains the gold standard that the other types of credit-scoring systems emulate, we'll focus on FICO's criteria here. You can bet that the scores provided by the credit bureaus entail a similar methodology. (The following is adapted from the information contained on MyFico.com, and is used with permission.)

Payment History—35 Percent

The largest factor in your credit score is, not surprisingly, your payment history. This includes all types of accounts, including credit cards, retail accounts (e.g., your Victoria's Secret and Bloomingdale's cards), utility and phone bills, installment loans, finance company accounts (e.g., your car loans), mortgage, and so on. Other factors include:

- presence of adverse public records (bankruptcy, judgments, suits, liens, wage attachments, etc.), collection items, and/or delinquency (past-due items)

- how long you've been past due on delinquent accounts

- how much you still owe on delinquent accounts or collection items

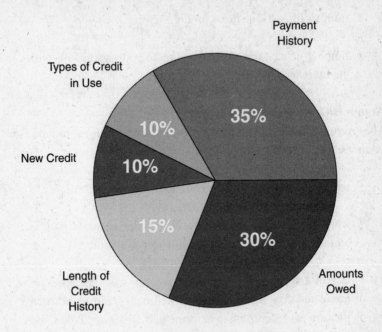

Copyright © Fair Isaac Corporation. Used with permission.

DECODING THE CREDIT SCORE FORMULA

- how much time has passed since the last time you were dealing with past-due items, adverse public records, or collection items (if any). For example, as of this writing, if you filed for bankruptcy in 2000, seven years have passed. If you filed in 2004, only three years have passed, which reflects more poorly on your record. Negative information loses its impact on your score over time. In another example, let's say you have a 60-day late payment on your record and a 90-day late payment. The 90-day late payment may appear to be the bigger mark on your record, but timing is also a factor. A 60-day late payment made just a month ago will affect your score more than a 90-day late payment from five years ago.

- number of past-due items on file

- number of accounts paid according to your agreements with creditors/lenders

Amounts Owed—30 Percent

The second-largest factor pertains to what you owe—today. This includes:

- what you currently owe on your accounts

- what you currently owe on specific *types* of accounts, such as a mortgage account versus a Home Depot account

- lack of a specific type of balance in some cases. Balances on home and auto loans can reflect well on a credit score when they are paid according to agreement. If all of your "loans" are in the form of credit-card accounts, however, you won't be nourishing your credit score as intensely.

- number of accounts with balances

- the ratio of your balances relative to your credit limits on certain types of revolving accounts

- the ratio of your balances on certain loans, such as a car loan (also called an installment loan), relative to the original amount of the loan

Length of Credit—15 Percent

This one is easy. Fifteen percent of your credit score is based on how long you've had your accounts open and how long activity on those accounts has been happening. Not every account, however, is treated as equal. As we'll see next, one type of account can weigh more heavily in your score than another type of account, whether for good or for bad. Having a home loan, for example, that you've consistently paid back in the past ten years according to the agreement will reflect very well on your credit, much more so than a regular credit card that you've had for five years. Having an eight-year-old credit card is better than having a six-month-old credit card. Your score considers both the age of your oldest account and an average age of all your accounts.

Type of Credit in Use—10 Percent

Do you have mostly credit-card accounts? Retail-store accounts? Do you have a car loan financed through your dealer? A mortgage with a bank? A business loan through a credit union? The number of various types of accounts constitutes 10 percent of your score. This also includes installment loans (e.g., car loans), mortgages, consumer-finance accounts, etc. As we just covered, different types of accounts bear different weights in your score. For another example, while a large debt such as a car loan may seem to hurt your score, if you make your payments according to your agreement, the debt is viewed as favorable. But if your debts are mostly on unsecured credit cards, this type of debt goes against your score. You want to have a healthy mix of accounts. The score also reflects the total number of accounts you have, but here's a little-known fact to keep in mind: For different credit profiles, how many is *too* many will vary. (More on this below.)

New Credit—10 Percent

This one is also easy to understand. How much of your credit history is based on new credit reflects 10 percent of your score. So this means the number and age of recently opened accounts relative to all other accounts and by type of account. Having a long history of credit with the same creditor is a good thing. Opening a flurry of new credit accounts, especially of the credit-card type or lines of credit without an asset attached, is not always a good thing. Anytime you make it look like you're overextended—or *about to become* overextended—you risk losing points.

Also included in this category are the number of recent credit inquiries made on your file, which are the requests a lender makes for your credit report or score when you apply for credit. Your score considers how long it's been since credit inquiries have been made, if any, and whether or not there's been any reestablishment of positive credit history following past payment problems. When you apply for a loan, you authorize your lender to ask for a copy of your credit report. On your report, you'll find an inquiries section, which contains a list of everyone who has accessed your credit report within the last two years (FICO scores consider only inquiries from the last twelve months). The report you see lists both "voluntary" inquiries, generated by your own requests for credit, and "involuntary" inquiries, such as when lenders order your report to give you a preapproved credit offer in the mail.

While you might have heard that it's not a good idea to check your report often, or that by accessing your report you get penalized via a drop in score points, don't worry about checking your credit report periodically to ensure that all the information is correct and to guard against your credit being assumed by identity thieves. FICO scores are designed to count only those inquiries that truly impact credit risk. Not all inquiries are created equal. In fact, the score does not count when you order your credit report or credit score. Also, the score does not count requests a lender has made for your credit report or score in order to make you a preapproved credit offer, or to review your account with them, even though you may see these inquiries on your credit report. Requests from employers are also not counted.

Just don't make a habit of accessing your report and score on a daily or weekly basis, as if you're watching the stock market. It's just not good for your peace of mind.

How often does your score change? It can change whenever your credit report changes, but it probably won't change a lot from one month to the next. In a given three-month time period, only about one in four people has a twenty-point change in their credit score. As you'll learn about shortly, a bankruptcy or late payments can lower your score fast, while improving your score takes time. That's why it's a good idea to check your score six to twelve months prior to applying for a big loan. This allows you the time to take action if needed. For those who are actively working to improve their score, it's perfectly fine to check it quarterly or even monthly to review changes.

When you shop for a mortgage or car loan, you may naturally cause

Inquiries Do Matter

According to FICO, one additional credit inquiry will take less than five points off your FICO score—for the most part. However, "inquiries can have a greater impact if you have few accounts or a short credit history. Large numbers of inquiries also mean greater risk: People with six inquiries or more on their credit reports are eight times more likely to declare bankruptcy than people with no inquiries on their reports."

multiple lenders to request your credit report, even though you're only looking for one loan. To compensate for this, the score counts multiple inquiries in any fourteen-day period as just one inquiry. In addition, the score ignores all inquiries made in the thirty days prior to scoring. So if you find a loan within thirty days, the inquiries won't affect your score while you're shopping for rates.

If any (or all!) of the above criteria sounds strange or confusing to you, you're not alone. Believe it or not, this is as close as we can get as consumers to understanding the inner workings of that credit score. Some of these criteria obviously correlate to positive marks on your score, whereas others point to potentially negative factors. Your score considers both positive and negative information in your credit report. For instance, late payments will lower your score, but establishing or reestablishing a good track record of making payments on time will raise your score.

Don't idle too much over trying to understand this breakdown. I'll help you extrapolate what you need to know so you can apply it to your own credit practices. From the above, we can draw several basic conclusions from which to create general guidelines that are relatively easy to understand and execute. I'll be with you every step of the way!

What's Not Part of Your Score
While some of the following items may be on your credit report, they do not get factored into your FICO credit score:

- your race, color, religion, national origin, sex, and marital status

- receipt of public assistance, or the exercise of any consumer right under the Consumer Credit Protection Act

- your age

- your salary, occupation, title, employer, date employed, or employment history

- where you live

- any interest rate being charged on a particular credit card or other account

- any items reported as child/family support obligations or rental agreements, unless a delinquency has occurred

- certain requests for your credit report, including your own inquiry into your report for the sake of checking it and inquiries by potential lenders, creditors, and employers

- any information not found in your credit report

- any information that is not proven to be predictive of future credit performance

What Is a Good Score?

The median FICO score in the United States is 723. *(Median,* by the way, isn't the same as *average.* This median number means half of the population scores higher than 723 and half scores below. The average credit score is actually slightly lower, at 678.) Although it varies from industry to industry, generally borrowers with scores above 740 receive the best rates. Here's the lowdown:

- mid-700s or higher get the best rates.

- low 600 to low 700s get good and bad rates, so shop around.

- less than 600 will require you to pay more for credit.

Today's lenders are more willing to provide information, so if you are seeking a loan, you can ask your lender what score you need in order to get his or her best interest rate. Also ask which credit bureau they use. It could be the difference between twenty and fifty points, which might affect your qualifying interest rate. If a lender pulls more than one credit score, it will often use whichever score represents the middle of the road. So don't assume you'll get the advantage if there's a wide fluctuation in your credit score across the different credit bureaus.

I'm going nuts! How many scores are there?

By now, you might be tearing your hair out trying to count exactly how many credit scores are out there on you. Here's the bottom line: We've all got three different VantageScores, one from each of the three different credit bureaus (using the same formula but different information); and we've all got three different FICO scores, each one based on a single formula used by Fair Isaac and employing the information provided by each of the three credit bureaus. So that makes six, and you should start by getting your three FICO scores and accompanying credit reports from the three bureaus. It's smart to check your scores as tabulated by the bureaus, too, but you can do that later. You don't want to overwhelm yourself with too much paperwork, and those per-score fees can add up. Also, be mindful of the different scoring systems and realize that a 750 from FICO is not the same as a 750 from VantageScore.

How Industries Evaluate Scores

Most people don't realize the extent to which their credit score can affect their everyday life—and even their sense of freedom. Your credit score can determine how much money you'll spend on finance charges, insurance premiums, and whether or not you can get your electricity turned on. As we saw with Deena, it can impact what jobs you'll be offered. And it can affect where you can live. Because so many entities use credit scores as a basis to assess risk, each situation is different. Advances in technology have given companies the ability to check creditworthiness in a few short minutes. The following are some examples of how scores might affect you in different scenarios.

Home Loans

A home purchase can turn from the American Dream to an American Nightmare when you're saddled with a high interest rate. If you have a low score of 500–559, you may get a $150,000 loan at a 9.29 percent interest rate and pay $1,238 a month. Interest over the life of the loan would be a whopping $295,811! With an excellent FICO score of 720–850, you could get the same $150,000 home with a 30-year mortgage at 6 percent and pay just $899 a month, with $173,757 in interest over the life of the loan—saving yourself $122,054. This example dramatically shows you in round numbers the importance of cleaning up your credit and improving your score.

Auto Loans

If you've ever sat in a dealership's "F & I" (short for "finance and insurance") office after picking out the car of your dreams and then getting down to the details of how you'll actually pay for it, you know that at some point your salesman runs a credit check on you to see if you qualify for that low, low APR he was talking about and that got you all excited in the first place. Granted, a car is much less of an item than a house, but buying one and financing it at a certain interest rate is pretty much similar to qualifying for a good home loan. The higher your FICO score, the better chance you have at landing the lower interest rate—whether you're buying or leasing. Annual percentage rates (APRs) can run from as low as 1.9 percent to more than 10 percent, which translates to the difference between paying $26,226 for a $25,000 car (at 1.9 percent) or nearly $32,000 for that same car (at 10 percent). Part of what decides your rate—besides your credit score—is how long you need that loan. The longer the loan, the higher the rate. (In March 2006, the average rate on a five-year new-car loan for a borrower with excellent credit was 6.53 percent.)

Keep in mind that you don't necessarily have to finance a car through the same place where you buy or lease it, but a lot of car dealers offer promotional financing programs that easily outdo what your bank or another lender can do interest-wise. To take advantage of those super-hot rates, however, you have to have a great credit score to start. Then you'll be in charge at the negotiating table! Buying or leasing a car can entail a lot of haggling, and having stellar credit can not only reduce that haggling but also get you the best car for the right money.

Landlord

In a competitive and busy rental and leasing world, landlords have begun to use credit checks as a tool for weeding out potentially problematic renters who might not pay rent on time or fully. If a credit screening returns poor results, landlords are legally permitted to reject a rental application, require that the applicant have a cosigner on their agreement, require an additional or larger deposit, or even charge the applicant higher rent. Ultimately, this means that having a poor credit score makes it much more difficult to have a choice in where you want to live. And if you want to live in an area where apartments go quickly and there are multiple people vying for the same great place, guess who gets first dibs on closing the rental deal? The one with the best credit.

Employment

Credit reports are a cheap and easy way to screen out applicants for those employers who do background checks. More and more employers are using them. A 2005 survey by the Society for Human Resource Management found that "19% of employers always do credit checks on job applicants, while 24% sometimes do. Findings show that the number of employers examining the credit histories of potential employees has nearly doubled since 1996." In America, the job market can often make for fierce competition among potential employees who all are jockeying for the same job. All other things being equal, imagine having the upper hand in a job application thanks to your credit score.

Insurance

Some studies have indicated that individuals with low credit scores perpetrate more fraud or file more claims even if those claims are legitimate. So individuals with long credit histories and high credit scores tend to get the best rates. The goal of every insurance company is to correlate rates for insurance policies as closely as possible with the actual cost of claims. Similar to a credit score, an insurance score is a numerical ranking that gauges how "risky" a potential insured is to an insurer. Studies show that how a person manages his or her financial affairs, which is what an insurance score indicates, is a good predictor of insurance claims. From this score, insurers figure out what kind of premium they will charge so it's equal to the risk they are assuming. In the future, some states may pass laws that prevent insurance companies from using a credit history to determine how much one pays in premiums. California has already passed such a law (Proposition 103), but who knows what really goes on behind closed doors at those insurance companies when they do their wild calculations? When you need car insurance, you need it, so it pays to have as much as possible working for you.

No matter where you stand today with your credit score, there is always hope for improvement. Don't get discouraged. I like to think of it as getting out of the victim mode and into the victory mode. It's all part of the "victorious" cycle we strive for in getting our credit straight: The lower your interest rates, the quicker you pay off your loans, the higher your credit score, the lower your new interest rate, the quicker you pay off your new loan, the higher your new credit score, and so on and so on. In fact, there are so many ways to improve your score that I've devoted an entire chapter to it (Chapter 5).

Discovering Small Slipups That Translate to Big Dings

In 2000, a real estate agent from the Bay Area formed a coalition with other real estate and banking professionals to help one million black people become first-time homeowners. They placed a two-page ad in *Essence* magazine and invited people to contact his group because they had money available to help. This agent received more than 700 applications, but amazingly was only able to qualify *thirteen* people! The others were disqualified on what's known as "thirty-day late," which means that they'd not paid bills until after they were overdue by thirty days and creditors reported it to the credit bureaus. Being thirty days late on a payment may not sound like a big deal, but it can result in a big ding in your creditworthiness.

Even if you have the money to pay your bills, it's not that hard for this to happen. One oversight or misplaced bill can easily lead to a derogatory entry on your credit report that takes years to remove. I have my own thirty-day-late story that happened a few years ago that left me so angry with myself I could hardly talk. Keep in mind my history! A decade earlier, I had been on the verge of bankruptcy with a credit report so negative, I was able to rent a house to live in only because of the generosity of a kindhearted landlord. After working extremely hard to turn my life and finances around in the ten years that followed, I was determined to keep my credit clean.

My thirty-day-late story happened in November 2003. It was a period where I was incredibly busy and highly stressed. A few years before, I had assumed the responsibility of handling my aging parents' finances after watching my elderly father have difficulty not only signing his name to a money order but struggling to get the check and bill in an envelope with the company's address showing through the window. At the same time my financial counseling practice continued to be active, I was traveling around the country doing speaking events, and on top of everything else, I was on deadline to finish the manuscript for my second book. I had been very conscientious about paying my parents' bills, as I didn't want them or my siblings to have any doubts about how I was taking care of their business. Instead, the oversight happened with my own bills.

At the time, I had a Discover Card with a $10,000 credit limit that I kept at a zero balance. The only reason I had the card was for the $100,000 travel and accident insurance policy that cost me $7.95 per month. I figured it wasn't a bad deal, considering I was in and out of airplanes and constantly traveling around the country. Every month the account was charged $7.95, and each month I paid the balance of $7.95.

Sometime around April 2004, I decided to run my semiannual credit report to ensure that everything was still in order and I was shocked to see a thirty-day-late notice showing up for Discover Card. I immediately knew it must be their error, because I hadn't been late on any bills for more than ten years. I called Discover Card and was indignant that they dare make that sort of mistake. Well, long story short, I was informed that my payment in October 2003 had never been received, and a subsequent check of my records indicated they were right. In November 2003, I had paid $15.90 and didn't think any more of it. It never dawned on me that the payment from October was actually thirty days late.

Suffice it to say, no amount of explanation, logic, and pleading could convince Discover Card or the credit bureau to remove the thirty-day late from my record. The bureau couldn't remove it unless authorized by Discover Card, and Discover Card wouldn't remove it because it was accurate information. The best solution they could offer was that I submit a 100-word statement that could be added to the credit report with my explanation.

It was hardly a satisfying resolution for me, given the drop in my credit score from the prior year. I had no need for any new credit, so I did my best to just let it go. But I was amazed at the range of emotions that resulted from this slip. The shame and embarrassment from years past came welling back up, and for a period of time I felt inadequate and incompetent once again—even though intellectually I knew it was an honest mistake.

My client Kenya is a sister who got her money straight and had a similar surprising revelation. Having paid off more than $12,000 in consumer debt and made her dream come true of buying her first home, she had come a long way in turning her finances around and was ready to see a reduction in the interest rate on her credit card. She was proud of herself—now accumulating assets and paying her bills on time. Or so she thought. To her surprise, when inquiring about the interest rate on her credit card, Kenya was told that she had been late nine times in twelve months. It took a while for this revelation to sink in. "I pay my bills every month. I never let the payments double up on the statements. And I haven't gotten any late fees," Kenya lamented. But eventually Kenya realized that her habit of mailing her payment in a day or two before the due date made it technically late, as it was received *after* the due date. This habit didn't affect her credit score, which has gone from 624 to 682 to 724 in a fourteen-month period, but because it affected her relationship with her creditor, she'll be paying a higher interest rate for a while to come.

The Universal Default Clause

Have you ever read the small print on a credit application before signing it? What about the card member agreement that accompanies your new plastic when it first arrives or when the card renews? How about the disclosure inserts that occasionally come with your monthly statements? I hate to admit it, but even though I tend to keep them, I never read them entirely. Of course, they're written in language that even experts in contract law don't fully understand. But there are traps in the fine print that you need to be aware of. One such trap is the "universal default" clause. Simply put, it allows credit-card companies to raise your interest rate if you're late making a payment, even if it's to someone else—for example, a misplaced bill for a $30 magazine subscription!

Though consumer complaints are on the rise, 39 percent of credit-card issuers apply the default rule to customers even if they have no late payments on their own card. Companies periodically check your credit report and determine if they are assuming more risk because of your payment history or higher balances with other companies and lenders. If so, your interest rate could go higher than 29 percent!

Today, some people say we live in an anticonsumer marketplace. It's easy to see why that's the sentiment in this country. With the universal default clause in effect, bankruptcy laws have changed, making it more difficult for overwhelmed consumers to erase debt. And as we'll see later, minimum monthly payments on credit cards have also increased from 2 percent to 4 percent of the outstanding balances, and late fees are assessed at $39. Who knows what's next? Let's make a commitment to position ourselves to be debt-free and minimally affected by whatever is coming down the pike.

Credit-Repair Companies

Patience. It's definitely a virtue. Unfortunately, most of us want what we want and we want it right now—including a clean credit report. Some folks will go to any length, including using credit-repair clinics to get the job done. But as you'll learn in the next chapter, you have to be very cautious with these companies and their services. You'll pay dearly for things you could do yourself. One company's fee is $599, with a one-year contract and $150 at renewal. Other companies could cost you even more.

The Federal Trade Commission warns about dealing with organizations that claim they can provide a new identity, a new file, and remove late payments, bankruptcies, or other information from your report. Remember: If the credit information is accurate, it will remain on your report for a period of time. For instance, if you were ten months late paying your cell phone bill and the cell phone company reported you, that negative piece of information is not considered erroneous or fraudulent. And it cannot be removed by you or a credit-repair company. It's part of your history. Relax. You don't need the help of an outside company to start doing the right thing. Make your payments by the due date, keep balances low, and your credit report will improve over time. If you choose to use a credit-repair company, I'll give you some tips to follow in the next chapter.

Credit-Monitoring Services

Ten years ago, no one in the general public had heard about these services. Now all the credit bureaus push for you to subscribe to one of their credit-monitoring services, which can cost more than $100 a year. These services allow you to have "real-time" information on who is accessing your credit. But these services do not necessarily give you the keys to unlock the doors to all of your credit reports and scores from all the bureaus every day. These services each have their own model for what they are providing you; for example, one service might examine all three credit reports, sift through the individual items, and rank them in order of impact on your credit report. It might also allow you to plug in a variety of credit behaviors, such as buying a car, paying off a credit-card balance, or closing accounts you don't use, and use its simulator to see how your credit score changes. Virtually all of these services have an alerting system in place for when something suspicious turns up on your credit report that can indicate identity theft, but nothing about these services is truly exceptional. You are basically paying for someone else to review and analyze your credit report. All of the services are based on paying for information that's available for free or at a very low cost.

For this reason, about the only time credit monitoring is worthwhile is when you've been a victim of identity theft or are at high risk of it. But even then, it's free and simple to have the credit bureaus flag your account and contact you when there's any activity. Bottom line: Don't be fooled into thinking you need a credit-monitoring service. Save the money and put it toward your debts.

Do Credit Scores Discriminate Against Minorities?

According to Fair Isaac, only credit-related information is provided on credit reports, so regardless of race or ethnicity, consumers with the same history would have the same score and would likely honor their financial obligations in the same way. The Equal Credit Opportunity Act also

prohibits lenders from using race, gender, or nationality when considering loan requests. But a recent Federal Reserve report based on 2004 data
indicates that blacks were more than three times as likely and Hispanics
more than twice as likely as whites to obtain higher-priced loans—1.75
percent to 2 percent above what banks normally charge their creditworthy customers. In 2004, only 8.7 percent of whites were in the higher-
priced category, while 20.3 percent were Hispanics and 32 percent were
blacks. The Fed researchers concluded that this discrepancy "may be
symptomatic of a more serious issue," but at the time of the report, more
evidence was needed to determine if banks were breaking discrimination
laws. Unfortunately, the same credit reports that keep track of these
higher-priced loans are used as background checks for employers and we
get stuck between a rock and a hard place—we can't get the job to
improve our financial status, to pay our bills on time, improve our credit
reports, and get better interest rates.

For now, we're forced to deal with the situation at hand. Our credit
history is going to be maintained by credit bureaus whether we like it or
not. But this can be seen as a blessing if you look at it like this: If racism
is still an issue with our lenders and creditors, the best way to combat it
is to use our credit reports to our advantage by making them as strong as
possible. The stronger they become, the weaker the credit industry's reasons for lending us money on poor terms. So it behooves us to be as diligent as possible in managing it properly. Once you know the rules of the
game, you can establish healthy habits that will get your credit score
straight and keep it growing!

Exercise One: Replace Old Trade-offs with New Beginnings

Go back to the list of trade-offs on pages 52–53. Review the list again, but this time write down any situation that applies to you in your journal. Next, I want you to write an affirmative "new beginnings" commitment statement that you can refer back to throughout the debt-recovery process. For example: "I am ready for a change. I know I have to make some sacrifices. I will do so with my eye on the prize. I embrace the prospect of financial peace of mind. I am worthy to receive it. I will make this my best year yet."

Exercise Two: Prepare to Meet Your Credit

It is extremely important to read and understand your credit report, but the process can certainly be daunting and anxiety-provoking. So let's begin by doing a five-minute relaxation exercise. First, find the most comfortable chair in your home. Sit down, close your eyes, and start to breathe slowly and deeply in through your nose. Imagine that your body is a balloon being filled with air as you breathe in. Then slowly breathe out through your mouth, allowing the balloon—your body—to deflate, and relax every muscle from head to toe as the air is released back into the atmosphere. Do this ten times, counting at the end of each exhale. Remember to breathe slowly, with the conscious intent to relax your mind as well as your body. When you have finished, slowly open your eyes and confidently move to the computer where you'll be ordering your credit report. Know that the credit report is merely a reflection of your past credit behavior and you are ready to review it but not "be" it. You have already chosen to improve it for the future, so there is no reason to beat yourself up no matter what is revealed. Note: If you are placing the order by mail or telephone, follow these steps when you have the actual credit report in hand.

Exercise Three: Your Credit Report

1. Order a copy of your credit report from each major bureau at least once per year. A three-in-one report is available from www.MyFico.com. Free reports are available, by law, once per year at www.annualcreditreport.com or by calling 877-322-8228. You'll receive the report, but not your credit scores. Even though it will cost you a few bucks extra to get the scores, it's worth it, so go ahead and order them to complete your analysis.

   Note: As I detailed in the chapter, the three credit bureaus have their own scoring systems now, so you may not be accessing your FICO scores when you order your free annual credit report and scores from the bureaus. Likewise, to view your VantageScores, you'll have to buy them from the bureaus themselves and not on MyFico.com. Focus on your FICO scores first. And keep in mind that you'll have three FICO scores, based on the three different credit bureaus reporting your information. For a recap of how many scores you should have and need, see the box on page (79).

2. Begin checking the report for inaccuracies based on your own recollection of accounts and your own records of statements and information. Use a colored highlighter pen and mark any information that strikes you as inaccurate or incorrect. At the same time, on a separate sheet of paper, make a list of any accounts showing unpaid collections (e.g., Mercy Medical, #555316 dated 11/02/03, balance = $888.60; Capital One Bank, #1234, $2,336.56 as of 04/16/04). Do read the entire report carefully to verify accuracy of the information. Common errors are (1) accounts that don't belong to you, (2) inaccurate information about your history, (3) outdated information, and (4) incomplete information.

   Check all the accounts, balances, dates, and credit limits. Also check the inquiry section at the back of the report; this tells you who has asked to see your credit report in the past two years. Other than the promotional inquiries (i.e., inquiries banks and credit-card companies make in order to offer you new lines of credit, such as a "preapproved credit card"), you should verify that you authorized the inquiry for any companies listed.

3. Now go back to the list of the unpaid collections and prioritize them by date. Determine if you want to pay those that are close to "expiring" due to the seven-year reporting period. You might want to consider how much is owed on the debt, the type of creditor you owe, and more important, what moral obligation you feel to satisfy the debt.

Note: Because the statute of limitations varies from state to state, you'll want to analyze your entire report before contacting creditors to update, acknowledge, or pay off old unpaid debts and collection accounts. You could end up "re-aging" your account and begin the seven-year reporting period all over again. "Re-aging" accounts is a tactic you'll learn about in the next chapter. It can be a good idea when you aim to pay your debt and clear up your credit.

I do not endorse letting old debts go no matter how old they are; you can't ever know when an old debt will come back to haunt you. Even though the credit-reporting industry has seven-year cycles (up to ten for bankruptcies), a creditor might keep you on *its* records forever and you may never be able to go back to that creditor again. This is why considering the type of creditor in question is important.

4. Correct errors and dispute inaccurate information. Write or call the appropriate credit bureau. Get an explanation of the entry. You may be referred back to the creditor for a more detailed explanation as to why the information was reported.

5. If you have a problem with the bureaus not resolving or responding to your credit issues, contact the Federal Trade Commission (www.ftc.gov), which regulates credit bureaus under the Fair Credit Reporting Act and by state law. Under "Consumer Information," you'll find a section devoted entirely to credit issues.

Getting Straight Do's and Don'ts

DON'T berate yourself or panic if the report reflects negative information. It may remain on the report for a number of years, but you can establish timely accounts and maintain a satisfying quality of life in the meantime.

DO spend time reading and rereading your report. Let your eyes get used to the layout and the organization of information. Revisit the report the next day to make sure that you digested everything.

DON'T order credit reports from companies that advertise they can obtain your credit report for free. They generally add your name and data to files and later sell the information for solicitation purposes or automatically sign you up for a free thirty-day trial membership in a credit-report information service. After you are signed up, if you do not cancel within 30 days you are assessed an annual membership fee of about $100 or more.

DO keep good records. Document everything you do. If disputing by telephone, remember to document the "who, what, when, where, and why": who you spoke to (name and employee ID number), what you spoke about (what's being disputed), when you spoke to them (date and time), where you called (telephone number), and why the item is in error.

 *Part Two*

Climbing Out of the Hole: Practical Tools and Debt-Reducing Strategies

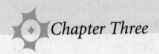

Chapter Three

Pay Off Debts and Get Your Priorities Straight

I get a kick out of it when I meet sisters who swear that when reading the stories and anecdotes I use in my books and magazine articles, I've somehow entered their private lives, witnessed their money dramas, and then shared the details of their innermost financial fears. But of course, these are women I've never met before or spoken to in my life! Suffice it to say, whatever money problems are described here, they are not unique to any one person. And no matter how isolated you feel, you are not alone in your suffering.

Perhaps you've picked up this book to simply work on paying down those credit cards in a more deliberate, organized fashion. And that's great. If you've never created an excessive debt problem for yourself, you can consider yourself lucky. But if you do have serious debt, the point is to not operate blindly or think you're standing alone out on some island.

As I mentioned in the first chapter, the average American family carried about $9,300 in credit-card debt in 2005. I suspect in many cases the amount is far greater than that, however. Maybe it's because the majority of clients I see have debt in excess of that figure.

In this chapter, we're going to begin taking action to start reducing your debt, so take a deep breath and sit down in a comfortable place. You may want to read this entire chapter first before you go back to reread and complete the steps. Try to avoid any distractions. Unlike other chapters that have multiple exercises at the end, you've got only one exercise to do here. If you flip to page 139, you'll see that I've created an outline of the steps detailed at length in this chapter. So if you read through and digest this material once, you can then go back and treat the entire chapter as a series of exercises.

Some of you may have to work simultaneously with this chapter and the next chapter, which details spending plans. You may, for instance, have trouble completing some of the debt-reducing strategies in this chapter because you don't know what available funds you'll have for making new payment arrangements with your creditors. It's okay if you come across instructions in this chapter where you say, "I can't do that yet because I don't know how much I can put toward paying that bill on a monthly basis." Just be patient. Between the information you take in here and in the following chapter, you'll have all you need to then see the big picture and consider your debt reduction strategies in relation to your spending plan. For purposes of having a starting point, however, it's important to know how to prioritize your debts and their eventual payoff.

Where to Start

When my new client, Morgan, shared her financial frustration, I had heard it many times before: "I just got paid. I have no money. I don't know where it went. And I don't know where to begin to deal with this." Then came nervous laughter, followed by the admission "Plus my mortgage is three months past due." Where did Morgan's money go? It didn't take long to figure out that a few months ago Morgan had panicked and sought out a quick-fix situation to her debt that came with a long-term devastating consequence: She now owed $2,000 to a payday-advance company, which was sucking her dry. (More on how these companies operate later; they can entail a more-than-900-percent interest rate!) Now, overwhelmed and disorganized, she was totally confused about how to even begin to tackle the problem. I told her right away, "First things first. You need to get clarity, find out where all your money is going, where it should be going, and when it needs to get there." Morgan then pulled from her tote bag a slew of envelopes and bills, some open, some not, and we got to work.

This is what you're going to do, too.

Step 1. Get Clear: Calculate Your Debt

If you've been avoiding your mail because you're afraid to face those bills and maybe even collection notices, it's time to put an end to that habit. Denial of debt is hurting you in more ways than you think. Once you take notice of those bills and acknowledge where your money goes, plus where your debt lies, a sense of calmness will begin to sweep over you. Why? Because you'll be gaining control of a previously out-of-control situation. The clarity that comes with knowing where your money goes and should go—even if it exceeds your income at this point—is tremendously powerful. Which is why **clarifying your debt** is step one. Shining a light into those previously dark corners will give you the strength you need to forge ahead and get your credit straight once and for all.

1. **Get clarity.** Gather all of your mail and bill paperwork, open *everything,* and sort by category in separate piles: credit cards, utility bills, student loans, mortgage, etc. Categorize to the best of your ability, based on what seems to go together naturally in one pile and what should be isolated from the rest. For example, if you've got medical bills and vet bills, you may want to file all the human medical bills together and your veterinary bills separately. Assuming you've already retrieved your credit report, you can use that to guide you as you hunt down all the

paperwork to support the bills and their accounts enumerated on the report. Dump all excess paper—advertisements, subscription renewals, solicitations, catalogs—immediately. If you've got a pile of old mail and unopened bills lying in a basket somewhere, go get it and sort through that, too. Leave no stone unturned. If you find multiple statements from one account, organize by date with the most current bill on top. Keep a stapler handy so you can keep all the materials for each bill or statement together and avoid getting pages mixed up. Remember, clarity will lead to power.

2. **List and assess the debts.** Now do a summary of your outstanding debts, including mortgage, credit cards, car loans, bank loans, and personal loans. List the creditor, balance, monthly payment, interest rate, and credit limit for each. Indicate the status of the accounts: current, thirty days past due, collection, etc. Verify the payment due dates and make a note of them.

Step 2. Prioritize Your Debts: Who Gets Paid First

You've got a gas and heating bill in your right hand and a Home Depot bill in your left hand. Which do you pay first? In this step, we're going to figure it out. When money is tight and you have to choose who gets paid and who doesn't, you don't just want to go with the squeaky wheel first. You'll need to prioritize payments to put the things necessary to maintain health and safety for your family at the top of the list.

No matter what you consider to be your biggest, most burdensome debt, here is the number-one rule you must follow: **Pay for absolute necessities first.** That means taking care of bills that put a roof over your head (i.e., rent or mortgage), heat and provide energy to your house (i.e., utilities, water, etc.), feed you (i.e., basic groceries), transport you to work and back (i.e., car payment), and allow you to communicate to the out-

Debt Summary

Month/Year _____

Creditor	Balance	Credit Line	Monthly Payment	Due Date	Proposed Monthly Payment	Finance/ Late Charges	% of Total Debt	Int. Rate	Status
TOTAL:									

side world (i.e., phone). Other necessities that should go on the top part of the list include child support, which, if forgotten, can land you in jail, and any medical emergencies you might have. If you have health insurance, you must pay that premium, too.

The Three Categories of Payment Priorities

Category 1: Necessities. Food, shelter, transportation, and dependent and personal care.

Food. It's important to nourish yourself and your family even if a financial crisis hits the household. Pay for basic food and essential medical expenses first, including health insurance. This does not mean dinner at fancy restaurants or a $5 frappuccino on your way to work! You won't have to avoid eating out forever, but for now, as you're getting started, you need to keep food expenses to a bare minimum. Don't spend $30 on Chinese takeout food or $20 on pork chops when the electric bill is unpaid. Think spaghetti or casseroles. Use coupons, buy groceries, and cook.

Shelter. Housing is essential for the health and safety of your family. Your mortgage or rent should be your next priority. Also included in this category are your utility payments, homeowner's insurance, and property taxes. You don't want the humiliation of eviction or foreclosure proceedings, and you also don't want to fear that the lights, heat, water, or phone will be turned off.

Transportation. You must have a source of transportation to your job in order to maintain a steady flow of income. If you need your vehicle for this purpose, make your car loan or lease payment next, along with automobile insurance. Nonpayment of a car note could lead to repossession and a major blemish on your credit report. Also, don't force your lender to put insurance on your vehicle, because it's too expensive, and in most states it's illegal not to have at least liability coverage. One thing to keep in mind is that you can save on payments, gasoline, repairs, insurance, and registration fees if you can limit yourself to one vehicle in the household. Work out a transportation schedule to meet family needs. It's worth the short-term sacrifice for the long-term gain of financial stability. Taking public transportation wherever possible will also help you save money on gas.

Dependent Care. Child-care expenses are important to pay so you can work without unnecessary worry about your children. Child-support payments are also essential because the possible alternative is wage garnishment and/or jail time.

Personal Care. Personal-care expenses are a priority—we all need to remain neat and clean for our jobs and families, especially if you are looking for work. However, at this time your personal-care expenses should include only the bare-bones minimums for hair care, toiletries, dry cleaning, and laundry. Visits to the hair or nail salon, or high-end cosmetics and beauty products, are now a luxury, not a necessity. Starting now, you must commit to spending only on things that are essential.

Category 2: Back taxes and student loans. These types of debts can feel most burdensome, especially if they are large. Luckily, debts with the IRS and your student-loan companies aren't like other kinds of debt, and as such they get treated separately.

If you owe unpaid taxes, the IRS can garnish your paycheck, take money from your bank accounts, or put a lien on your house and other property. However, the IRS will work with you to come up with a schedule of payments. Whatever you do, don't avoid filing when taxes are due. Not filing can result in penalties and interest of up to 25 percent of what you owe.

Student loans represent another special category. Because most student loans are backed by the government, the government can come after you in ways other creditors can't. If you're delinquent on paying back your student loans, Uncle Sam can seize your tax refunds and garnish your wages and, in some cases, your Social Security benefits. Fortunately, the government offers many solutions if you can't afford to make those student-loan payments, which we'll get to shortly.

Category 3: All other debts. Credit cards, store cards, gasoline cards, payments for furniture or appliances, personal loans from family and friends.

Some of these loans may be secured by an asset, such as furniture, boats, expensive electronic equipment, or anything you signed a security agreement for as collateral that can be repossessed by the lender. (Don't forget that homes and cars are secured debts unless you own them outright. They should be considered top priority because they relate to basic necessities—unless you've got more than one home or car.)

Hopefully, family and friends will be the most understanding of your creditors. Keep communication open, be honest, and confirm your commitment to repay the debt in full. Failure to do so will likely create anger and resentment, and possibly destroy the relationship.

Edgar and Emily

Clarifying their debts helped two of my clients, Emily and Edgar, enormously. For years, this fifty-something couple had focused on maintaining a steady base of clients for their janitorial business. Married twenty-five years, they became parents to a daughter, Alicia, only twelve years ago. In addition to expenses for private school and braces, they did a pretty fair job of keeping three employees and the occasional subcontractors paid on time while slowly growing their business over the years. At times, they were compelled to use personal credit cards to keep things operating smoothly. "We have good credit and everything is paid on time," Edgar remarked during their first financial counseling session after being referred to me by their accountant. However, anxiety and feelings of being overwhelmed began to show on Emily's face. "Yes," she declared, "but I feel our personal finances are beginning to spiral out of control." Then she went on: "It's the blizzard of bills that land in our mailbox every month that has me worried," she said, referring to the nine credit-card accounts they maintained.

Within the next two hours, we clarified their debts and then went on to map out which debts needed to be paid first, second, third, and so on. It was evident some changes could be made to simplify their bookkeeping. None of the nine accounts carried balances at the maximum credit limit, but they each had interest rates ranging from 3.9 percent to 23.9 percent.

Edgar and Emily immediately implemented a consolidation plan. At their next appointment they were confident and calm, having reduced their nine credit-card balances down to just four.

Prioritizing debt is the natural second step once you've clarified your debt. With the dollar amounts and bills in front of you, it's time to start taking action. Simplifying debt entails designing a plan for each type of debt you have, starting with the most important debt and considering basic bills that support your general health and everyday life. You'll also base your plan on what each debt is costing you, such as a credit card that charges you 13.9 percent interest versus another one that charges you 29.9 percent interest. Edgar and Emily implemented a formal consolidation plan to get rid of the balance on the cards with the highest interest.

Before you can really start tackling your debt, however, you'll need to have a clear sense of your resources, which will then work in tandem with your debt-reduction efforts. This exercise will also help you configure your spending plan in the next chapter.

Step 3. Figure Out Your Resources

Now it's time to figure out what resources you have that can reduce and eliminate your debt. Grab a pen, open up your journal, and list your assets and all sources of income due in the upcoming month that can off-set your expenses and debts. Here's a list to guide you:

Sources of Income

>   Average net monthly take-home pay, considering net wages, salary, commissions, and overtime
>
>   Income from operating a business or profession
>
>   Income from real estate (such as a rented room in your home)
>
>   Income from interest and dividends
>
>   Alimony, maintenance, or support payments
>
>   Social Security, unemployment, or other government assistance
>
>   Income from a trust or other such financial vehicle
>
>   Income from disability or life insurance
>
>   Income from miscellaneous activities, such as selling goods on eBay or freelancing

Assets

>   Cash
>
>   Checking accounts
>
>   Savings accounts
>
>   Certificates of deposit
>
>   Stocks, including options, and bonds
>
>   Money market funds
>
>   Mutual funds
>
>   Automobiles (calculate your equity by subtracting what you still owe on each vehicle from its current market value)
>
>   Primary real estate (list your equity only—its current market value minus what you owe your mortgage lender)
>
>   Income property (include equity only)
>
>   Retirement accounts (IRAs, 401(k)s, SEP, Keogh, etc.)
>
>   Business interest, partnerships, and joint ventures
>
>   Cash value of life insurance

Annuities

Money owed to you by others

Household furnishings, including audio, video, and computer
   equipment

Art or other collectibles, including antiques

Clothing, furs, and jewelry

Sporting and hobby equipment, including firearms

Tax refunds

Unimproved land

At the very least, this exercise should give you a rough estimate of your monthly *liquid* income—the cash that comes in for your disposal without you having to sell anything or cash out an investment account. Calculate your total liquid income and write it in your notebook.

Looking at Your Assets as Sources of Money

Not all assets are created equal. If you find a stash of cash somewhere among your assets, such as an inheritance or a retirement fund, that can save the day and take care of serious debt, let me warn you that unless you work toward changing your behavior with money and spending, you'll quickly wind up back where you started from and you'll have lost valuable assets that you may never be able to recoup again. Draining a retirement fund, for example, for purposes of paying down debt should be a carefully thought-out decision. Family money you've inherited and that was originally meant to help pay for a home can also vanish in the blink of an eye if you use it toward debt and then don't change your habits.

The lesson: When you evaluate your assets as potential sources of money to pay down debt, consider how difficult it will be to replace those assets in the future. In other words, think about the replacement cost of those assets and if you can really afford to lose them. (See "Top Ten Sources to Put Toward Debt.")

Your best source of money to put toward debt is your liquid monthly income and any extra income you can generate (the topic of Chapter 7). It's also okay to dip into savings, as long as you keep a small cushion—enough to cover your most important living expenses for a

Top Ten Sources to Put Toward Debt

Money owed to you by others

Extra income from current employment

Supplemental income from additional employment or freelance work

Money saved from downsizing living expenses

Sale of underutilized household goods, including furnishings, audio, video, and computer equipment

Sale of art or other collectibles, including antiques (*not* family heirlooms)

Sale of items you've got too much of, including clothing, shoes, accessories, jewelry

Sale of sporting and hobby equipment you rarely use (rent skis in the future, don't own them)

Savings

Stocks sold from a trading account (*not* a retirement account)

month or more. It doesn't have to be an all or nothing approach. If you have $5,000 in savings, for example, and you have a credit card balance of $20,000, you don't have to put all of your savings toward your balance if that makes you uncomfortable. It's okay to allocate a percentage, such as half, toward your debt and keep the rest in savings. Think about selling some of your less desirable assets and applying those proceeds to your debts. If, for example, you've got three extra televisions and appliances or gadgets you never use, consider selling them on eBay or the online classified ads at a site like Craigslist.com, or have a weekend garage sale. This may give you some much-needed cash to pay down some of those balances.

Okay, now let's get right to debt organization.

Step 4. Get a Plan

Planning your debt repayment starts with taking that inventory of your debt and assets, which you've done in Steps 1–3, and setting forth a way to synchronize paying down the debt using what you've got and in a responsible, timely manner. In this step, you're going to map out how you're going to address each and every debt, one by one, according to each one's priority. If your electricity and water is about to be shut off, you must take action quickly. As we've discussed, you must take care of your most immediate concerns first.

It's far too easy to think the creditors and lenders are out to get you when you're in debt up to your earrings, behind in payments, or you've got bad credit. On the contrary, they don't want to see you swallowed up by debt and will work with you if you take the steps to address the problem and treat it seriously. Getting on the phone and broaching the conversation is a courageous step in the right direction. Create a telephone log section in your journal that documents all your conversations. Set aside a page or two for each account, and keep them all separate. At the top of the page, record the account name, number, balance, and the account's corresponding lender or creditor's contact info. Include any identifying details you want that help you know what you're looking at. For example:

> Account name: Mercy Medical (visit on 11/15/05)
> Account number: 40016X
> Balance: $485
> Contact: 800–123–4567

> Account name: MBNA (credit card)
> Account number: 1234–5678–9123
> Balance: $6,788

Your first order of business is to attend to any accounts related to basic necessities, then back taxes and student loans. You must get current with basic bills before you establish a debt-repayment plan for past-due loans and credit cards. By now you should know which of your debts you need to address first, given your circumstances. Contact your mortgage and car lender, for instance, and explain your intention to get back on track, and that you need to reach an agreement with them over the terms of your payments. If you have an asset that you deem a necessity, such as a car, you'll need to keep up with payments or risk losing possession of the item. If a debt relates to a service you need, such as a gas card to fuel your ride to work and back, make it a priority to bring those accounts up to date. If these accounts are unpaid, you could temporarily lose privileges, have the accounts closed, or possibly be sued if the unpaid balance is high. In fact, paying for gas might be something you'll want to do with cash rather than a card. Later in the book I'm going to show you a cash-only system that can help you reduce your expenses, especially those that vary month to month and are typically paid out-of-pocket. If you've got unpaid bills for legal and accounting services, you'll want to contact the creditor and work out a minimal payment arrangement. If unpaid, these bills can be turned over to a collection agency and show up on your credit report.

Mortgage lenders and car-financing companies have a different relationship with you than do your credit-card companies. (The same goes for the IRS and student-loan companies, which I'll explain how to handle in a moment.) Foreclosing homes, repossessing cars, and garnishing wages is not a goal of any financial institution; remember that when you speak with them on the phone. They are not your enemy; they are, in many ways, co-partners in your journey toward freedom from the debt (and toward homeownership, car ownership, etc.). Share with them what you can realistically afford to pay them regularly each month, and ask if they can lower your interest rate for a period of time and waive any fees or charges related to your late payments or nonpayments. You won't be the first person who's called with such a problem, so don't hesitate to ask how they typically handle a situation like yours. Stress your goal of fixing the debt. They will likely work with you in a way that's mutually beneficial.

If your utilities account is past due, contact your local utility company and request a payment arrangement based on your ability to pay. In some cases, a down payment may be required before a bill can be divided for a number of months, but you must stay current on future bills. If you have a large bill and are considered a low-income customer, you may qualify for a number of special programs. Check the brochures included in your monthly billing statements. Utility companies often run budget programs where you pay a set amount each month. The annual bill is averaged over a twelve-month period so you can avoid extremely large bills during winter months. If you're in a dire situation and can't work out a solution with the utility company, contact your local Social Services Agency, Salvation Army—(800) SAL-ARMY—your local church, United Way, or Society of St. Vincent de Paul for budget or emergency assistance programs.

Don't be afraid to negotiate a payment plan with your doctors and hospitals for medical bills, especially if you've got a balance due that's impossible to handle in one payment. Suggest a three-month or six-month arrangement. If the bill is especially large, you may be requested to make a financial disclosure (provide a tax return, pay stub, and savings balance) to determine an appropriate payment. If you communicate your financial status with your hospital or physician, and sincerely try to work out an arrangement that ends in full payment, you can usually prevent collection and/or lawsuits. To find resources, ask questions of doctors, nurses, social workers, and your local United Way. There are many private organizations and foundations with funds to assist you.

How to Take Care of Back Taxes and Student Loans

Once you've cleared up any debts related to basic needs, category 2 debts must be addressed. Here's the action you should take, step by step:

For taxes: Go to www.irs.gov and locate the nearest IRS office so you can have a face-to-face conversation with someone or set up an appointment. The IRS operates a number of offices nationwide. You can also start by making a phone call (1–800–829–1040) and asking what your best course of action should be, which may include setting up an appointment to speak with a representative who can create a payment schedule for you. If there is no IRS office close to you, definitely start with the phone call. A list of contact numbers is located on the IRS Web site (go to "Contact IRS"). Another option is to consult with a professional tax advisor, an enrolled agent, or attorney who can help you deal with the IRS. Ask family members and friends for referrals. You will likely pay a fee for this service, however.

For student loans: The ball and chain of many otherwise debt-free sisters, student loans can feel like an inescapable nightmare that won't ever go away. The good news is that student loans financed one of your greatest assets—your education, which will finance your future and reward you in ways that no other "debt" can do. It's been estimated that over the course of a lifetime, the value of a college education is about $2.1 million in earnings. So the pros definitely outweigh the cons to getting educated and taking on that debt. The other good news about student-loan debt is that there are specific systems in place for helping you deal with this debt, including the ability to get your loans deferred or canceled.

Here's how you can take charge of student loans in five easy steps:

1. Locate your loan paperwork. If you don't have a clue where it is, use the National Student Clearinghouse's loan locator at www .studentclearinghouse.org (click on the Students & Alumni tab). You can also locate your loans through the National Student Loan Data System at www.nslds.ed.gov, which the U.S. Department of Education maintains.

2. Contact your lenders and start discussing your options. Because loans can be resold to other lenders, you may not be dealing with your original lender. That's okay. Find out if you can qualify for getting your loans (1) canceled, or (2) deferred, with or without interest accruing. Your options will depend on the type of loan you have and other factors, like what kind of a job you have and whether or not you are disabled or have a dependent who is disabled. For example, some loans allow full or partial "forgiveness" if you are a teacher in a low-income public school, serve in the military or Peace Corps, or have a career in law enforcement.

3. If you can't get your loans partially or completely canceled based on your circumstances, ask for a deferment. This means you request that you delay your loan payments. Again, you have to meet certain criteria to qualify for this grace period, but it's automatic if you do. If your loan was subsidized by the government, such as a Stafford loan, you won't accrue interest during that grace period. But interest will accrue on unsubsi-

dized loans that, while not due during your deferment, will be due eventually.

4. If deferment isn't an option for you, ask for forbearance. This is the next-best thing to a deferment. It delays your payments but does entail interest accruing during your grace period whether or not your loan was subsidized. You'll also have to qualify for this arrangement, but ask your lender if it can apply to you.

5. Consider student-loan consolidation. Having multiple student-loan accounts can make simplifying debt an extra challenge. Added to that frustration is the fact that those loans each carry variable interest rates that change once a year—July

Which Loans Can I Consolidate?

The types of loans that you can consolidate include:

Federal Stafford Loans (both subsidized and unsubsidized)

Federal PLUS Loans (for parents)

Federal Family Education Loan Program and Direct Loan Program

Federal Insured Student Loans

Federal Nursing Student Loans

Federal Supplemental Loans for Students

Loans for Disadvantaged Students

Health Professions Student Loans

Health Education Assistance Loans

Note: If your loans are all from the same lender, you must consolidate with that lender. Otherwise, you can choose where you want to consolidate, shopping for the best loan source. Points of contact for student-loan consolidation: Sallie Mae, www.salliemae.com or call 800-448-3533; and the Department of Education, http://loanconsolidation.ed.gov or call 800-557-7392. And for more detailed instructions on managing student-loan debt, check out *Take Control of Your Student Loan Debt* by Robin Leonard and Deanne Loonin (NOLO).

1—based on the going Treasury bill index rate. Although these rates tend to be cheap relative to other loans, no one can guarantee that they'll remain low. With a loan-consolidation plan, however, you lump all of your student loan accounts together into one and lock in a fixed interest rate for the life of your loan. This approach does have some caveats: (a) you no longer qualify for deferment or forbearance, (b) you lock yourself into a steady repayment plan that you can't easily change, and (c) if you do qualify for loan cancellation based on a future type of employment, you won't necessarily be able to apply for that cancellation.

If your student loans were from a private lender who won't allow you to consolidate, request a new repayment plan. Ask about different repayment options and consider each option in light of your limitations and goals. Make sure you're aware of how much you'll owe each month, what interest you are being charged and if that will change, as well as how long you'll need to make payments to complete the contract.

The most lenient aspect to student loans is that they allow you to choose a repayment plan that fits your budget, no matter how long it takes to pay it all off. Depending on how much you owe, you can take five, ten, or even thirty years to pay back your loans. Obviously, it would be nice to pay it off as soon as possible to avoid those interest payments. But keep in mind that student loans are of a different breed from, say, consumer-debt loans. Student loans typically have low interest rates and can still exist even when you take on other large debts, such as a mortgage. I will say, however, that having enormous student loans can affect your ability to afford a mortgage. So keep that in mind when increasing student loan balances. Don't be a professional student; start early to seek scholarships and grants. There are lots of programs out there—you just have to find them. Check out www.FastWeb.com for 1.3 million scholarship opportunities, or check the Women's Resource Center at your local university.

One sister, Kiki, asked her lender to automatically deduct a loan payment from her bank account once a month, and was rewarded with a deduction of .25 in her interest rate. When another sister, Tami, kept up with her payments for a full three years, her lender rewarded her with another decrease in her interest rate by a full percentage point. The lesson: You can negotiate anything once you begin to work with your lender and show proof that you're willing to meet your obligations to the best of your ability.

One final note about student loans: You may be eligible for a tax break by deducting up to $2,500 a year in interest payments that you make on your loans. For example, if you're single and make less than $50,000 a year, or if you and your husband file jointly and your combined income is less than $100,000, you'll probably qualify for this deduction. Ask your tax advisor for details.

Step 5. Negotiate with Creditors

With basic needs, taxes, and student loans under wraps, now it's time to determine how much money is available to pay on each of your other debts by adding all expenses *except* debt repayment. By "expenses," I mean what it costs you to cover your regular living expenses and basic bills. If you have only $500 left over but your monthly payments toward debts, including loans and credit cards, add up to $1,000, then you must begin a process of negotiating with your creditors for the fair amount of the $500 each creditor should receive. For example, let's say your debts in category 3 total $18,386. If your Visa balance is $3,670, that's roughly 20 percent of the *total debt* (3,670 ÷ 18,386 = 20%). Propose a temporary payment of $100 ($500 x 20%) for three to six months until you get back on your feet. You may get some resistance, but most creditors would rather settle for a lower payment that can be consistently met than have delinquencies pile up.

Unlike mortgage lenders and car financers, credit-card companies aren't really copartners in your journey. They love someone who carries debt and has a problem with credit. Why? Because that's how they make money off you! Your debt is their money in the bank—because of interest. And your bad credit gives them reason to keep raising your rates and charge you enormous fees when you're an hour late on a bill or can't pay the minimum.

Well, sister, here's the most thrilling part of straightening out your credit: You get to stand up for yourself and become empowered in the process, by requesting better terms from your creditors. The credit industry is rife with fierce competition. Credit-card companies want your business, so you have more leverage than you think. You can negotiate just about anything you wish, including interest rates and limits, or threaten to move on over to a new creditor. This is the part I love most about helping people make amends with their finances. But, of course, there is a right way to approach this challenge. In a moment, I'm going to show you how to prioritize your credit-card debts so you pay them down in a practical and efficient manner. But first, you must negotiate better terms so you can slow down your accumulating debt that seemingly grows with every tick of the clock.

Using your journal, line up all your creditors' phone numbers and have your latest statements on hand. (This is probably when you also realize that even though you may have nine credit cards, you've got only four different creditors for those cards. The consolidation in the banking industry in recent years has made for fewer parent companies of gazillions of different kinds of credit cards. So you might have three Visas and two MasterCards all under the same credit-card issuer! In a recent ad for Chase, the company boasted about the fact that it offers more than 900 types of credit cards.)

Before you figure out which cards you're going to pay off first, you're going to contact all of your creditors and make a few requests.

Your three main goals when you're on the phone include

1. Bringing your accounts up to date

2. Getting a lower interest rate, and

3. Getting them to waive fees.

Let me give you some information on each of these goals and then I'll explain how to be a good negotiator.

1. **Re-aging.** If you've fallen behind in payments and are being charged up the wazoo with late fees and over-the-limit fees,

you need to get your card(s) "re-aged." This means you bring your cards up to date so you're no longer getting slapped with those delinquent charges. Perhaps you've funneled all your money to one card in an attempt to bring that card up to date; meanwhile, your other cards have become delinquent, thus deepening the problem. It's like building multiple sand castles too close to the surf. You pay attention to one while all the others get buried by the incoming waves. Fortunately, some credit-card companies are willing to reclassify your account as current—in exchange for regular payments. By bringing your accounts current and making on-time payments, you will automatically improve your creditworthiness. The longer you can show continual on-time payments, the quicker you can improve how a lender views you as a credit risk. If your account, however, has gone severely off course because you're significantly past due (approximately 120–180 days), you might be dealing with a "charge off" account, which means your account has been written off by the creditor as a loss.

2. **Interest rates.** Credit-card interest rates can be as low as zero percent and as high as 40 percent annually. As I write this, the average credit card in America has an interest rate of about 13 percent. Your statements will tell you what your current rates are, which might have changed significantly since you first got those cards. Cards with zero percent interest rates don't last long; those are usually "introductory rates," which can then skyrocket overnight to more than 20 percent a year. (Remember that credit-card companies can change your interest rate at *any* time, as long as they notify you in writing before the new rate takes effect. You might have thrown out that letter before reading it, thinking it was junk mail when it arrived.) Request a lower rate, and don't be afraid to keep requesting a lower rate (don't accept their first offer!). You might be able to cut your rates in half, if not more. Remember: They don't want to lose your business.

If interest rates don't faze you and you don't think they make a huge difference in what you owe over time, think again. An $8,000 debt at 19.9 percent interest will cost you about $12,690 over five years. That same debt at 7 percent will cost you about $9,504—nearly $3,200 less! (And if you can pay off the loan quicker with larger monthly payments, you'll save even more money.)

With your credit-card statements in one hand and a computer mouse in the other, go to a Web site like www.lowermybills.com or www.bankrate.com and comparison-shop competitive offers. Yes, you get to *shop* for the best rates. But before you switch your debt to another card with a lower rate, start with your current card issuers. They'll likely want to negotiate. In fact, you might not be able to get off the phone with them until they get you to say yes to a new low rate that works in your favor.

3. **Late fees.** It's been estimated that nearly a third of the credit-card business revenue today comes from late fees, which can range anywhere from $15 to $39. Some companies require your payment to reach them by a certain time on the due date to avoid a late charge. So if your check arrives at 1:01 P.M. and it was due at 1:00 sharp, well, you get slapped with the fee. Here's a secret the credit-card companies also don't want you to know: Some will waive your late fees if you simply call and ask them to do so. What's the incentive for them to waive your late fees? They keep your business. If you know you may be late on a bill, call in advance and ask for a grace period. Also ask the person you speak with to "document" your record, so you have proof you called in advance of the bill's being late. Be sure to document your records as well.

Annual fees are a different story: They can be difficult to get waived, especially if your cards are linked to bonuses like airline-mileage or rebate offers. It doesn't hurt to ask for these fees to be waived, however. If you've never taken advantage of those bonuses (which you're actually paying for to some extent with those "membership" fees), it may be time to con-

Dealing with a Charge-off Account

If your account has been "charged off," your creditor has taken it off the books so the creditor can declare a loss on that account for tax purposes. Your account is then reported to the credit bureaus and the charge-off will remain on your credit report for seven years plus 180 days from the date of the first nonpayment, according to the Fair Credit Reporting Act. That the creditor has charged off the account doesn't mean you are excused from the debt; the creditor will likely attempt to collect the debt with either an in-house collection program or with a third-party debt-collection service. For instance, if you find out that your debt has been "sold" to another company, it's probably been passed on to a debt-collection service. Because you defaulted on your original contract for the debt with your creditor, now you can be asked to pay it in full. A charge-off is a huge red flag for lenders, and paying it off will not remove it from your credit report. But your credit report will indicate a "paid charge-off." Sometimes a creditor will accept a partial payment of the debt and the account will be reported as "settled charge-off."

Here are the steps to take on a charged-off account:

1. Contact the original creditor. Ask if your account information is accessible and who is responsible for collecting the debt. You may be able to deal with your original creditor directly.
2. Find out the balance of your account with the company handling the debt. Explain that you intend to pay back the debt. Here's an example of what to say: "I am making plans to pay back this debt, and want to discuss optional payment terms that I can meet given my budget. In looking at my paperwork and financials, $_____ is an amount I can manage on a regular basis. Can you make that work for me?" Suggest a number that you can afford. (This amount may be easier to figure out once you've done your spending plan.) Don't promise to pay more than you can afford, even if they ask you to. If they counter with a higher number, say, "I considered payments in larger sums, but I just can't promise that much at this time. $_____ a month is the best I can do right now, but we can revisit this in about three months, at which time maybe I can agree to larger payments. I'm working very hard on this to get it taken care of quickly."

3. Once you have paid the charge-off in full, request that they remove it from your credit report.

4. If the company won't remove the charge-off from your credit report, make sure it's been updated to "paid charge-off" at the least, by checking your report with each of the three bureaus.

5. If you cannot locate your account information at all, and your original creditor is of no help, submit a statement of up to 100 words to each of the credit bureaus, explaining that you have contacted the creditor in an attempt to take care of the debt but your account information was not available.

sider a card without such fees or that has benefits you'll use. (It may not be a good idea to cancel a card and close out the account if you've had it a long time. Old accounts can be credit boosters, which you'll learn about in Chapter 5. However, if you can cancel your membership in the program that calls for the fee—while still holding on to that same card—then that's the best option.)

Negotiating 101

Being a good negotiator is all about practice. Your first call to the first credit-card company might make you queasy in your stomach, but don't feel intimidated! You'll be a pro in no time at all. If you've been a good customer in the past (i.e., you have at least some history of paying bills regularly), your negotiating room is enormous. If your record isn't so good-looking, don't panic. There's still plenty of negotiating room.

If you're just looking to lower your interest rate, start by explaining to them that if they're not able to meet your expectations, you'll reluctantly have to close your account and transfer your balances over to another card. (You won't actually close your account, but threatening to do so is your leverage tool.) You can even name a few other competitors who've been slamming you with fantastic offers every day in the mail. If you get a quick "No, sorry, but I'm not authorized to do that," then ask to speak with a supervisor. And if the supervisor gives you problems, you simply continue to explain that you've got several offers from other companies and that you'll be forced to close your account today.

Here's a script you can follow for just negotiating a lower interest rate credit card. This script assumes you've given your account number already, using the automated system you hear when you first place the call. Get the customer service rep's name and employee ID or badge number, and document the call yourself in case they fail to do so.

Hi [state his/her name], do you have my account in front of you?

The representative will probably say yes, because you've entered your account using the keypad on your phone. The rep will ask for verifying information for security purposes. Then you can proceed.

As you can see, I have an account with you that has a balance of [give the amount]. My interest rate is [give the rate]. The reason I'm calling is because I've had my account with you since [give the date], I've never been late [if that's the case] and as a courtesy I'd like to get a lower interest rate. [If you don't get a positive response add the following]. I have many offers from other banks sitting here with great interest rates, and I'm tempted to move my account. I've always liked your company and the service I've received, but now I need a creditor who will work with me to at least match the other offers that I have. Is there anything you can do?

In many cases, it's as easy as that—they'll offer you a lower rate. If you like, you can ask if that's the absolute best offer they can make, just to ensure you get the lowest rate available. On the other hand, if you're someone who has had trouble meeting your obligations and needs to restructure payments and fees, be sure to show deference and be courteous. Remember, the old saying, "You can attract more bees with honey than with vinegar." The person on the other end of the phone is not obligated to help you, so be respectful. Here is the script to use with the creditor.

As you can see, I have an account with you that has a balance of [give the amount] and a minimum payment of [give the amount]. My interest rate is [give the rate]. The reason I'm calling is because I need your help, [state their name]. I'm requesting three things: 1) I need to negotiate a new payment plan that meets my current capabilities. I cannot afford to pay more than [give the dollar amount] on this debt each month over the next [give the number of months]; 2) I'd also like to discuss my options to reverse some of the extra fees and charges that have been added to my account; and 3) I would like a lower interest rate. I've been a customer for a long time [give the number of years if it's impressive]. Recently I've had some temporary financial difficulties and I'm working very hard at paying down this debt. Can you help me, please?

If the representative says he or she's not authorized to help you in any way, you say:

Okay, then please transfer me over to your supervisor or someone who can help me.

Then you repeat the above script again. If you still run into trouble, ask to speak to that person's supervisor. And if you hit another wall, kindly and calmly say:

Thank you, for your time. I'm sorry we couldn't reach an agreement.

More than likely, you won't get this far and the representative will give in. (Oh, and if it does, in fact, get as far as you hanging up the phone after this last statement, just call back again! You won't get the same person on the phone. Try another round.)

I'm confident that you'll be able to arrive at a fair agreement. The trick is to be strong and keep in mind that they don't want to lose your business. You have more leverage than you think.

Again, no matter what transpires when you make these calls, make sure the call is documented.

Pay Cards with Highest Interest Rates and Lowest Balances First
Now that you've negotiated better terms to your agreements with your credit-card companies, it's time to sit down and prioritize those credit cards. For some people, balance on credit cards comprises the largest debt of all.

The goal, obviously, is to lower the amount of your debt on your cards as fast as possible and with the least amount of extra cost in interest, fees, etc. To figure out which cards you're going to tackle first, review your Debt Summary worksheet, which lists each account with its corresponding outstanding balance and interest rate. If you've negotiated new interest rates on your cards, write down those rates. Now look at the cards that have the *highest interest rates* and aim to pay down the ones that carry the *lowest balances* first. Why do you do this? Well, I find that when you can eliminate the debt on a card quickly, you'll get an emotional boost that will in turn motivate you to keep going. If you devote the most money to the card with the highest interest rate and lowest balance first, you'll get down to the cards that may take more time to pay off, but they will have lower interest rates (especially now that you've renegotiated those rates). If you've got two cards that have very similar balances and interest rates, just use your best judgment when deciding which one you want to pay down first. Don't get too technical about it when you set your priorities. Revise the list in the new payout order and stay the course. Eventually you'll be debt-free.

I'll share with you my advice for how many cards you should have in Chapter 5. DO NOT, however, cancel any cards until you learn which ones you should keep. As you'll find out later, you don't want to close out your credit cards that have the longest history.

Dealing with Harassing Creditors and Debt Collectors
I mentioned in the previous chapter that you have rights as a consumer *and* debtor. Hopefully, all of your negotiations will go smoothly and you

won't run into mean, unfriendly creditors and collectors—especially once you've started to take action on paying down your debts in a methodical fashion. However, given your priority of debt repayment now, you may have to deal with harassing creditors and collectors who think they should be paid first. Even though you may have contacted them to negotiate better terms and find a better payment plan, that doesn't mean you won't find yourself fielding phone calls from them once in a while as you focus on your most pressing debts. Thus, you need to know how to handle the conversation. Here's a script you can use to get through any difficult conversation:

> *I appreciate the information you're giving me and I'll add that I am aware of my rights under the Fair Debt and Fair Credit Collection Practices Acts. I'm also very aware of this particular debt and I'm doing my best to rectify it through a plan. If you don't stop calling and harassing me like this, I'll formally write a letter requesting that you cease all communications with me, which I know falls under the law. I'll also report any violation you make to the Federal Trade Commission. Please be patient with me as I work on my plan and address this debt in a responsible manner.*

If, after you've said the above statement, the caller continues to bother you, simply repeat the same statement one final time. If that doesn't work, say, *"Excuse me, but I'm going to hang up the phone now and write that letter."* Then hang up and follow through. In all likelihood, the conversation won't reach this point.

Step 6. Get Support and Be Accountable

Helen, a thirty-eight-year-old hairstylist, was overwhelmed with debt and in hot water. "I have destroyed what used to be solid credit," she said. "All of my credit cards are maxed out and past due, some for ninety days or more. Now I'm worried that I won't be able to move into another apartment, get a mortgage, and lower my interest rate on credit cards." Then she continued, "And I have no idea how to save in the midst of all of this." She was right—that is, until she took some decisive action.

Over the years, Helen had accumulated $47,000 in credit-card debt and personal loans. Much of it was old debt from a past business that wasn't profitable. But to be fair, she had to admit some of it was from, as she calls it, "stupid" spending—clothes, lifestyle, furniture, and travel. Her monthly payment on this debt was in excess of $2,400, and interest ranged from 15.9 percent to 27.98 percent.

Helen had tried negotiating with her creditors for lower interest rates, to no avail. They agreed on a payment strategy to get her current, but wouldn't budge on reducing interest rates. When I explained to Helen about the services offered through the National Foundation for Credit Counseling, she took action immediately. Helen called the toll-free number and was referred to a local agency, where she scheduled an appointment for the following day. After careful analysis, Helen was able to consolidate $38,000 of debt into a single payment of $940 and reduce her interest-rates. They now ranged between 6 and 9.9 percent!

"I feel better now," states Helen, beaming with pride. "I'm also reducing my daily expenses. I have no cable and no long distance on my home phone." At this rate, with continued discipline, she'll be able to have that savings buffer in no time at all!

At this point in the book, you should know that you're not alone when it comes to having less-than-perfect credit. I hope you also realize that you don't have to—and shouldn't have to—go at fixing your credit all by yourself. It might take some extra help and support from others to get you back on track. And that's nothing to be ashamed about.

Credit counseling and debt management are booming industries, especially since the Bankruptcy Reform Act became law in 2005, mandating that anyone contemplating bankruptcy receive a certificate from an approved, nonprofit budget and credit-counseling agency within 180 days of filing. But the fact that the government has released a list of approved counselors doesn't mean there aren't any shady, dubious counselors out there who prey on debtors. Many credit counselors will lure you in and then smack you with excessive fees, poor services, and promises to help you in ways that they just can't deliver. For example, no one can erase a bad mark on your credit report if the negative mark is legitimate—no one! In 2004, AmeriDebt, once one of the largest credit counseling agencies in the business, paid $170 million in fines for misleading customers.

The trick, then, is finding a good credit-counseling service that you can trust and that won't leave you in a worse-off position. When you Google "credit counseling," more than 13 million Internet links are found. That's pretty daunting, isn't it? Debt-management companies, which typically go hand-in-hand with credit couselors and which I'll cover in detail below—are up 467 percent since 1998. Not only has the Reform Act created an instant market for this industry, but people who seek help—even without thinking about bankruptcy—are also fueling a growing need.

Credit Counselors

Certified credit counselors can help you make budgets, cut spending, and even create debt-management plans where the agency negotiates with creditors on your behalf to lower payments, reduce your interest rates, and sometimes eliminate interest entirely. Reputable agencies tailor payment plans to each individual's circumstances, sometimes offering services for free.

Some programs allow you to use a period of interest reduction to pay down your debt. You won't, however, get a reduction or discount on your principal debt. Many of these plans require you to deposit money each month with the counseling service. The service then pays your creditors.

The best place to start is the National Foundation for Credit Counseling, which aims to set the national standard for quality credit counseling, debt-reduction services, and financial literacy training. Founded in 1951, the NFCC is America's largest and longest-serving nonprofit credit-counseling organization, with 120 member agencies and more than 1,000 local offices throughout the country. Many NFCC members are known as Consumer Credit Counseling Service ("CCCS"). To reach the National Foundation for Credit Counseling's 24-hour hotline, call 800–388–2227 or access it on the Internet at www.nfcc.org. Another reputable organization to check out is the Association of Independent Consumer Credit Counseling Agencies (AICCCA). They can be found at www.aiccca.org or by calling 800–450–1794.

Debt Management and Debt Reduction

It's easy to confuse credit counseling and debt management. They can be very much one and the same. A credit-counseling firm that helps you negotiate new payment terms with your creditors and assists you in dealing with your debt can also be called a debt-management firm. Be careful, however, if a certain firm uses "debt management" to mean "lightening your debt load." If your counselor says he can reorganize your debt entirely by contacting your creditors and negotiating *settlements* on each of your debts so you pay less of the entire bill . . . you're not dealing with basic debt management. You're likely dealing with so-called debt reduction, debt relief, debt workout, debt settlement, or a host of other names implying they help actually lower your debt liability. They do so by reducing your debt down to 30 to 50 cents on the dollar. Most plans last three years or less, but in some cases credit-card-debt-management plans may last up to four years or longer. Costs are generally 8 to 15 percent of your total outstanding debt. Firms can calculate your fees based on the money they save you, taking 25 to 33 percent of those savings. Just understand that you can negotiate settlement offers yourself and eliminate paying fees for this service.

Note also that a debt manager who can actually lighten the weight of your debt burden will *not* help your credit score—even if you pay off your settlement. You're better off working off your entire debt load and not taking shortcuts, because shortcuts will shortchange your credit score. But if your debt is significant and options for repayment are minimal, it can be worth it to make a settlement and then be patient, as your credit score will improve over time.

Most debt-reduction firms work with basic credit-card debt (unsecured commercial creditors), but some may also work with medical bills, auto deficiencies, and other similar unsecured debt. If you're in need of help with secured debt, such as your mortgage or car loan, you'll need to find a firm that specializes in these kinds of secured debts. Be sure to ask any debt-reduction firm that's working with you what it does when one of your creditors refuses to negotiate.

Beware of Scams: You've seen television, radio, Internet, and billboard ads on the highway that target debtors with seemingly unrealistic promises. *No credit? Bad credit? No problem! We'll get you out of debt and erase those negative marks on your credit report today!* Some of these advertisements read like a fad diet that promises you all the rewards with little or no work involved. The credit-counseling and debt-services industry is fraught with suspicious activity. Any advertisement that makes wild promises to get you out of debt quickly may be a method for obtaining a large, up-front fee or a disguised way of stealing your identity. In addition, it is illegal to represent that negative information, such as bankruptcy, can be removed from your credit report. Promises to "help you get out of debt easily" are a red flag. Be especially wary of these offers.

The Red Flags: Agencies to Avoid

The following red flags were published in a 2003 report by the Consumer Federation of America, a nonprofit association of consumer groups, and the National Consumer Law Center, a nonprofit organization specializing in consumer issues on behalf of low-income consumers. This is an adaptation of that publication.

- **High fees.** If your setup fees and monthly fees seem expensive, they probably are. Generally, if the setup fee for a debt-management plan is more than $50 and monthly fees exceed $25, look for a better deal. If the agency is vague or reluctant to talk about specific fees, go elsewhere.

- **"Voluntary" fees.** Some agencies offer a suggested rather than a set fee. Don't be bullied into paying these fees in their entirety. If the full fee is too much, don't pay more than you can afford. If there's a required "voluntary contribution," it may come with high monthly service charges, which can add to your debt and defeat your efforts to pay your bills.

- **The hard sell.** If a representative talks from a script and pushes debt "savings" or says your *only* way out is a consolidation loan, hang up.

- **Employees working on commission.** Most credit-counseling agencies are nonprofit organizations that are supposed to consider your best interests when offering you information. Employees that receive commissions for placing consumers in debt-management plans are more likely to be focusing on their own wallets than yours.

- **They flunk the "Twenty Minute Test."** Any agency that offers you a debt-management plan in less than twenty minutes hasn't spent enough time looking at your finances. An effective counseling session, whether on the phone or in person, takes a significant amount of time (thirty to ninety minutes).

- **One size fits all.** A good agency should talk to you about whether a debt-management plan is right for you rather than assume that it is. If the agency doesn't offer any educational options, such as classes or budget counseling, consider one that does.

- **Aggressive ads.** Don't respond reflexively to television and Internet advertising or telemarketing. Get referrals from friends and family. Find out which agencies have been subject to investigations and complaints. Your local Better Business Bureau might be helpful here.

Remember, get references and don't give out your personal information until you are confident that the counselor works for a legitimate company.

Support Groups

Let's be honest: Getting a handle on your spending habits and dealing with debt and poor credit sometimes requires more than rigid programs and counseling down to your dollars and cents. Debtors Anonymous, for instance, is a nationwide twelve-step program that helps you deal with your spending problem and gives you the guidance for "compulsive debting." Debtors Anonymous, whose support program works similarly to Alcoholics Anonymous, offers support via others who've incurred serious debt and have routinely abused their credit. Check out www.debtors anonymous.org for more information and to find a meeting near you. You can also dial directory assistance or request information by sending a self-addressed envelope to Debtors Anonymous, General Service Office, P.O. Box 920888, Needham, MA 02492–0009. Phone: 781–453–2743; fax: 781–453–2745. Or e-mail the office at new@debtorsanonymous.org and indicate your city, state, and proximity to larger cities. Several Debtors Anonymous meetings happen online; meeting times and access numbers change periodically.

Financial Coaches

Think of a financial coach as you would any coach—someone you can trust like a mentor to guide you from where you are today to where you want to be tomorrow. Oscar-winning actors have acting coaches; top athletes have coaches; singers have their voice coaches. You, too, can have your own financial coach who can help you avoid dangerous pitfalls while accelerating your financial journey. With a coach, you have both reliable support and also immediate accountability. A coach can be used as a sounding board before financial decisions are made. Because so many of us wrap too many emotional issues around money and finances, sometimes a financial coach is exactly what's needed.

Finding the best financial coach for you can be like finding the perfect psychotherapist. In other words, you want to find someone you can develop a good rapport with. Start with referrals from friends, family members, and coworkers. If you have an accountant, he or she can probably give you some leads. Or get a referral from a friend for an accountant who can then lead you to a coach. If you don't want to pay for private, one-on-one sessions, which can cost upward of $100 an hour, you can look into coaching packages (e.g., a three-month package for $500–$1,000), group sessions, or seminars that are offered in your community. Pay attention to advertisements in your paper for large-scale financial tours that come to town once or twice a year. You can usually sign up for classes or go listen to a series of speakers. Just be careful not to spend too much money once you're *at* those events and seminars. Glean the free knowledge but don't feel pressured to spend hundreds of dollars in packaged products such as tapes, CDs, DVDs, books, and so on.

Family Members

One topic seldom discussed when talking about climbing out of debt and boosting credit scores is family relations. Embarking on a debt diet isn't easy, and for many sisters, it ain't fun. If you've ever been on a diet before, you know the power of choice, free will, and yes . . . discipline! You know that you have to cut back, if not entirely give up, a few of your favorite things.

Coming face-to-face with your debt and credit problems takes guts and courage. Pat yourself on the back for getting this far and reading this book! But I encourage you to also go farther than just admitting your problems to yourself. Open up about your situation to selected family and friends. Tell them what you are doing and where you plan to be three months, six months, and a year from now. Just like being on a diet, letting your family and the friends with whom you like to lunch and shop know about it can make this process a whole lot easier. Ask for their encouragement and support of your financial goal. The confession can be a humbling, sometimes embarrassing experience for some people. It might make you cry and feel bad or guilty about yourself when you fess up to your problems, and that's okay. Let the emotions move through you and be strong. You'd be surprised by the amount of support you'll get just by sharing your goals and how you plan to reach them. Plus, by telling your family and loved ones about what's going on, you'll no longer be able to keep your situation a secret, which can have the negative effect of promoting your own self-denial.

Step 7. Get Loans? Maybe, Maybe Not

Debt-consolidation loans can be a good option for many people, but you need to consider them very carefully. And I'm not referring to student-loan programs here; I'm talking about loans for consumer debts, which allow you to consolidate many of those debts into one loan with one payment each month. You may be advised during your counseling—or even from friends and family—that you should choose this option, so let me explain briefly how it works.

Generally, interest charged on consolidation loans falls far below the interest charged on most credit-card debt, thus allowing easier repayment of the debt. But these loans are often secured by your home or some other asset that you can use as collateral. You must be able to make those monthly payments or you risk going into deeper debt . . . and losing your home. That said, you may be able to find and qualify for an unsecured loan from a reputable bank or lender, such as a credit union, that offers a great interest rate without having to put up an asset as collateral.

The advantage of consolidating your debts is that you only have to deal with one creditor. However, if you must secure the loan with an asset, you should weigh the risks of losing that asset. Refinancing mortgages and home-equity loans has been heavily marketed in recent years due to the record-low interest rates in the mid-2000s. You've seen these ads on television as well: "Cash out the equity in your home to pay off high-interest debts" or "Get cash today to use toward those mounting credit-card bills with a second mortgage." Some firms even offer people loans equal to 125 percent of the value of their home. When you refinance, for example, you replace your first mortgage with a new one that's for more than your home is currently worth, so you can pocket the difference. This all sounds spectacular—but these loans come with costs that can be very high to bear. The decision to use your house as a piggy bank should be made carefully. Each option bears its own costs. But you have to consider what your interest rate will be, and if it's not lower than the interest rate on a home-equity loan, then it's usually not the ideal option. You also have to consider closing costs, which you have to pay when you refinance but not when you get a home-equity loan or line of credit.

Home-Equity Loans and Home-Equity Lines of Credit
In your counseling sessions you may also run into a strong argument for getting either a home-equity loan (HEL) or home-equity line of credit (HELOC). You may also hear success stories from friends and family

members who've been pulled out of the financial hole using these types of loans. The low interest rates in the early to mid-2000s that made for a hot real estate market also encouraged many to apply for home-equity loans and lines of credit. But understanding these loan vehicles should precede any decision to apply for them.

When you're strapped for cash to pay off soaring debt, and you look around—you might smile when you think about the biggest asset you probably have: your house. Both HELs and HELOCs are secondary loans on your home based on the equity you've built up in it. With a home-equity loan, you get a lump sum. A HELOC gives you a revolving credit line, much like a credit card. But these two loans do not always share the same interest rate. The interest rate on HELOCs typically involves variable rather than fixed rates. The variable rate is based on a publicly available index such as the "prime rate" published in some major daily newspapers or a U.S. Treasury bill rate. Thus, the interest rate for borrowing under a HELOC changes, mirroring fluctuations in the value of the index. Most lenders cite the interest rate you will pay as the value of the index at a particular time plus a "margin," such as two percentage points. Because the cost of borrowing is tied directly to the value of the index, it's important to find out which index is tied to your HELOC, how often the value of the index changes, and how high it has risen in the past as well as the amount of the margin.

Home-equity loans, on the other hand, are second mortgages that usually come with a fixed interest rate that you lock in when you get your loan. Because you receive the entire amount of the loan up front, interest charges start right away.

So how much credit can you get on a HELOC? Many lenders set the credit limit first by taking a percentage (say, 75 percent) of the home's appraised value and subtracting from that the balance owed on the existing mortgage. Then the lender will consider other factors, like your ability to repay. This is determined by . . . you guessed it: by looking at your income, debts, and other financial obligations as well as your credit history. Many HELOCs set a fixed period during which you can borrow the money, such as ten years. At the end of this "draw period," you may be allowed to renew the credit line. If your plan does not allow renewals, you will not be able to borrow additional money once the period has ended. Some plans may call for payment in full of any outstanding balance at the end of the period. Others may allow repayment over a fixed period (the "repayment period")—for example, ten years.

Unlike a HEL, which gets you all the money right away, you don't have to draw from your HELOC until you want to, and you won't owe any interest until you do so. You might, however, have some restrictions. For example, there may be limitations on how you use the credit line. Some plans may require you to borrow a minimum amount each time you draw on the line (for example, $500) and to keep a minimum amount outstanding. You may also have to take an initial advance out when the line is set up. You access this loan with checks, credit cards, or an electronic transfer.

Using these two vehicles—HEL and HELOCs—to cash out some equity in your home to put toward other debts can be a dicey game. Why? Because you've got your home tied to these loans as collateral. Whether you've got a HEL or HELOC, if you fall far behind in payments (or, in the case of a HELOC, can't keep up with rising interest rates that raise your payments), then you can lose your home. What's more, because these plans can give you relatively easy access to cash, you might find you borrow money more freely. You might end up in deeper water and then not qualify for refinancing when you need it most. Remember that credit-card debt is unsecured, which means the credit-card company can't force you to sell anything to pay it off, including your home. With a HEL or HELOC, you basically attach your home to your unsecured debt in a way that can force you to sell your home to pay off that (unsecured) debt.

If you need to borrow money, home-equity lines may be one useful source of credit. Initially at least, they may provide you with large amounts of cash at relatively low interest rates. And they may provide you with certain tax advantages unavailable with other kinds of loans. (Check with your tax advisor for details.) At the same time, however, having revolving credit based on your home can fuel already existing problems with abusing credit. Using a HELOC to pay for last year's vacations, holiday shopping, and luxurious trips to the spa is a bad idea. HELOCs

With HELOCs, Go Beyond the Minimum Payment

If you opt for a home-equity line of credit and apply it carefully to your serious debt, try to pay more than the minimum each month. Minimum payments on HELOCs are interest-only, which is why those minimum payments are so small. You can end up ten years down the road still owing the principal. Then what do you do? Some people do roll their debt into a new HELOC, but this just creates a vicious cycle you might never climb out of.

should be saved for serious matters, such as medical bills, home repairs and improvement, and education. Keep in mind that if you sell your home, you'll have to pay off your credit line at that time.

Similarly, using home-equity loans in a frivolous manner is also a bad idea. People who take out traditional second mortgages on their homes (i.e., home-equity loans) do so to pay for their kids' education, to add on to their homes, or in some cases to fund a business venture. They often have a clear idea what they're going to use that loan for when they apply for it, and they don't freely spend that lump sum on past consumer debt or what can easily become future consumer debt.

When contemplating either a HELOC or a HEL, be sure to ask your lender the costs related to these loans. Besides their interest rates, ask about annual fees, closing costs, and any balloon payments owed at the end (more typical of a credit line). Home-equity lines of credit typically are a good deal for those who want a lower up-front rate and access to money at un-predictable times. However, home-equity loans are better suited to those who need a specific amount of money and payment stability.

This final piece of advice should be obvious: If you already have one of these loans, either as a HELOC or HEL, and it's part of your debt pile, it should be high on your payback priorities so you maintain as much equity as possible in your home, but lower than your high-interest-rate unsecured credit-card debt. You may be able to negotiate better terms with your lender, so it never hurts to ask. Set up an appointment with the bank at which you have your HELOC or HEL and see what they can do. If they know that you're working hard to resolve your credit and debt problems, chances are they will want to work with you. The bank doesn't necessarily want you to lose your home, either.

The Family Loan

Just because you share your financial struggles and your plan to fix them with loved ones doesn't mean you can accept loans from any of them! If anyone offers money to help you clean up your credit and get out of debt, be very careful and think through your decision. You have to quit borrowing money to really take control of your own finances. Here's my rule if you're tempted to accept such an offer: If you have seriously made a commitment to get your credit straight and are following the steps in this book, and a relative offers you an interest-free loan enabling you to pay off a 24.99 percent credit card, you may have ample reason to say yes. But please be cautious and brutally realistic in mulling over this decision. If you do reach a loan agreement with a relative, put it in writing and treat it like any other business transaction.

My Thoughts on Bankruptcy

The decision to file for bankruptcy is a serious one. It should be considered a financial protection of last resort. Even if you have so much debt that you can't fathom ever paying it all back, bankruptcy may still not be a good option for you. The rules of bankruptcy changed vastly in 2005, with the Bankruptcy Abuse Prevention and Consumer Protection Act taking effect, which made it more difficult to discharge debt in a classic Chapter 7 filing. For starters, your income in relation to your living expenses goes through a "means test" to determine whether or not you can (a) file for bankruptcy, or (b) pay back a percentage of your debt. More than likely, if you file for bankruptcy and actually qualify, it can hurt you for a long time. The new law also puts a cap on homestead exemptions, meaning there is no guarantee that you can save your home in a bankruptcy filing. Moreover, bankruptcy will not help you if your debt is largely from items like student loans, back taxes, and child support.

Counseling is also now a requirement under the new law for anyone contemplating bankruptcy. Before you can even file, you must receive a certificate from an approved nonprofit budget and credit counseling agency within 180 days prior to filing. The certificate states you have received a briefing on opportunities for available credit counseling, and you have been assisted in performing an individual budget analysis. Then, before you receive your discharge, you'll have to go through another education course in personal financial management. It's highly likely that if you get good credit counseling, your counselor will be able to provide information to you about bankruptcy and whether it should be a consideration given your circumstances. But I'd think long and hard about this option before taking this route.

A bankruptcy filing stays on your credit report for ten years, during which time you'll find it difficult to apply for credit, get a home or car loan, and obtain competitive rates on things like insurance and interest on those loans. It may even impact your ability to get a job. The ding in your credit, however, is not the only downside to a bankruptcy filing. Bankruptcy can entail the seizure of many of your assets, including your car that you haven't finished paying off yet. If student loans are killing you and you want to file for bankruptcy just to get rid of an incomprehensible balance due, let me say that the new bankruptcy law makes it even tougher to erase those types of loans. Unless you can prove that repaying a student loan would create an undue hardship on you and your dependents, which is very difficult to prove without a severe disability, all student loans are now nondischargeable, even if your lender is a nongovernmental, commercial (private) entity. Again, with all the options available these days to deal with student loans, the best solution is to follow my five-step process for getting those loans managed in a way that doesn't have a negative impact on your credit score.

How much is too much debt when it comes to thinking about using bankruptcy as a way out? Unfortunately, there is no hard-and-fast rule on this. I've seen people climb their way out of hundreds of thousands of dollars in debt, and I've seen people file for bankruptcy with less than $10,000 in debt. Generally speaking, the bankruptcy court will probably deny your petition to file Chapter 7 if for six months before filing you have income of $100 or more left over per month after paying your living expenses. Regardless of your debt or living expenses, if your income exceeds the median income level for your state, chances are you'll have to reorganize your debt under Chapter 13 and pay back a large portion of your debt.

My bottom line on bankruptcy is that you should consider it your last and final option. If you do go this route, it pays to speak to a counselor first who can help you evaluate your particular situation and weigh your individual pros and cons. Make sure this person has no financial incentive in your filing for bankruptcy, either—as may a bankruptcy attorney who simply wants your business.

Exercise One: Actions and Affirmations

Remember: Little steps amount to big leaps. You can chisel away at a mountain of debt and still reach the summit! One of my clients, Violet, was heavily burdened with $45,900 in old debt from thirteen different accounts. After following my seven steps, then planning and tracking her expenses for the last two years, eight of the thirteen accounts have been paid off. But Violet is most proud of the $50-per-month payment arrangement she made on each of three high-balance credit cards. It's a small, yet important step toward a growing self-worth. "It is so satisfying to sit and pay bills first," she says. Although her situation is not perfect, Violet is definitely making progress.

Now it's time for you to go through these steps. Follow the seven steps outlined in this chapter one by one, and say an affirmation to yourself at the start of each step. I'll give you those affirmations here. Write them in your GIRL journal as you say them out loud to yourself in the mirror, and repeat them when necessary.

Step 1: Get Clear: Calculate Your Debt

I will stop denying my debt, which ultimately denies my future. I have the courage, strength, and fortitude to look at each and every debt with resolve and then address them as necessary. God, give me the strength to accept my debt and not be afraid of it.

Step 2: Prioritize Your Debts: Who Gets Paid First

I will understand my debt and be able to see through this mountain once I simplify it and make sense out of which bills should be paid first, second, third. There is order to this chaos, and I am in control of creating that order.

God, give me the strength to see past this mountain of debt and find the pathway that will take me far beyond it.

Step 3: Figure Out Your Resources

I will accept that the power of my income is as great as I want it to be. No matter how many resources I have, I can make my money work toward paying down my debt as long as I choose to use it wisely.

Step 4: Get a Plan

I will formulate a plan that meets each and every debt in a methodical fashion.

Step 5: Negotiate with Creditors

I will approach my lenders and creditors with resolve, patience, and deference. I will be honest with myself and about my ability to pay. And I will approach them as though they are copartners in my journey. I will treat them with respect and not with an attitude.

God, give me the strength to remain patient and confident when I speak with my creditors. Let me see them as humans and not targets, for they—as individuals—are not the reason for my situation.

Step 6: Get Support and Be Accountable

I will be open to letting professionals help me deal with my debt if that's the best course of action.

God, give me the strength to open up to others about my debt situation and follow their lead in counseling me back to financial health.

Step 7: Get Loans? Maybe, Maybe Not

I will look honestly at my options and consider loans if they are the right choice, given my circumstances. I will not jump into any loan, however, without doing my homework and making sure that it's in my best interest.

God, give me the strength to look rationally at my debt situation and find the best course of action. Give me the foresight to see the best road to take, even if that may not seem like the easy way out today.

Getting Straight Do's and Don'ts

DO accept responsibility. You received goods or services and should rightly pay for them.

DO open your mail. Respond even if only to say you don't have the money to pay, but will contact them next week for a status update.

DO be proactive and inform creditors of your situation. Answer the telephone and don't avoid them. Don't lie about payments—that "it's in the mail" when it's not—and don't promise anything you can't deliver.

DON'T become overly anxious. An account may need to go to a collection agency before a creditor is willing to lower payments enough to fit your budget.

DO prepare a script of what you plan to say when you speak with the creditor. Acknowledge the debt, explain that you plan to repay it, state what you can or cannot do today, and agree to keep them informed.

DON'T curse agents or lose your temper. Be humble and talk to the creditor as a person, not as the source of your troubles. Consider saying, "I've got a problem. Is there any way you can help me?" People tend to feel good when they are helping someone—but not when you take the approach "You owe me."

DON'T forget about student loans, even if you defaulted on them long ago. Explore consolidating them into one if you can.

DO document conversations with creditors: date, time, phone number called, name, specifics of the conversation, and promises made.

DO respond to any court summons, regardless of what the creditor says. You need to explain your situation to the judge and show a willingness to repay. By not showing up, you appear irresponsible and will likely have a judgment placed against you.

DON'T beat yourself up about letting old habits get you in this position. Vow to do better in the future.

DO remember to be patient with yourself. You didn't get here overnight, so don't expect everything to be resolved quickly.

DO pray before you pick up the phone. Ask God to give you favor in the eyes of the creditor.

DO bless your creditors. Thank them for having confidence in extending credit to you.

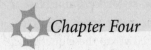

Chapter Four

Establish a Spending Plan That Meets Needs and Ditches Debts

A few years ago, I spoke at a women's conference in Florida. Another speaker, Deborah Owens, author of *Nickel and Dime Your Way to Wealth,* was discussing money and relationships with the group. She asked a very profound question: "What would you rather have, a man who earns $100K per year and spends $125K, or a man who earns $50K and spends $40K?" It's an important question to ask as you consider choosing a mate, but it's also critical when contemplating your own finances. Think about it. What would you rather be: a sister who earns $100K per year and spends $125K, or a sister who earns $50K and spends $40K?

You might also ask yourself the following questions right now if you're really serious about getting your credit straight: Am I ready to make some tough choices regarding my current lifestyle? Am I willing to modify my spending and be disciplined, understanding I don't have to go into deprivation? Can I develop a mind-set of "consume less" as opposed to "consume more"? Am I willing to make some short-term sacrifices for a long-term gain? If you answered yes to these questions, then you're probably ready to free up money to pay down your debt and increase your credit score. If you answered no to these questions, then keep reading, enjoy the anecdotes, but realize you likely won't see much improvement in your present financial circumstances. You make the choice.

Remember: Life is a series of choices. You can decide to stay in debt and maintain poor credit. And you can make the decision to get out of debt and improve your credit. Debt and credit are immune to what you look like and how old you are. But you are not immune to debt and poor credit if you don't make good decisions. In other words, you choose debt and poor credit—they don't necessarily choose you.

In *Girl, Get Your Money Straight!*, I devoted a lot of attention to creating a spending plan. It's the cornerstone of personal financial recovery and long-term success in financial management. Having one in place is essential to reducing debt, boosting credit, and giving you the foundation for building wealth. In fact, a spending plan is perhaps more critically important to have now than at any other time, or under any other circumstances. You must establish a plan that frees up as much extra money as possible to put toward your debts. The exercises you've already gone through—or partially gone through—in the previous chapter will be very useful and helpful in this chapter.

Here's the reality: If we *have* money, we'll find a multitude of uses for it—uses that weren't as pressing during our cash crunch but are tremendously pressing if dollars are at our disposal. If we *don't* have much money, on the other hand, we will usually modify our spending to accommodate the cash that's available. The lesson: Learn to reduce your spending *despite* excess cash today and you'll not only get out of debt quickly and recover your creditworthiness, but you'll also have a whole lot of excess cash at some point in the future with which to invest and finance your wildest dreams. This is key to building wealth.

A Spending Plan Is Not a Budget

Which sounds better and more empowering: *I have a spending plan* or *I'm on a budget*? The former statement has a sense of ownership, the latter does not. To say *I'm on a budget* sounds as if you're forced to be on someone else's plan. I prefer to use the term "spending plan," because "budget" holds so many negative connotations. When you think "budget," the words "limitations," "inflexibility," "sacrifice," and maybe even "deprivation" come to mind. These can fuel ill feelings on the inside that can backfire over time and lead to more excessive spending. It's like going on a no-carb diet and then craving bread and pasta so badly that you give in and lose all sense of control.

Women especially don't like to have any ceilings placed on their spending. But a spending plan is empowering and proactive. It entails choices, and you get to arrive at your own plan based on your needs as well as your debts. The purpose of a spending plan is not to limit spending, but rather to map out a way to achieve a quality of life that has a sense of balance and well-being—that respects your personal needs as well as your debts.

I love the tagline for the television program about law enforcement called *The Closer*. It says, "Confession is good for the soul." Although in the case of the TV drama it's about confessing to murder so a case can be closed, confessing to excessive or inappropriate spending—no matter how minuscule—can have similarly positive effects. If you haven't already pinpointed where you spend excessively based on previous exercises in the book, then establishing a spending plan will enable you to see where your weak spots are. Once you are willing to come out of denial and admit to those weak areas, you can design a treatment plan and let the healing begin. (Your wallet will thank you!) In order to free up money to pay off debt and improve credit, you must get honest about your expenditures and decide what's acceptable and what's not. You have to draw certain boundaries and stick by them. Depending on your situation, this might entail making a few minor lifestyle modifications, or it might call for sweeping changes in how you live and what you value.

For example, a habit of buying magazines from the newsstand every other day or junk food at the grocery checkout line can add up over time. Internet shopping, including cheap music downloads, can sneak up to big numbers on your credit-card statements. Going out to lunch every day or participating in happy hour three times a week can also excavate your wallet.

I'm not asking that you give up all that makes you happy and helps you lead a balanced life, but the key word here is *balance*. You must balance your lifestyle in relation to your money. We all know what eating Twinkies would do to us if we ate them every single day. But that doesn't mean you have to nix them entirely from your diet if they are a source of pleasure and comfort. You simply have to balance them out in the context of your overall diet. The same holds true for splurges and excesses related to money.

In this chapter, I'm going to help you create a practical, realistic spending plan with debts in mind, plus teach you tricks for continuing to reduce your expenses and finding that all-important balance. I'll also share with you a technique that I've found very useful for those struggling to rise above their debt pile; it's called the cash-only envelope system, and it can be an eye-opening experience. Use any of the work you did in Chapter 3 to assist you here. For example, the inventory you took of your income will help you create a reasonable plan.

Before I dive into explaining the exercises you'll complete to make your own spending plan, let's take a look at two sisters' experiences with their plans and how they worked.

Deena's First Spending Plan

Deena, the young sister in Chapter 1 who was turned down for the bank position because of her negative credit report, later found employment in the office of a neighborhood car wash where no background checks were done. She also participated in Tupperware parties as an independent consultant for extra income. When she came to me, Deena had a number of financial goals: to graduate with no bills, have $1,500 in savings, improve her credit score, and save for a car and her children's education. But she had a fetish for shopping and no concept of how to budget her money. When she had a financial windfall from overdue child-support payments, she *almost* fell back into a familiar pattern of splurging on wants before taking care of her needs. Luckily, she came to see me before all that "extra" money actually got into her hands. At the time, she had a credit-card collection account for $1,034 and a cell-phone collection account for $424. According to Deena, the creditors were calling seven times a day.

Deena was somewhat stunned that her first monthly spending plan revealed $5,550 in income but $6,097 in expenses—or a $547 shortfall. But the shortfall wasn't the only surprise. Sounding perplexed, she explained, "It's hard to believe I'll bring in this much money and I'm still wanting to spend more!" Her income that month had broken down as follows: $450 child support, $1,700 office assistant job, $1,800 back child support, and an anticipated $1,500 from hosting Tupperware parties.

It's amazing how quickly we forget the pain of pressing debt. We pray to God for a blessing to deliver us from the evil creditors; then a chunk of money comes in and we renegotiate with God about our priorities. Deena's frivolous and dysfunctional spending showed in the first draft of her spending plan. Her monthly expenses included: $200 in electronic equipment for her daughter; $200 on pets; $400 on kids' clothes; $250 on toiletries; $150 payment on a credit card (the balance was $350); $200 toward savings; $1,200 on clothes, shoes, and accessories for herself; and $0 toward the collection accounts. Clearly, it was unreasonable for her to spend $1,600 on clothes for herself and the kids in one month when she had creditors hounding her for unpaid bills.

After I initiated a heart-to-heart dialog with her about financial responsibility and what it takes to achieve financial peace of mind, Deena revised her spending plan. She came to her follow-up financial-counseling session reporting payment of the following: $540 settlement to the credit-card collection; $424 to pay off cell-phone collection; $350 to pay off current credit card; $168 accessories for self; and most important, she put $2,000 in savings! That $2,000 she managed to put into savings was made possible by the windfall of extra money she finally received, as well as a few modifications to her spending that resulted in excess cash. Had I not intervened when I did on her financial outlook during our first session, she probably would have spent that money and created more debt. "It was an emotional roller coaster, but I'm happy I paid off the bills," Deena confessed before going on to say, "Now everything is falling into place."

Thank goodness she was willing to wisely change the allocations, pay off her nagging old debts, and save some money first. This gave her immediate peace of mind. She felt in control of her life, so much so that when her car died and she lost her office job unexpectedly two months later, she survived. That saved money came to her rescue.

Candace's Tracking Her Ins vs. Outs

Another sister who learned the value of a spending plan is Candace, a thirty-five-year-old divorced project manager from Detroit. "I want to get my money straight, but it's overwhelming and I don't know what the hell I'm doing!" she declared when she first came to see me. Then she went on in frustration, "I feel like I'm spinning my wheels. I need someone to say, 'Do this . . .'" Since the onset of her financial problems six years ago, Candace, who has no children, had always reluctantly counted on the generosity of her parents for a monthly bailout.

What precipitated Candace's financial problems initially was a habitually unemployed spouse. She had a mortgage that was $5,300 past due; accounts in collection, including a student-loan balance of $2,500; medical bills of $266; and miscellaneous bills of $355. When she filed a Chapter 13 bankruptcy, which is the type that works out a payment plan with creditors for most of the debt, she restructured about $10,000 of debt. The bankruptcy filing also allowed her to restructure her payments, save her house, and pay off the outstanding collection accounts. Later on, the bankruptcy was discharged or paid in full—again with the help of her parents.

But Candace's money troubles didn't end with the bankruptcy or her divorce. She continued to fall into the trap of overspending and relying on her parents for the bailout. Aside from the guilt and feelings of failure she carried as a grown woman, Candace dealt with their fluctuating attitude that went from nurturing and supportive to critical and judgmental. It, too, was a heavy burden to bear. Her parents obviously wanted her to succeed financially as much as she did. Even as she fought through her fear to show up for her first financial-consulting session with me, she admitted to being an emotional wreck as she ran her credit report in preparation for our meeting. Candace wanted to be a responsible adult; the memory of her bankruptcy experience loomed large in her mind.

The week before our first appointment, Candace took a major step by downsizing her vehicle—with her parents cosigning—from an Explorer to a Focus, thus reducing the monthly payments, gasoline, and insurance expense. Other important steps for Candace included developing a strong will to get out of her parents' pocket, living within or even below her means, and not creating new debt that would lead her back into bankruptcy. She wanted nothing more than to avoid going to her parents for money between paychecks, but she knew that on her own she couldn't master the art of creating a budget that worked month after month.

We started by looking at her upcoming month and creating a detailed spending plan, estimating her needs based on her expectations. In our first draft, her expenses totaled $4,030. With her set income of $3,088, her shortfall would be $942. Candace acknowledged, "That's about right, because currently I'm borrowing about $1,000 monthly from Mom and Dad." Then I asked her to review each line item and ask herself, "Is this a need or is it a want? Can this expense be held off a month or two? Can I reduce this expense by $5, $10, or $20 to help cover the $942 shortfall?"

Candace managed to reduce her food costs from $495 to $295 by lowering her expenses on groceries and opting to use what she had already stored in her freezer. She eliminated buying breakfast by deciding that she'd make coffee and a bagel at home, and canceled dinner plans with a departing coworker since she'd already contributed to the office's going-away gift. Candace reduced self-care from $579 to $249 by choosing to do her own hair and nails for the month, and postponed an expensive teeth-cleaning with a cosmetic dentist; she decided that she'd reschedule that appointment later on with a regular dentist. She did, however, keep her waxing appointment, which was the one indulgence she didn't want to go without. Candace also realized that she could avoid a fancy birthday gift for her boyfriend, since she knew he'd prefer a home-cooked meal and a rented movie anyway. She canceled charity for the month. Finally, a tax bill of $366 couldn't be paid, so she decided to pay $100 and ask for a payment plan for the balance.

When Candace finished with her revisions, she had reduced her expenses to $2,954 and eliminated the $942 shortfall. She was thrilled at the prospect of having a positive cash flow of $134! Not only would she *not* need to borrow money from her parents, but her plan included a $100 payment to them! Candace would now operate on a cash basis and use the "envelope system"—separate envelopes containing the appropriate monthly cash allocation for items such as groceries, gasoline, eating out—to ensure

Candace's Monthly Spending Plan

	Old	Revised
FOOD	495	295
HOUSING	645	645
UTILITIES	307	307
CABLE	110	110
PHONE + DSL	130	130
NEWSPAPER	36	36
CELL	50	0
SELF-CARE	579	249
PETS	20	20
TRANSPORTATION	842	842
ENTERTAINMENT	50	20
INVESTMENTS	200	100
MISC. (BIRTHDAY GIFT)	50	0
MISC. (CHARITY)	50	0
BACK TAXES	366	100
PARENTS	100	100
	$4,030	$2,954
In	$3,088	3,088
Out	-$4,030	- 2,954
	$- 942	$134

she stayed within the spending limit and even saved some money each month. I'll explain how to use this system a bit later in this chapter.

Spending Plan Basics

If you completed the exercises in the last chapter, you should now know how much money comes in and gotten some of your debts in order. In this chapter, you'll chart your day-to-day expenses to find out exactly where your hard-earned cash is going and where you need to be cutting back. But knowing what's draining your income daily, weekly, and monthly isn't just a one-time exercise; it should be habitually on your mind every day as you make decisions about whether or not to buy certain items.

Creating a spending plan for the upcoming month doesn't start on Day 1. A critically important financial strategy is to identify your upcoming needs for the month at least *fifteen days before* it starts so that if you anticipate a negative cash-flow situation, you have a couple of extra weeks to find additional income. Or you can move a purchase from one month to the next, or even shift priorities, so you don't take up the slack by charging items. Not every month will necessarily be exactly the same, but a new spending plan should be developed for each month, as detailed as possible with your actual month's expenditures, and be completed at least fifteen days before the month starts. If you've got lots of birthday celebrations in your family in May, for instance, when you chart out your budget for that month in mid-April, you'll want to make room for any gifts should you choose to give them. This might entail cutting back in another area of your expenses to make up for the additional expense. Or you might decide that you can't afford real gifts, so you'll be able to plan ahead and think about what you can do instead that doesn't cost much. (More on gift giving below.)

Though it's more ambitious, you might also consider devising three additional spending plans: a barebones minimum, an average month, and an ideal month. The barebones minimum plan provides a road map for the worst-case scenarios by identifying the least amount of money you can get by on during a given month and still remain current on all bills. The average-month plan allows you to factor in a certain amount in every category of spending. For example, you may not buy new clothes each month, but let's say that over the course of a year, you generally spend $1,200 on clothing. In the average-month plan, you would calculate $100 each month to be set aside to cover the cost of new clothing when the purchases are actually made. Then, under the ideal plan, you complete the worksheet using the ideal amount you would like to spend in each category. This is when you can accelerate your debt repayment *and* maintain two hair appointments for the month. Although this figure will likely exceed your monthly income, it will reveal how much money you need to make to assure that your wants and needs are met monthly.

Guidelines for Typical Spending Plans

Do you know how much you *should* be spending on housing, food, and entertainment each month? Looking back at past bills tells you how much you're spending, but how do you decide what's okay and what's not?

According to surveys done by the National Foundation for Credit Counseling, to determine national averages, the chart on p. 153 shows the breakdown of where people's money typically goes. The chart is a rough guideline. If you live in a metropolitan area like New York City, Detroit, Chicago, Atlanta, San Francisco, or Los Angeles, you should expect to devote more money toward housing. You may, for example, have to plan on housing taking up 40 percent of your income, and trim your other living expenses down to 20 percent.

Be Realistic About Costs and Expenses

As you begin to think about your various expenses for each month, be as specific and realistic as possible. You'll avoid a significant amount of stress if you're proactive and detailed from the get-go. Instead of saying, "I expect to spend $200 next month for food," break it down, because the reality is you'll likely spend $200 on groceries, $40 on coffee and muffins on the way to work, $60 on lunch, $30 on chips and soda for your afternoon break, and $150 on dinner. All of this comes to a total of $480 rather than $200. One sister, Lisa, called in to a radio station talk show to describe how she saved $200 on groceries and a total of $500 per month

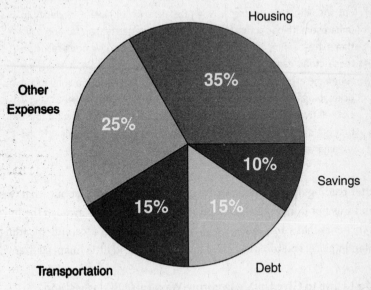

Housing: 35%
Mortgage/Rent
Repairs
Taxes
Utilities
Insurance

Transportation: 15%
Car payments
Gas
Insurance
Repairs
Parking/Tolls
Train/Bus fees

Debt: 15%
Student loans
Credit cards
Personal loans
Installment loans

Other expenses: 25%
Groceries
Eating out
Vacations
Entertainment
Clothing
Phones
Dental

Savings: 10%

> **Murphy's Law of Money.** It's always safer to build in an extra cushion of about 10 percent into your budget—even if you've conservatively figured out your monthly expenses. Why? Because we all have a tendency to underestimate our actual expenses, and it's better to plan for and have that extra cushion available to us when we need it so we don't resort to those credit cards. Another reason: You're likely to have at least one "one-time expense" every few months that you didn't plan on—a parking ticket, plumbing problems, or the cost of buying a plane ticket to visit a sick relative. Having that money available to you when you need to cover that one-time expense is vital to maintaining your financial health and keeping you above water.

after reading my first book. By being incredibly detailed about what was and was not in her monthly allowance, she successfully avoided the hidden items that can sabotage a spending plan. With a careful spending plan in place, you too can expect few surprises and little financial drama.

Do I Have to Give Up My Eyebrow Wax, False Eyelashes, and Hair Highlights?

Although that's the question one sister articulated at our first session together, she had already decided she was willing to let go of the lashes and hair highlights in order to get financially stable. The eyebrow waxing was up for discussion.

Numerous strategies to reduce expenses can work for you if you're willing to be open to a little sacrifice and inconvenience. It's up to you to decide what you're willing to give up and what you're not willing to give up for the sake of your wallet as well as your sanity. You can, for example, learn how to highlight your own hair from a box and scatter salon appointments throughout the year so overall you go less frequently. You can also learn how to wax your own eyebrows or team up with a sister-friend and schedule evenings once a month when you get together for dinner and wax each other's brows. Remember, try not to equate cutting back with totally depriving yourself of the things that contribute to your well-being and sense of self. Simply evaluate your methods of self-care and look for cheaper alternatives. Just because you visit the spa once a month for the full treatment doesn't mean you can't get those same treatments elsewhere for a fraction of the cost. Besides, once you get used to being frugal with your self-care, you'll enjoy those times when you decide to splurge on yourself and go for the deluxe version!

Small Indulgences That Add Up Big
Many of our favorite things cost cents on the dollar but add up to a substantial amount over time based on the quantities we buy. You don't have to scratch them off your favorite-things list completely, but cutting back on the individual item purchases, buying them in bulk, and searching for discount rates can add money to your savings instead of cash registers.

Keep in mind, also, that pricing may vary drastically depending on where you purchase goods. Here are five examples of things we often buy without much thought:

Snack foods	Candy, cookies, chips, crackers, vending-machine goods; anything processed, packaged, crunchy, salty, and sweet!
Beverages	Soda pop, coffee drinks, juice, and bottled water
Reading material	Newspapers and magazines
Meals-on-the-run	Fast food, supermarket buffets, and salad bars
Lucky chances	Lottery and raffle tickets

Tithes and Offerings

Tithing and church contributions are a very sensitive subject to deal with in the black community. Even though it would technically go under "other expenses," in many cases it is without question the first disbursement of funds people make. In fact, African Americans attend religious services more regularly than the general public. While it's a major source of strength, inspiration, and community spirit, it can also be a source of cultural pressure and financial expectation for black people—especially if you feel obligated to tithe when you've got bills you can't pay. You might think that tithing is your way to get into heaven. If this is a non-negotiable area, then fine; make the cut somewhere else in your expenses. But consider this: if you get your debt under control, you'll be able to tithe comfortably and meet all of your needs and wants consistently.

Charity

If you're in debt and facing an uphill climb back to creditworthiness, I strongly suggest that you hold off on making regular contributions to charity until two things have happened: (1) you've gotten your debt under control by making regular payments for at least six months, and (2) you've managed to create a small emergency fund for yourself so you won't fall back into debt at the drop of one unexpected bill. That said, let me offer some guidelines for when you reconvene those contributions.

Charity Support Guidelines

It wasn't until she was preparing for a tax meeting that Constance realized how much she had given to charities. Fortunately, she had obtained and filed the proper receipts. She had checked the receipts for accuracy when she'd originally received them; nonetheless, the numbers really surprised her when she added them up. "Throughout the year, I gave cash donations here and wrote checks there without realizing how much was spent for charitable contributions," she recalled. "Since then, I have logged all of these types of donations and reviewed them periodically throughout the year."

When charity appeals tug at your heartstrings, don't forget what you have in your pocketbook and bank account. Charity is a wonderful thing, but you should give these charity support guidelines some consideration:

1. Check up on the charity. You can request copies of annual reports. Visit sites such as Smartmoney.com and Charitynavigator.com, where you can obtain independent ratings on many of the largest charities. Charity Navigator also rates top metropolitan areas on how effectively charities located in their area

operate. You don't want your hard-earned money going to a charity that won't use it as promised. It's better off in your pocket than that of a crooked charity.

2. Don't automatically pay the same amount you paid previously or the minimum a solicitor requests. When your salary changes, the amount you can really afford to give does, too. That may mean some years you have to give less—or even not at all—to some charities.

3. Regularly check to see how tax laws have changed. (I'm not suggesting that you become an expert in tax laws, but stay tuned in to new information that's often broken down easily in articles and newspapers come tax season.) The rules change periodically. If you don't know what they are and what their impact will be in light of your financial status, your charitable contributions might not qualify for deductions.

4. Collect the proper receipts/documentation when charitable donations are made and file them for easy access later. Those tax deductions can equate to money you need for other things, including debt repayment. It is much easier to get receipts close to when donations are made than to backtrack and retrieve them later. Depending on the amount of your charitable donation and tax bracket, additional documentation may be required if you are audited and want to retain credit.

5. Don't pledge more money than you will be able to afford when the bill arrives. Putting down a big amount on a pledge form means that charity is counting on you to fulfill the commitment. You don't want a commitment to charity to result in more debt for you and then a further drop in your credit score.

6. Monitor how much you spend on tickets for fund-raisers and related expenses, including auctions. The expenses for elegant

dresses, accessories, getting hair/nails done, parking, and cash bars can add up. I suggest that you avoid such fund-raisers entirely while you are paying down your debt and working to get your credit score up. Don't use a fund-raiser as an excuse to spend frivolously and fall back into the debt hole for a while—even if it is for the sake of charity.

7. Determine whether taking mileage deductions for charitable work is appropriate for you. Then keep the required data in mileage logs. If you are audited, you don't want to lose this deduction due to missing documentation.

8. Consider supporting charities in ways other than always making a payment. Many charities create wish lists indicating items they need for core service populations or projects. Sometimes those items can be purchased at a discount—for example: canned goods and blankets for drives. Or you can volunteer your time to assist with the running of the organization—such as helping out with mailings, or doing fund-raising—or offer your own companionship to young children, the elderly, or even animals at shelters.

Gift Giving

Attention, generous gift givers! Even though you've probably heard "it's the thought that counts," your gift-purchasing habits may not reflect it. It is important for your gift-related expenses to be appropriate for your income level. Otherwise, you will have less money for paying bills or adding to your savings. Here are some suggestions:

- **Do** comparison-shop. Check for the best price when purchasing gifts available from a multitude of retailers. If retailers have a price-matching policy, ask them to honor it.

- **Do** add up all the costs related to ordering from catalogs. Make sure postage or shipping and handling plus other costs listed on order forms don't offset savings on selected items. Try not to request express or overnight delivery options.

- **Do** plan ahead. Just as with personal purchases, you can shop at the end of seasons for gifts. Items marked down in after-holiday sales can be purchased at substantial discounts and stored away. Some of these sales reflect 50 percent or even 75 percent markdowns. But don't lose your mind and overspend due to the adrenaline rush of bargain shopping.

- **Don't** lose track of how much you spend on items accompanying your gifts, such as paper, ribbons, and cards. Use creative options for wrapping gifts. Some people wrap gifts in newspaper or containers with practical uses—for example, toiletries in a dollar-store shower tote. Recycle gift bags and bows. Make or purchase economical cards and gift tags. Use computer software for creating greeting cards.

- **Don't** think that every act of kindness or gift must be reciprocated with a gift from you. Sometimes just showing appreciation by saying thanks or sending a thank-you note is enough. You can also utilize Web sites with e-mail cards and save postage.

Tracking and Analyzing

Successful dieters are known to keep food journals where they tally up their calories for the day and keep track of their eating habits. It's a very effective weight-loss and weight-management tool, because it's too easy to eat more than we realize unless we're keeping track of it all. That way, when we find that we've overspent our calorie budget for the day, we can plan to eliminate something the following day to make up for that excess. Having a spending plan and tracking your expenses works the same way. Creating a clear spending plan is only half the battle; testing it out and seeing whether or not you can measure up to your intentions is the other half. In the exercises at the end of this chapter, you're going to start tracking your spending and watching carefully for what routinely drains your accounts. This will allow you to plan for excesses and splurges smartly.

One of the first things new clients tend to tell me is, "You know, Glinda, I make good money, but I don't know where it goes." When it comes to recovering from debt and building a better financial future, it's not about how much money you make. It's about how you spend it and what's left. Often we think, "I've got to make more money—that will solve the financial problem." But more money is usually not the whole answer. Instead, you'll need to go through the process of tracking your expenditures—that is, actually adding up how much money was spent and where. With more attention to purchases, you will find how much "minor" daily splurges add up to big bills over a year. Eating a "cheap" $6 lunch every day in the café by work translates to an annual lunch bill of about $1,500. I encourage you to ask yourself, "How do I feel about spending that much on lunch while I complain that my bills are late and I never have money to take a vacation?" If you were to brown-bag your lunch four days a week, you could save $1,200. Now imagine that $1,200 going toward a credit-card bill.

It's one thing to spend your cash on superfluous items like Starbucks and lunch cafés, but it's a whole other thing to pay for them with borrowed money. Erika Lim, director of Career Services at Seattle University School of Law, goes so far as to distribute coffee-consumption charts on campus that show if you refrained from buying a $3 latte for thirty years, you could save $55,341 (with interest). Similarly, a five-day-a-week $3 latte habit on borrowed money—i.e., credit—for one year can cost $4,154 when repaid over ten years with interest. Feel free to plug in your own numbers and calculate what your daily coffee consumption or other daily or weekly habit is costing you.

As newlyweds, my husband Edward and I tracked our food and grocery expenses for one month. The total came to $947 for just the two of us! Further analysis exposed how lots of eating out and champagne with dinner can be very costly. We were still in wedded bliss and happily indulging our champagne tastes—but on a wine cooler budget! It took no time at all for us to shift our champagne tastes to special occasions only. And besides, with our respective weights headed in the wrong direction, we thought it was better to cut down on such elaborate meals and drink more water anyway!

Food Shopping Tip: Shop the Perimeter, Not the Center Aisles

Grocery stores can be like toy stores for grown-ups—especially for those who love to eat, snack, and cook. The vast majority of packaged and processed foods are found in the inner aisles of supermarkets. All the fresh vegetables, meats, fruits, fish, dairy, and bread products typically line the outer aisles. If you avoid the inner (dangerous) sanctum and instead shop the perimeter, you'll avoid a lot of those extra costs related to packaged goods and achieve the added benefit of avoiding a lot of empty calories, too!

A financial planner friend of mine once contacted me regarding a family that was still perplexed after tracking their expenses. This family of five from southern California got a rude awakening one year at tax time when they looked to see how much they'd spent on food during the prior twelve-month period. Surprisingly, it was more than $26,000, or almost $2,200 per month! That's more than a mortgage payment for most Americans! This family had no clue as to what they *should* be spending, but they knew that $26,000 was not a healthy number. I recommended a guideline for food expenses that I'd read in *Money* magazine several years before. It stated that you should spend $200 per month for each adult and $150 per month for each child. Given that, this family should have been spending around $850 each month—a far cry from $2,200.

Another working-class couple that came to me with $85,000 in outstanding credit-card balances began creating monthly spending plans and tracking their expenditures consistently. After using a portion of their inherited stocks to pay off the high-interest-rate debt, this couple committed to operating on a cash basis that they have now maintained for over six years. Giving attention to their finances, planning, and knowing where their money goes has kept them from running those credit cards up again. I'll explain the cash-only system below; it's a technique I encourage everyone to try at least once.

There are many benefits to analyzing your expenses and making appropriate changes. Remember Markayla from Chapter 2, the sister with a $2,800 monthly debt repayment—$2,000 of which was paying for interest? She had many other ideas and uses for her money. But until she tracked and analyzed expenses, she never understood how much she was paying for her debt and how much it was impinging on her goal of saving money for her children's education. I think Alfred Edmond from *Black Enterprise* said it best. He suggests you ask yourself, "Am I using money to buy things or accomplish things?" Buying things refers to purchases like a new car or a plasma television. Accomplishing things means spending money on opportunities that move you forward—like homeownership or an education.

The Cash-Only Envelope System of Tracking

Want to really reduce your monthly expenses by a lot? When my client Vonnessa came to me stating that she charged everything because she got mileage points and liked to have all of her bills come on one statement, I asked her what her monthly tally amounted to. She said between $2,500 and $3,000. She did pay off this balance every month, but when I encouraged her to go on a cash-only basis using an envelope every day with a predetermined allowance, guess what? She dropped her monthly spending down to $1,500! That's just $50 a day. Even though Vonnessa went back to using her credit card for convenience's sake, the lesson paid off. She knew that she had to stay within a $50-a-day limit to come out a winner at the end of the month. That one exercise over the course of a month resulted in saving more than $12,000 a year!

Exercise Three at the end of this chapter will get you started on using the cash-and-envelope system for yourself. It is quite simply the best way I know of to track and save money at the same time. You'll start by learning to rely on cash to get through your day. No credit cards. No store cards. No debit cards. You'll figure out how much of an allowance you can give yourself—based on your spending plan—to cover certain categories of expenses, such as household items and personal care, and you'll divvy up your dollars among those categories using separate envelopes. This forces you to stay within your plan and avoid frivolous, excess spending. When the money is gone, you can't buy anything else. This is an incredibly powerful exercise to get you to see exactly how much you can limit your spending by resorting to cash only—and not having any other means of payment.

Kwanzaa Concepts

Getting from Thanksgiving to New Year's can entail a slow, burdensome drain from your wallet. But a great way to reduce your year-end expenses is by celebrating Kwanzaa instead of getting caught up in the commercialism of traditional holiday spending. Kwanzaa is a holiday celebration linked to our African heritage. According to the *New York Times*, more than 18 million people worldwide now celebrate Kwanzaa. Founded by Dr. Maulana Karenga in 1966, it is celebrated each year from December 26 to January 1. Kwanzaa is derived from the Swahili phrase "matunda ya kwanza," meaning "first fruits," and is linked to the traditional celebration days for African harvest festivals.

During the celebration of Kwanzaa, families and friends are encouraged to spend quality time together each day acknowledging diverse skills and talents. Thus, gifts are made for one another reflecting creativity and ties to our ancestors. An important lesson is that gifts do not have to be expensive in order to have value. In fact, the gifts of Kwanzaa are unique treasures to be enjoyed all year long.

Exercise One: Create Your Own Spending Plan

Your goal as you begin to set your credit straight will be to develop a new plan each month—fifteen days in advance. Each plan will detail your estimated upcoming monthly expenditures. By following this timeline, if you have a shortfall—more money going out than coming in—you'll have time to cut expenses or generate additional income. To free up as much money as possible for debt repayment, you'll want to create a barebones spending plan.

As you begin to map out your plan, don't forget to ask yourself: What can I hold off on doing for a month or two that costs money, such as getting a teeth cleaning? What can I stop doing temporarily that costs money, such as weekly manicures? What can I cut back on without totally eliminating? For example, let's say your daughter's school tuition is due very soon. You may want to wait on scheduling her orthodontic appointment for braces until you've paid that tuition. Use the following worksheet to get started and follow these easy steps:

1. Check your calendar and note any special events that may cost money. Examples: festivals, town fairs, birthdays, and anniversaries. Create specific funds for those special occasions, or consider ways to give a gift without its costing anything.

2. Complete your spending plan by making the best estimate of your upcoming bills and other needs for the month using the worksheet on the following pages. Tweak the payments in all categories to determine the minimum amounts that can be spent without creating a sense of deprivation.

3. Try to include an amount for your savings cushion so you have a resource available for emergencies. If this is too much to bear right now as you focus on debt reduction, that's okay. You can build this reserve later.

4. If possible, include the "Murphy's Law of Money," which means that anything that can go wrong will. Add an extra 10 percent to the spending plan once it's done—if you can. That figure is realistically what you're going to spend if something goes wrong (like car problems, plumbing, falling and getting hurt, etc.).

5. Calculate your cash flow. What is the amount left over after you subtract the total expenses from the net income you will have for the month?

6. Apply remaining cash to your debts according to the priority payment plan in Chapter 3.

If you have a mentor or friend whom you trust and with whom you can share your personal financial life, ask that person to review your spending plan with an objective eye. Ask for suggestions in modifying or tweaking the plan for the better.

Monthly Spending Plan

	mo. plan	wk. 1	wk. 2	wk. 3	wk. 4	wk. 5	mo. total
Food							
Groceries							
Breakfast							
Lunch							
Dinner							
Snacks							
Guest							
Totals							
Shelter							
Housing							
Phone							
Water/Garbage							
Gas and Electric							
Cable							
Newspaper							
Household Items							
Insurance							
Housekeeper							
Totals							
Self-Care							
Clothing							
Shoes							
Accessories							
Hair Care							
Toiletries							
Manicure							
Massage							
Medical							
Dry Cleaners/Laundry							
Life/Disability Insurance							
Totals							
Recovery/Self-Improvement							
Spiritual							
Therapy							
Financial Counseling							
Totals							

	mo. plan	wk. 1	wk. 2	wk. 3	wk. 4	wk. 5	mo. total
Dependent Care							
Clothes							
Child Care							
Pets							
Totals							
Transportation							
Car Payment							
Gas							
Maintenance							
Parking/Tolls							
Bus or Other							
Insurance							
Totals							
Entertainment							
Movies							
Video Rental							
Concerts/Theater							
Dating							
Totals							
Investments							
Savings (Cushion)							
Vacation							
Retirement							
Totals							
Monthly Allocations							
Taxes							
Car Registration							
Totals							
Miscellaneous							
Totals							

	mo. plan	wk. 1	wk. 2	wk. 3	wk. 4	wk. 5	mo. total
Debt Repayment							
Totals							
One-Time Expenses							
Totals							
Business Expenses							
Rent							
Phone							
Office Supplies							
Postage							
Totals							
Income							
Totals							

MONTHLY CATEGORY RECAP

	mo. plan	mo actual	
Food			
Shelter			
Self-Care			
Recovery/Self-Improvement			
Dependent Care			
Transportation			
Entertainment			
Investments			
Monthly Allocations			
Miscellaneous			
Debt Repayment			
One-Time Expenses			
Business Expenses			
Total Expenses			
Income			
Cash on Hand +			
Income +			
Total Income =			
Expenses −			
Cash Flow			

Exercise Two: Begin Tracking Your Expenses Daily

Creating a sound spending plan and tracking your expenses always go hand in hand, so even if tracking and analyzing isn't normally your thing, do your best to be extra meticulous for at least three months. It's a lesson that has big rewards. Keep all your receipts.

Write down every cent you spend, no matter how insignificant it may seem. Carry a small spiral notepad in your purse to jot down the amounts, or write the expenditures on the envelope you carry with the day's cash in it if you're on the envelope system (see the next exercise).

To track your spending, use the worksheet on the following pages. You can also download the abridged version of *The Basic Money Management Workbook*, which includes worksheets, from my Web site (www.BridgforthFinancial.com). Another option is to create a spreadsheet on your own in a program like Excel, using the categories on my worksheet. Drop your data into it daily. You'll be able to draw basic conclusions about where your money goes. And then you can more confidently take the proper action.

If you run your own business, you should do this same exercise for your business. Be sure to include office supplies, shipping and postage, rented or leased equipment, and any other expenses related to your business that are not listed on the spending plan.

Daily Tracking

	mon.	tue.	wed.	thur.	fri.	sat.	sun.	total
Food								
Groceries								
Breakfast								
Lunch								
Dinner								
Snacks								
Guest								
Totals								
Shelter								
Housing								
Phone								
Water/Garbage								
Gas and Electric								
Cable								
Newspaper								
Household Items								
Insurance								
Housekeeper								
Totals								
Self-Care								
Clothing								
Shoes								
Accessories								
Hair Care								
Toiletries								
Manicure								
Massage								
Medical								
Dry Cleaners/Laundry								
Life/Disability Insurance								
Totals								
Recovery/Self-Improvement								
Spiritual								
Therapy								
Financial Counseling								
Totals								

	mon.	tue.	wed.	thur.	fri.	sat.	sun.	total
Dependent Care								
Clothes								
Child Care								
Pets								
Totals								
Transportation								
Car Payment								
Gas								
Maintenance								
Parking/Tolls								
Bus or Other								
Insurance								
Totals								
Entertainment								
Movies								
Video Rental								
Concerts/Theater								
Dating								
Totals								
Investments								
Savings (Cushion)								
Vacation								
Retirement								
Totals								
Monthly Allocations								
Taxes								
Car Registration								
Totals								
Miscellaneous								
Totals								

	mon.	tue.	wed.	thur.	fri.	sat.	sun.	total
Debt Repayment								
Totals								

One-Time Expenses

	mon.	tue.	wed.	thur.	fri.	sat.	sun.	total
Totals								

Business Expenses

	mon.	tue.	wed.	thur.	fri.	sat.	sun.	total
Rent								
Phone								
Office Supplies								
Postage								
Totals								

Income

	mon.	tue.	wed.	thur.	fri.	sat.	sun.	total
Totals								

Exercise Three: Try the Cash-Only Envelope System

Here's how the cash-only system works:

1. Based on your monthly spending plan, in which you've identified all areas where you need to spend money in the upcoming month, you know what your expenses will be and what you can expect to have to pay at various times during the month. Determine what bills will be paid by check or direct debit from your checking account, taking into account *when* they need to be paid—first of the month, middle of the month, or end of the month. Obviously, you can't pay for everything with cash. Pay your basic bills (i.e., rent/mortgage, utilities, phone, cable, water, etc.—anything that you'd normally mail) by check, online, or by an automatic debit from your checking account. Also consider which paycheck should go toward which payment. For example, if the cable bill is due on the twentieth of every month and you get paid on the fifteenth, that particular paycheck should go toward that bill.

2. Determine what can and should be paid for with cash in order to stay within your spending limit. Any purchases you make in person, for instance, should be paid with *cash only*! This includes groceries, personal items paid from your wallet, a trip to the mall or Home Depot, lunches, toiletries, household items, gasoline, and so on.

3. Create separately labeled envelopes for the categories of cash-only expenses you have—for example, "household items," "personal care," "lunches," and so on. Then determine how much cash to allocate for these purchases, using your spending plan as a guide. You will pay for these items using that set amount of cash from each envelope. This prevents you from spending more than the allocated amount when you're in the store. You cannot use credit cards, debit cards, checks, or store cards. If you run out of cash, you can't buy anything else.

4. Aim to make only one visit to the ATM per week. You can allocate the money by day, week, month, or pay period. For example, if you set aside $80 for lunch money a month, you can take $40 cash per pay period or $20 per week or $4 per day. If you've got a spouse, you need to agree to a per-person allowance. For example, if you agree that you and your partner can allocate $200 total to lunches a month, that's $100 per individual, which boils down to $25 per person each week, or $5 per day.

You don't have to stay on the cash-only system forever. I've had many clients who fall in love with this system, though, and remain on it for many months. It's an eye-opening experience that can reduce your overall expenses significantly. Try it for at least one month and see what happens!

Exercise Four: Celebrate Your Bills

Try making bill paying a time for celebration. After hearing about how one of my clients enjoyed it, another client, Beverlee, vowed to have Bill Payment Celebration Days. Instead of dreading the experience, she would light a candle and put on a favorite CD that hadn't been played for a while. Sometimes plans would be made for doing other fun things after the bills were paid. Either way, the celebrations always ended with a prayer thanking God for all of the blessings in her life—including the ability to pay her bills.

In this exercise, try to come up with your own ways of making paying bills a pleasure rather than a chore. Try planning a night with friends, or a favorite activity as a reward—a hot bath, or cooking a fabulous meal for afterward. If you choose to pay your bills on a weekend, do it first thing in the morning and then plan the rest of your day around activities that make you happy. For example, you can meet friends for an afternoon hike or picnic. Once you've done your bills, avoid doing any other type of "chore" or "errand" that day that wouldn't be on your list of your favorite things to do if given a choice.

Exercise Five: Continue to Revisit Your Plan and Find New Ways to Cut Expenses

Spending plans should continue to evolve and change according to your needs and obligations. This is why it's important to create a new plan two weeks prior to the upcoming month. Don't know where else you can cut your expenses? Use the following list of ideas to see what else you can do. If you find at least ten more ways to whittle your expenses down, you'll accelerate your debt reduction and your credit mending at the same time. Get out a highlighter and mark the ones you'll plan to do.

Fifty Ways to Whittle Away Common Costs

1. Collect recipes from Mom, friends, and coworkers for stew, spaghetti, casserole, and chili. These dishes are dollar stretchers and filling choices with many tasty variations. If you cook up a pot of chili on Sunday, you instantly have a meal ready to go all week long for some lunches and dinners.

2. Cook more. There are cookbooks for all levels, from basic cooking for those who can barely boil water, to those used for becoming a gourmet chef. Check out *Dining on a Dime* by Tawra Kellam and Jill Cooper. For an even cheaper route, go online and download recipes for free!

3. Buy store-brand products instead of brand names.

4. Do your own hair and nails except on special occasions. Purchase products at beauty supply stores, as some carry spa-quality items on the cheap. Invite friends over to join you for pamper or makeover parties, rather than going to a salon.

5. Buy a water purifier and eliminate bottled water. And keep some bottles filled for emergency use. That way, you'll always be prepared.

6. Eliminate cable or reduce premium cable channels. You might have to miss some of your favorite programs, but the savings will be worth the sacrifice. (You can rent them on DVD later.)

7. Eliminate iTunes, TiVo, satellite radio, and pay-per-view. Check to see if special events or concerts can be viewed at a friend's house or places you can go for free or a minimal cover charge.

8. Limit your number of movie rentals per month and return them on time to avoid fees. Make sure to check out only the number of movie rentals that your schedule allows time for viewing.

9. Limit your number of CD purchases. Check before buying new releases by your favorite artists for duplication of songs on CDs already in your collection.

10. Limit your number of DVD purchases. Remember, movies just sitting in a rack year after year don't entertain anyone.

11. Reduce phone features and phone lines. Check your bill if you forgot what features came with your plan or how much they cost. It might be time to eliminate some of them or switch to a less expensive plan with minimal features. Reduce phone lines if you don't really need them, or buy new technology that could eliminate them entirely. For example, you could purchase a multiline telephone or fax machine that intercepts fax signals, eliminating the necessity for a separate phone line. If you have a high-speed connection to the Internet, you can now buy a virtual line that operates through the Internet (actually, it's called "voice-over Internet protocol") and you can drop the more expensive service offered by traditional phone companies with standard phone lines. Vonage is one example of a company that offers voice-over IP. You may even be able to keep your existing phone number.

12. Return library books on time to avoid fines. Keep a list of the items you and your children check out so no one forgets about them.

13. Cancel subscriptions for newspapers and magazines you are not reading. Those unread stacks are a waste of money and just take up space.

14. Use the telephone book and not directory assistance. Making several calls to directory assistance during the month adds up. This is true for your cell phone, too.

15. Bundle telephone, cable, and Internet services. Signing up with or switching to one company for all of these services can result in substantial savings.

16. Downsize your vehicle. Gasoline, car insurance, car payment, and repair bills can all be reduced with a switch such as one from a Lincoln Town Car to a Taurus or Jeep to a Jetta.

17. Consolidate errands, thereby reducing gasoline. Try to schedule everything requiring a trip to another part of town on the same day. Making that trip several times during the week is a waste of time and money. Complete some errands on workdays if stops are along the way, rather than waiting for your day off.

18. Know how to get to your destination and reduce gasoline usage. Map out your route before leaving home. Get directions or check with Mapquest.

19. Drive less. Do business by phone and Internet when possible.

20. Set up or join a car pool with your coworkers.

21. Set up or join a neighborhood car pool for taking kids to their activities or practices.

22. Don't drive during the hottest time of the day. Reduce A/C use and save gasoline.

23. Stop buying gas-guzzling cars and SUVs.

24. Purchase gas during the early morning or late afternoon during the summer. You'll get slightly more gas when it's cooler than when it's hot. And don't buy premium gas.

25. Check the Internet for sites that list local gas prices. Seek the cheapest gas station—it's all the same.

26. If you catch a cab, make sure the taxi driver takes the shortest route.

27. Ride a bicycle. Cut some expenses and burn some calories.

28. Walk more. One sister realized the value of walking when she gained ten pounds after getting her driver's license!

29. Eliminate health club memberships, especially if you're not using them.

30. When making purchases at conferences, malls, or home parties, pay only with cash and bring along only the cash. Vow not to yield to the temptation of using credit cards or checkbooks. This way you can avoid spending more than you plan for ahead of time.

31. Bundle insurance. Use an insurance company that handles property, casualty, and life insurance so you can get those discounts for using the same insurer.

32. Increase insurance deductibles and see a reduction in premiums.

33. Pay bills on time and avoid late-payment fees and interest-rate increases. Don't pay extra fees for making payments by telephone.

34. Ask creditors to lower interest rates on credit cards.

35. Cut back on postage by using your e-mail account more.

36. Resist that new-car purchase. Consider a moderately priced used car.

37. Sell something on consignment at a resale shop. Have a garage sale once a year. Sell items on eBay and Craigslist.com.

38. Let your presence be a present instead of always giving gifts or money.

39. Say "no" to others—grown folks and kids. Don't enable.

40. Limit dining out to once per paycheck.

41. Limit dry cleaning. Use a product like Dryel (the home approach to dry cleaning) or get a bottle of Woolite. Take better care of your clothes by hanging up suits at the end of the workday as opposed to throwing them on a chair for two or three days.

42. Clip coupons from the Sunday newspaper.

43. Check for coupons and deals on the Internet. Airline-ticket deals are frequently available. Some companies, such as Dell Computers, offer huge discounts for online purchases.

44. Check for in-store coupons and sale announcements.

45. Check for bargains and special sales in newspapers before going shopping.

46. Mail in rebate forms. Don't forget about these opportunities to get checks in the mail.

47. Avoid purchasing extended warranties for low-cost appliances, such as toaster ovens, microwaves, blenders, small televisions, and cameras under $200.

48. Wait forty-eight hours before committing to any purchase or service exceeding $100.

49. Buy generic medicines.

50. Buy cosmetics at the drugstore—not the department store.

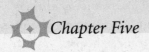

Chapter Five

The Secrets to Boosting Your Creditworthiness

Becoming disciplined with spending can have some unexpected benefits. As we've seen, we are often conditioned to relate to money in certain ways based on our upbringing. And it can take years to recondition our habits. Some people, however, learn to change their habits quite quickly, as the gratification that comes from successfully managing your money can be extremely powerful.

Take Julia, my forty-one-year-old client, as an example. Julia grew up one of four girls in the household with her single mom. They never had new clothes and had to make do with hand-me-downs. She remembers many meals where they had cereal for dinner, and vividly recalls feeling embarrassed while standing at the cash register with her mom, watching the clerk subtotal items one by one, as they tried to get as much as possible for the few dollars they had to spend. As an adult, Julia refused to add up items when she shopped. If she didn't have enough cash, she hoped there was enough available credit on her cards. Julia knew it was a disservice to her children when she lavishly spent in an effort to compensate for her own childhood poverty. But sometimes she couldn't help it.

In our first meeting, Julia described how she and her husband paid bills separately from their respective paychecks. But previously, bill paying shifted back and forth between them because each thought he or she could do a better job. They even refinanced their home a couple of times just so they could pay off bills. Julia readily admitted she was out of control with her credit cards and had a habit of charging them up to the limit. She confessed that on one outing, her twelve-year-old son even declared, "Mom, you are spending *too much* money!" Although she rolled her eyes and said, "Boy, be quiet," the guilt and embarrassment welled up in her as she continued making her purchases.

After just one financial-counseling session, however, Julia saw the other side of her habits. Later, when she and her fifteen-year-old daughter went grocery shopping with a set budget of $100, her daughter exclaimed, "Mom, that was good!" when the clerk hit the total button on the cash register and the amount $100.71 appeared. By focusing on needs and not falling prey to impulse shopping for her wants, Julia had been able to accomplish her goal of staying within a limit—*and* she'd taught her daughter a valuable lesson about discipline. This was the turning point for Julia's money management.

As you begin to tackle your debts and spend more wisely, you'll automatically be giving your credit score a booster shot. You'll reach your own turning point and experience an "Aha!" moment that will inspire you to keep going. But you have to do more than just pay down your balances and follow a spending plan if you really want to get that credit score up and holding steady.

In this chapter, I'm going to give you a rundown of all the ways in which you can inject points into your score and keep it moving up. Some of this advice might sound familiar. Why? Because you probably learned some of the secrets in Chapter 3 when I talked about the process of debt reduction. Many of the techniques go hand in hand. Now, however, let's go deeper into `is complicated place where we have to accept credit cards and credit bu-
s as a part of life and learn to use them to our benefit! The banking in-
ry continues to evolve at the same speed as technology, which can be a

good thing for making quick purchases and payments at the click of a mouse, but a bad thing if you're not keeping track of account balances—especially when your deposits are not as frequent as those quick withdrawals and automatic debits. It takes only a few seconds to suffer a significant drop in your credit score. It generally takes a while to see a significant change in your score for the better.

Just understanding the system and making a few choice moves can effect positive change in your credit score. Some of the strategies are no-brainers; some are logical and you'll say, "Oh, that makes sense." But some are counterintuitive and might make you want to say, "Gee, that's weird." Nonetheless, they are worth taking seriously and can help you get the results you want.

The No-Brainers

Pay Bills on Time

If you've made it a habit of being late with your bills, aim to change the way you send payments in so you don't ever become delinquent again. You want to eliminate thirty-day delinquencies on your credit report at all costs. Missing one payment might not seem like a big deal, but that simple oversight can reduce your score in an instant if it becomes delinquent. Two or more delinquencies in the past twelve months is a big red flag to lenders, and it shows in your lower credit score. If you're making your payment online, you need to be conscious of the cutoff time for same-day payment processing, too. Being even *one minute* late can throw your payment into the next business day's processing and generate a late charge. Even worse, if you wait until day twenty-nine to make the payment (meaning it's twenty-nine days late and on the cusp of being officially delinquent), that small delinquency will be reflected on your credit report for seven years. It's okay to pay bills close to the due date, but be watchful of when on your calendar those dates land. Don't push the limits and expect the clock to tick backward for you in those final moments. Have a buffer zone. If you mistakenly send in your payment late (or you *think* you sent it on time but it wasn't received in time), ask your creditor to waive the late charge.

Establish a Method for Paying Bills and Stick with It

There are lots of ways to keep track of bills and make payments these days. To increase the likelihood of making on-time payments month after month, be organized and aim to pay virtually all of your bills the same way. Be consistent. Here are some ideas:

1. A very effective way is to sign up for online or direct-pay services, timing the withdrawal from your bank account a certain day a month when you know the funds will be there. Here's another great tip: If those credit-card statements arrive at the worst time of the month for you financially, call and request a new closing date so you can schedule payments that are more in tune with when you have available funds. For example, if your Visa card closes on the fifth of the month and the bill arrives soon thereafter, around the ninth, but you don't get your paycheck until the fifteenth, contact the creditor and ask that they move the closing date to the twelfth so when the bill arrives, you're ready to pay it.

2. Plot payments by due dates, as well as paydays, on a month-at-a-glance calendar. Based on those dates, plot out the days and times that you will devote to sitting down and making payments, such as writing checks.

3. Buy an accordion-style folder with pockets numbered from 1 to 31, and insert each bill on the day it needs to be sent out. Get into the routine of checking each day's pocket for bills that must go out.

Consider Easy Ways to Make Payments Using Today's Technology

If you're not good with checking your mail, opening your bills, and then sending in a traditional check, you can thank technology for all that's available today to make bill paying automatic. Sign up for online banking and pay your bills through automatic transfers from your checking account to your creditors and other vendors that you owe. Many computer programs have calendars now that you can fill with appointments. Use those calendars (or an old-school one in your organizer, on your desk, or in your GIRL journal) to record when bills are due so you can be sure to make those transfers on time.

You can also set up automatic transfers to occur on a weekly, monthly, or quarterly basis. This is especially helpful for bills like insurance premiums for auto, home, and health. That way, you know you won't miss a payment and you won't risk losing coverage. BUT, if you can't remember to record that deduction from your checkbook, then you may be better off making those payments yourself from your account when they come due. Otherwise, you can tell your insurance companies when you want them to deduct from your account for payment, and request a day that you know is when you typically have enough funds available.

You can actually schedule payments and transfers way in advance, sometimes up to a year. Say, for example, you want to be sure you roll some money over into your savings account every month from your checking account. All you have to do is set up a "recurring" transaction with your bank and pick which date you want that transfer to happen each month.

Online banking takes the backache out of personal financial management, but it doesn't mean you can skip out on balancing your checkbook. Go through your transactions online at least once a month and make sure everything looks a-okay. Check for any errors, fees, or deductions

Caution: Using a Credit Card to Pay for (and Keep Track of) Everything Can Be Risky

Credit-card companies now want you to use their cards to pay for just about everything—from your new pair of undies to your water and sewage bill. They claim this not only allows you to avoid missing a payment, but also makes it easier to keep track of payments because they all come on a single statement. For some people, this can be an excellent way to simplify and streamline their bill-paying system. HOWEVER, if you've got problems already with your credit cards, you don't want to pour more salt into this wound until it's healed. This can be an option a bit later on. At that point, you can designate one credit card to handle certain bills (your most important living expenses, like utilities and insurance) automatically as long as you can pay that one credit-card bill in full each month.

you don't recall, such as overdraft fees and mysterious bank charges. Reconcile your checkbook register. Report any errors to the bank, and ask questions if you don't understand a transaction that's listed.

For more on balancing a checkbook and tips to managing your money, see Chapter 5 of *Girl, Get Your Money Straight!*

Don't Bounce Checks

In the old days—before we had online banking and automatic bill pay—you could write a check today knowing that it wouldn't get cashed (or "go through your account") for about three days after you sent it. In other words, you could take advantage of "the float"—the time it takes for banks to deduct from your account. Well, not anymore! Even if you write a check today and drop it in the mail, it will be cleared electronically and probably destroyed as soon as the recipient gets it. In some cases, this means tomorrow if you're sending it in the mail locally—or right on the spot if you're handing over a check to a vendor in a store. This new system also allows for digital images of checks to be deemed legal representation of payment, and you no longer receive your original, canceled (handwritten) checks back in the mail with your bank statement each month.

Why did this new system emerge? The events of 9/11 had a lot to do with it; when flights were grounded after the attacks, banks became paralyzed and unable to process checks that had previously been flown around the world to various banks for clearance. The need for electronic clearings to keep commerce moving was evident. You may have heard of this system as Check 21, short for Check Clearing for the 21st Century Act, which permits anyone, including banks and customers, to deposit, present, send for collection, or return a paper reproduction of an original check, called a "substitute check." Under Check 21, any bank or financial-service provider may remove an original paper check from the check-clearing process and send a "substitute check" to the next financial institution. Alternately, the bank may send an electronic image of the check if both the sending and receiving financial institutions have agreed to this. This process is called "truncation."

Electronic check processing also means consumers can't play games with cash flow related to the checks they write. When you write checks, be sure you carry that amount in your bank at the same time. Otherwise, you'll likely bounce the check and be slapped with fees.

Manage Overdraft Responsibly

Overdraft protection is a service many banks offer to protect you when you need some cash to cover checks you've already written. The cash can be transferred from your savings account, a credit card, or a line of credit. If you don't have protection, fees related to an overdraft can be hefty, and they add up quickly if multiple checks come in at the same time. If your overdraft protection is tied to a savings account, you can deplete that account rapidly. If it's tied to a credit card, you can run up that bill pretty quickly, too. You should decide whether or not you want overdraft protection, and if so, be extra cautious about relying too much on it. Overdraft is never a free service. Each transaction is related to a fee (and sometimes an interest rate, depending on what kind of overdraft protection you have), so it's not the savior it's touted to be and should not be used on a routine basis. Avoid overdraft by properly managing your checkbook, and use the coverage for peace of mind as a good backup *just in case.*

Remember to Watch Out for Universal Default

If you've got one of those credit cards with a very low introductory rate, and you've transferred debt over to that in the hopes of paying it down more easily, be careful about letting your other cards go unnoticed. As I mentioned in Chapter 2, a record number of credit-card companies have built "universal default" clauses into their agreements, which allow them to raise your interest rate if you're late making a payment—even to another credit-card company. So if you've got a card with nearly 30 percent interest and you're only making regular payments on the one with zero percent interest for the first six months, you might find that low-interest card is suddenly charging you 30 percent interest, too. The provision, generally buried in the fine print of your credit-card agreement, basically says that if you are more than thirty days late on any payment to anyone, the interest rate on your credit card could shoot up and your credit score may be damaged.

Reduce Outstanding Debt and Pay More Than the Minimum

You want to see your balances moving downward, not upward. Makes sense, right? Of course, it's best if you can pay the bill in full each month, but if not, pay as much as possible. In 2005, minimum monthly payments increased from 2 percent to 4 percent of the total amount owed, thus causing payments to double. While in some cases this requirement causes a financial hardship for those who can barely pay the 2 percent, in the long run it's better for the consumer. If they stop incurring new charges, the balance will pay off much sooner and they save significant dollars from interest on debt. Some creditors are now sending notes with their credit-card statements indicating that you can call them and they will keep the 2 percent minimum at your request, but you must declare financial hardship and close the account.

To really understand how much your debt is costing you when you pay just the minimum, consider the following: Let's say you have a $10,000 debt on a credit card with an interest rate of 16 percent. If you make a monthly minimum payment of $400, which is 4 percent, it will take you 168 months, or 14 years, to pay off the debt and you will have paid $4,931.02 in interest. (And if you pay only 2 percent, or $200, a month, it will take you 531 months, or 44.25 years, to pay it off! That will cost you $19,328.23 in interest.)

However, if you up your payments to $450 per month, it will take you only 27 months to get rid of your debt, which is 2 years and 4 months. You will pay only $1,939.25 in interest over that time. The lesson: If you can pay more than the minimum and put more toward paying down your debt every month, you'll be debt-free sooner and not have to give up so much money in interest. In this example, adding just an additional $50 a month to the minimum payment makes a huge difference in the time it takes to pay off the balance and the total cost you bear in interest.

Lower Your Utilization Ratio

By paying down your debt you lower the "utilization ratio," which is the gap between your credit limit and your actual balance. Keeping the utilization ratio down is a big credit-score booster, so show as much available credit as you can. Definitely don't max out or go over limit on accounts. Lenders prefer it if you don't go beyond about 30 percent of your total limit. And ironically, 30 percent of your credit score is based on this utilization ratio. If your limit on a card is $10,000, but you've just bought a 60-inch plasma television with it, your credit score just took a hit.

Mike Schiano, vice president of InCharge Education Foundation, suggests 50 percent as a threshold; that is, if you have a credit line of $10,000, don't go over $5,000 in debt. Jeanne Sahadi, staff writer for Money.Com, suggests 30 percent, and Liz Pulliam Weston, author of *Your Credit Score: How to Fix, Improve, and Protect the 3-Digit Number That Shapes Your Financial Future*, recommends between 20 and 30 percent.

I say start with 50 percent, then go for 30 percent, then 20 percent, then 10 percent, with the ultimate goal of paying your bills off monthly. Take baby steps, if necessary. And if you're not sure what your credit limit is, find out—and make sure it's accurately reflected on your report. If your statement says you've got a limit of $10,000 but the credit-reporting company indicates you've got only $5,000, your credit score is unnecessarily suffering as a result because your debt-to-available-credit ratio increases.

I once noticed an inaccurate credit limit on one of my accounts. The creditor had been automatically raising my credit limit throughout the years, but the report didn't reflect the increase. So when I made a large purchase and didn't pay the balance off right away, it made my utilization ratio 85 percent when it should have been 37 percent. I simply called the credit bureau, filed the dispute by telephone, and a letter arrived a few days later showing the correction had been made. Just one more reason why reading your credit report and fixing errors is important!

Minimize New Applications and Inquiries

Even getting insurance quotes or changing your cell-phone service can generate inquiries on your report. Remember, your score reflects how many inquiries and which type have been made on your report. Recent inquiries that herald new lines of credit can go against your score. Don't impulsively sign up for retail-store credit cards during holidays to grab extra discounts on merchandise. Anytime it appears you're about to overextend yourself, you risk losing a few points. As I mentioned in Chapter 2, this is a fuzzy area in the scoring system. If you're a responsible consumer, opening new lines of credit won't be a big deal in terms of your credit score. If you have a history of credit problems, however, new lines of credit—especially of the unsecured-credit variety—might hurt your score. Inquiries that *you* make when requesting your credit report do *not* count against you or have an effect on your score. But a flurry of inquiries from potential creditors and lenders that you've authorized for purposes of getting more credit can send your score down a notch.

In addition, shifting debt from higher-interest-rate accounts to other new accounts may cost you. This strategy may lower your interest rate, but it can also lower your credit score, because the length of the credit histories is averaged and a new credit line shortens the average age of accounts.

For example, let's say you've got five credit cards, each with a $5,000 limit. Cards A and B are ten years old; they carry about $8,000 of debt. Cards C and D are two years old, and they carry a total of $2,500. And card E is a card that you just got today with a low introductory rate and a higher limit, $10,000. You decide to roll your balances over from your ten-year-old cards to this new card, and you close out those older accounts. You also add another $2,000 from Card C so you can close that account, too. You're left with Card D, which holds $500, and Card E, which now holds the limit of $10,000.

You might think this was a smart idea for two reasons: (1) you got rid of three cards, and (2) you moved the balances over to a new card with a lower interest rate and higher credit limit. Well, what you really did was punch a big fat hole in your credit score. By transferring those balances and closing old accounts, you got rid of cards with credit-boosting age and you weighted your new card down to its limit. Now you've got a card with a utilization ratio of 100 percent! Not a good thing.

What you should have done was the following: (1) *avoided* opening a new line of credit, (2) called and requested a lower interest rate on your old cards, and (3) started to pay down those old cards and kept those accounts open. If you wanted to get rid of a card or two, you should have aimed to pay down that one card with $500 on it and then closed that account, which was only two years old. You would have been left with three cards, all of which were working in your credit score's favor due to their age. (Remember, establishing a history with the same creditor is a credit booster, a tip I'll reiterate in the next section.) And once you paid off those balances, you would have gotten another boost in credit.

Perfectly Sensible and Logical

Establish Credit History

Although most would agree that giving a young person his or her first credit card is taking a huge risk and is stupid in some cases, in actuality it's a blessing in disguise—if that person can use the card responsibly. Why? Credit cards help us establish a credit history, without which we'd be unable to apply for any loan or even buy things like car insurance. We'd also have a hard time renting an apartment, landing the dream job, and navigating through life. Blank credit reports are credit-score sinkers. You need to establish a good credit history, which entails using credit responsibly, and preferably with creditors and other businesses with whom you can establish a long-term relationship.

Minimize Accounts, but Vary the Types

Consider having a mortgage, an auto loan, two major credit cards, and one retail store or gasoline card. That should be enough accounts to show a pattern of on-time payments without getting overextended with debt. However, it's been reported that some insurance companies, for example, offer their best rates to those with five credit cards. So this isn't a one-size-fits-all rule of thumb. If you have a compulsive debting and spending problem, I find five cards to be a bit too much temptation! See if you can get down to just two credit cards, then consider applying for new lines of credit in the future once you've gotten a handle on managing your money.

Unfortunately, there is no golden rule for how many accounts and which type of credit are best for getting the highest credit score. This is a gray area in the credit industry. Recall from Chapter 2 that part of your credit score is based on how much you appear to be overextending yourself. If you've never had a problem with credit and paying down balances in the past, then opening up a few lines of credit won't be such a big deal and won't necessarily cause a drop in your score. On the other hand, having several lines of open credit, especially new credit, can look like you're standing at the edge of a cliff and about to jump into new debt. The exact calculation of this risk in terms of your credit score is one of the secrets in the credit-scoring industry. Suffice it to say that you don't want to appear vulnerable to abusing your credit given your history. Keep your access to credit in line with your needs and you'll be okay. As you also know from Chapter 2, variation among types of credit is good because different types of credit carry different types of risks— and rewards. Clearly, there's a difference between the debt carried on a home loan and the debt burning on a credit card filled with purchases from long-ago must-haves for depreciating assets. As an aside, a new program to check out is BrightScore at www.brightscore.com. The company InCharge Institute of America has created BrightScore to help consumers better understand their credit scores. Among the services and information they provide is a breakdown of the point system, which can help clarify your specific questions about the scoring formula.

Think Twice About Closing Old Accounts

For reasons similar to why establishing a credit history is a credit booster, maintaining a history with the same creditors is also a credit booster. Closing old accounts shortens the length of your credit history and lowers credit scores. Recall the example I just gave above. Having old accounts on your credit report helps balance the newer ones, even if those accounts carried outstanding and delinquent balances in the past. In fact, keeping an old account in good standing, but relatively inactive, can be a boon to your credit score. Remember that part of your credit score is based on the age of your oldest account and the average age of all your accounts.

Some situations do merit the closing of accounts, however, and thus a slight decrease in credit-score points—especially when keeping the account open carries too much risk of running up the balance. The state of your balances weighs twice as heavily in your score as your length of credit history. How well you manage your balances reflects 30 percent of your score, whereas how long you've had your accounts reflects only 15 percent of your score. So if you can't keep a good, clean record of maintaining an account, closing it so you don't continue to overextend yourself will help you mend your credit in the long run. I suggest that you

Good vs. Bad Debt: There Is a Difference!

As I mentioned briefly in Chapter 1, the types of credit you have correlate to the types of debt you carry and how your score reflects those debts. "Good" debt helps finance long-term investments like an education or a home. These investments increase over time. "Bad" debt, on the other hand, helps satisfy short-term gratification and does not usually appreciate over time. Vacations, new gadgets, nights out on the town, and routine visits to your favorite store are outdated or used up in the long term.

In terms of your credit score, those debts that appear to be "bad" have a tendency to drop your score. Conversely, debts considered "good" can boost your score.

That said, I do want to add that *any debt* can be bad if you have too much of it or if it prevents you from having a balanced life and a sense of well-being. If one particular debt haunts you, focus on paying down that debt more quickly than others, and do what you must to regain a sense of well-being despite the debt. Few debts can go away overnight; learning how to live with them as you work toward paying them down is part of your healing process. And this is when positive affirmations and prayer can be especially calming and powerful.

focus on doing your best to keep your oldest accounts (i.e., clear up their balances and any delinquencies) before closing them out and relying on newer lines of credit.

Many sisters ask me whether closing an account that had negative marks on it can erase those bruises from the credit report. Until the negative marks are seven years old, they will remain on the report even if the account has been closed. This is yet another reason to save your old accounts, even if their history is negative. Once you turn your accounts around and reestablish a good payment history with those creditors, you'll soon meet that seven-year point, at which time you'll be in great shape. You'll have accounts more than seven years old and those negative marks will have dropped from your report. Two big boosters to your credit score.

Keep Accounts Active

Use at least one credit card per month. The consistency of purchases and payments continually adds new positive information to your credit report. I don't mean you should charge more for the sake of keeping your accounts active, though. You can pay for a small necessity using a card, such as gasoline to get to work.

Beware of "Interest-Free" Loans or Lines of Credit

Don't be fooled by the deferred-payment programs that promise "No payments and no interest until the next millennium." What this means is that if you don't pay up in full by that date, you will then owe all that interest that's been accumulating plus the balance. And if you can't afford it, you can face expensive penalties. It's best to avoid these "deals" even if they are enticing. Buy when you can afford to make regular payments from the beginning. These promotions get people to buy items they cannot afford now, banking on future income. This is a recipe for trouble.

Use Debit, Not Credit

When you use a debit card instead of a credit card, you're forced to stay within the limits of your account's balance. Debit cards are just as convenient and they won't increase your debt. You can only spend what you have in the bank.

Counterintuitive Strategies

Spread Balances Over a Number of Cards

Many sources recommend carrying smaller balances on several cards instead of a large balance on one card. This prevents you from going past that 30 percent utilization ratio and establishes a history with more than one creditor. For example, if you have three credit cards with a $1,000 credit line on each, it's better to keep each balance below $500 rather than consolidating everything onto one card. However, don't open up new credit lines simply for the sake of spreading out your balance! This one I learned the hard way. One time I thought I'd use this strategy to spread my debt around instead of having everything on one card with a utilization ratio at 75 percent. I opened a new credit card with a 0 percent interest introductory rate and shifted part of the debt to the new card. That's when my score went down. In hindsight, it would have been better to spread the balance over the two credit cards I already had with zero balances and high credit limits. After that, I decided to leave well enough alone until I had more time to analyze my entire report.

Don't Have Too Many, but Don't Have Too Few

How many "preapproved" credit-card applications do you get in the mail? A lot? Their offers can be enticing, but 10 percent of your score is based on new credit. If you're applying right and left for new credit because your old credit got you into trouble, this can work against your score, as I've already mentioned. If you've got 10 credit cards, fish out which ones are the oldest and mark them as "keepers." Then try to pay off the balances on the newer cards (or transfer balances if they are too large for you to handle in a reasonable time frame) and consider closing only those newer accounts. See if you can get your credit-card inventory down to fewer than five, and use your oldest cards regularly.

Having too *few* cards can also hurt your credit score. If you've had problems in the past, you might need to add new secured credit cards or installment loans to help rebuild credit. A *secured* credit card is an account you set up backed by a deposit of savings. The required savings deposit for a secured card may range from a few hundred to several thousand dollars. Your credit line is a percentage of your deposit, typically 50 to 100 percent. Usually, a bank will pay interest on your deposit. In addition, you also may have to pay application and processing fees. Before you apply, be sure to ask what the total fees are and whether they will be refunded if you're denied a card. A secured card can require an annual fee and a higher interest rate than an unsecured card.

An *installment* loan, on the other hand, is a loan that you repay with a fixed number of periodic equal-sized payments. A car loan is a classic example of an installment loan. The finance company or bank pays for the entire car and you pay back the finance company or bank in monthly installments per your agreement, including interest. These loans can vary tremendously based on their length and interest rate. It also depends on the source of your lender. While hard-money loans can be especially troublesome because of high interest rates, loans from established, reputable lenders are typically good. Let's say a lender offers you $10,000 today in cash to help you settle your debts, and charges you an interest rate of 11 percent on that loan over five years. Your payments back would be $217.42 each month. And here's what that loan would really cost you: $13,045.45! But at 6 percent it would cost $193.33 per month and only $11,600 for the same five-year period. With installment loans, you have to be careful because such a loan can give you access to large sums of money today to disperse as you choose.

While both secured credit cards and installment loans may not be the best option because they can cost you more in the end, they do come in handy for those who are denied credit as a result of their history. But don't open too many accounts, since as we discussed before, that also works against you.

Convert Secure Credit Cards to Unsecured

If you've got secured credit cards, convert them over to unsecured cards after twelve to eighteen months of on-time payments. Be sure that those companies provide reports of your diligent payment history to the credit bureaus. (Simply call and request it if you don't see a record of your relationship with them on your credit report.) As mentioned before, secured cards are a short-term remedy when you can't get good credit terms or are denied credit entirely. Most secured cards, however, have annual fees and higher interest rates than regular, unsecured cards.

Watch Timing of Spending

When someone pulls your credit report to gauge your creditworthiness, where your balances stand *at that moment* becomes a factor in your report. In fact, the balance on your most recent statement is what gets reported and incorporated into your score, so timing is key. If you normally pay off your credit balance in full every month, but sometimes make purchases that take your credit limit to, well, *the limit*, your score can go down. How? As discussed, the credit-scoring formulas like to see a nice, big gap between the amount of credit you're using and your available credit limits. Aim to keep your balances below 30 percent of your limits if you can.

If you make a purchase that, say, requires using 60 percent of your credit limit and that balance hasn't been paid yet when your report is sent in, creditors will think you've overstepped your boundaries. For this reason, it's suggested that large purchases be avoided within 60 days of applying for a loan. Another solution is to ask for more credit so when you do make those larger purchases you won't step outside that 30 percent box so easily. But be careful of this option. The more credit you have, the more temptation to overspend.

Upgrade Basic Cards to Premium Cards

Once you've reestablished a good financial reputation again with your credit-card companies, you'll likely be eligible to apply for premium bank cards (i.e., "platinum" or "gold" credit cards that offer you rewards in return for your purchases). One client, Kara, was surprised to find that when she checked her credit score after getting her financial house in order, it said she had "too few premium bank card accounts" and that "not enough premium bank card accounts has a negative impact on your credit score." Kara had to laugh at this negative mark on her report, because at least it was something she could take care of immediately by contacting her credit-card companies and requesting that they offer her an upgrade.

This sounds like a strange way to boost credit, but chalk it up to the mystery of the credit-scoring system. To convert your current cards to premium cards, call your creditors and ask what premium bank card programs they have available for which you can qualify using your current card. You won't have to close your basic cards and open new accounts, however. They can simply upgrade your current account. You'll probably get a new card in the mail with a different design on the face, indicating your elevated status. (For security purposes, some credit-card companies have stopped making credit cards that say "Platinum" or something similar right on their faces. The only way to tell the difference between a basic card and a premium card is by how your account is labeled on file.) Try to avoid programs that entail an annual fee or rewards that you know you won't use, such as mileage points. Do your homework to find a premium bank card that meets your needs. With all the credit-card programs available today, you're bound to find an appropriate one.

Gain Some Experience with Debt

This might sound like the strangest strategy yet, but taking on debt—especially good debt—and then slowly but diligently paying it off is a great way to boost your score. It shows that you can handle debt in a professional manner. Let's say, for instance, that Erika just finished college and needs a car to get to and from her new job. Other than a few periods when she carried some small debt on her credit cards to help get through school, she's had absolutely no experience with huge debt and has a pretty good record.

If Erika buys a $20,000 car with no down payment and finances that debt through a loan—paying it off as planned in monthly installments over four years—she will, at the end of her loan, have given her credit report and score some serious nourishment. In the future, a potential lender will look at that huge debt that she took on and see that she managed to pay it all off. But if, for the sake of argument, she had paid for that car without any reliance on credit (as in she pays cash for it from an inheritance or lets her *father* buy it, and she then pays him back personally over time), then her credit report never would have seen and recorded that debt and that payoff. Her financial feat would have gone unnoticed in the credit-reporting world.

Revolving debt, even if it's attached to unsecured credit cards, does help your score in the long run. As you begin to pay down those balances, you start to show a payment behavior that can work in your score's favor. As indicated in one client's credit-score report, "More revolving accounts, containing longer credit histories, provides more payment behavior information," which positively impacts your score. Not enough revolving-debt experience, on the other hand, negatively impacts your score. So there's something positive to be said for the debt that you carry.

Exercise One: Schedule Weekly or Monthly "Mind Your Own Business" Days

This chapter gave you a lot of ideas for boosting your credit score and managing your creditworthiness in the long term. Some of these strategies won't be available to you based on your current circumstances, such as applying for premium bank cards. Many of these strategies are for your consideration at a later date, once you've paid down more of your debt and gotten your credit straight. So keep your personal circumstances in mind when you think about which strategies you want to practice today and which ones you should plan to do in the future.

Because it can be hard to remember all these ideas on a regular basis, especially as you continue to pay down your balances, it's helpful to create focus sessions where you sit down and review these strategies. You can schedule time either once a week or once a month when you commit to evaluating these strategies and choosing which ones are relevant to you at that time. For strategies that you cannot do yet, decide on a future date when you hope to be in a position to practice or implement them. This makes you more accountable for your overall plans, and mindful of the techniques in general. For a step-by-step action plan, consider the following:

1. Set aside a section in your journal called "Mind Your Own Business Focus Sessions." This will be where you take notes based on the sessions you schedule. You'll assess which strategies you are already using, and which ones you can start doing.

2. Get out your calendar and mark "focus session" on the same day either each week or each month. For example, you can choose to schedule a focus session every Sunday night or Monday morning. Or you can choose to write down "focus session" every first Monday of the month. However frequent you choose to make these sessions, commit to them now by marking them down on your calendar.

3. Now review the ideas in this chapter and pick out the ones that you think you can consider doing starting today. Write them down in your journal. For example, you might write "Pay bills on time, avoid new lines of credit, pay more than the minimum on credit cards, and watch timing of spending." Be as specific and thorough as you'd like. Writing these goals down is also a positive affirmation of your intentions.

4. Go back to the list of strategies in this chapter and pick out ones that you'd like to review at your next session. Write those down in your

journal. It will prepare you for starting your next focus session. Make sure you evaluate how well you practiced your current strategies.

When you sit down for these sessions, you may or may not want them to coincide with your bill-paying. It's up to you. This exercise should not feel like a chore. View it as a way to empower yourself and gain a stronger financial footing. And, like paying your bills, you can celebrate your sessions by playing your favorite music or planning a fun activity for afterward.

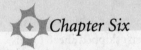

Chapter Six

Couples in Credithood

Luckily, the strategies you've already learned up to now, including how to reduce debt, create a spending plan, and track accordingly, also apply to couples. If you've got a significant other, you can go through the same steps outlined in the previous chapters as any single sister would, and factor in one important difference: a partner who shares the responsibility of getting your debts reduced and your credit straight. Whether you and your partner share debts together or each carry individual debts, straightening out your financial lives should be a team effort. It comes with the territory of being in a partnership. But here's the catch: It's not always so easy to accomplish financial harmony in a relationship. That's why couples need more than just the step-by-step debt-reduction and credit-boosting strategies. They need guidance in finding that harmony and working together so they not only keep their financial goals aligned, but they also synchronize their efforts to successfully achieve those goals in the future.

In this chapter, we'll delve into those strategies for achieving financial harmony in couplehood. Hopefully you haven't skipped ahead to this chapter just because you're in a relationship. You'll need all the lessons you've already learned up to this point to proceed and know exactly what to do. Go back and read how to reduce debt and create a spending plan if you haven't acquainted yourself with those techniques. You'll be applying many of them here, but I won't rehash the process; I'll simply give you added guidance that's specialized for couples.

Credit and Couplehood

Any conversation about couples and money is bound to include the fact that money—or the lack thereof—is commonly thought to be the number-one cause of divorce in this country. In my sixteen years as a financial counselor, I see the *failure to communicate* as the primary cause of rifts in relationships and eventual divorce. Granted, it's usually the failure to communicate *about money* that feeds the statistic—especially when money can't be discussed in a noncritical or nonjudgmental way. Many couples are challenged on a daily basis because they not only lack the skills to address and resolve money matters effectively, but they are invariably stuck—unable to talk about money without rehashing the same old argument time after time.

Take Cassie and Theo, for example. Their relationship is at a crossroads and money is one of the issues driving a wedge between them. Married for five years with one son, the couple has been close to divorce twice. They are currently living in separate households but trying to work through their issues and reconcile. She is a computer programmer and he is an entrepreneur. A big part of Cassie's frustration is that Theo knows about her finances but she doesn't know about his. Although Theo has explained many times that his money comes in unpredictable waves and he's forced to put money back into his business to keep it going, Cassie is resentful because she thinks he should be doing more for her and their son. Cassie remarks that after spending her paycheck and the $600 per month she gets from Theo, she sometimes feels "like a crack addict, wondering 'How do I get through the next fourteen days?' "

Although they were both scheduled to come to the first financial-counseling session together, Cassie ended up coming alone. Frustrated with being asked for money, Theo said to Cassie, "You need to go and get *your* thing straight!" So he chose not to show up. But soon thereafter, a resistant Theo came to the next session. The air was thick with tension and he sat with his arms folded.

Ironically, both Cassie and Theo admitted to having concerns about communicating with each other. And justifiably so. At times I felt like a traffic cop, frequently insisting that one person be quiet so the other could finish making their point. It was evident they were stuck on finding fault with each other. I heard the same points brought up two and three times, each criticizing the other person and rehashing the same hurtful experiences from many years past in their relationship. Obviously, these same arguments happened over and over again with no forgiveness, acceptance, or resolution.

There was plenty of blame to spread around. For example, Cassie was furious that Theo had bought another house without her input. Theo was irritated that Cassie didn't share the $1,200 income-tax refund. Theo also was upset that Cassie found an old savings account with $400 in it and used that money to buy computer equipment for their son when she complained she doesn't have enough money to meet her monthly budget. Cassie was angry that Theo claimed to never have more money to contribute to her household when she frequently saw new items and fixtures at his house. The list went on and on. Cassie felt miserable, disrespected, taken advantage of, dogged, and bullied. Theo shared similar feelings, including resentment and entrapment.

Factors evident in this relationship and many others that lead to marital discord include power plays that create sabotage, control issues that create resistance, stubbornness that builds an impasse, and secrets that destroy trust. These factors collide and amount to irreconcilable differences that characterize millions of unhappily married or divorced couples. Many psychologists agree that money issues are generally more difficult to talk about than sexual dissatisfaction. In fact, couples are more uncomfortable talking about their differences with regard to money than almost any other issue. So what happens is they don't broach the topic, and if their spending and saving behaviors are not in synch, at some point problems arise and the futile quarreling and bickering ensues. While it's nice to hope that we choose partners who are similar to us and who share a similar value system, that's not always the case when it comes to money. Indeed, we inherit money behaviors and attitudes from our families and other influential people in our lives, but we don't necessarily hook up with a partner with exactly the same sets of money values.

If you've gotten to that place where quarreling and bickering over the differences in your spending habits is a new daily issue, chances are you've been hibernating under indifference and apathy for a long time; you were placating and practicing appeasement because you just couldn't communicate verbally with your partner over money. For example, newlywed Lynn admits to being very spoiled when it comes to shopping. Her husband, Danny, never says no. And even if he did, she knows she can still go to Mom when she feels a need. Prior to the marriage, she *really* took advantage of that option. Danny's mouth literally fell open the first time he saw her closet. Continuing this lifestyle while living paycheck-to-paycheck may keep her happy for now, but it's a calm before the storm and a disaster waiting to happen.

Debt in particular can slowly erode and ultimately destroy a marriage if it spins out of control and cannot be managed by both partners together as a team. Debt can be the underlying cause of chronic tension that rears its ugly head eventually when one partner decides the marriage isn't working and gives ultimatums. It's human nature, unfortunately, to deal with excessive debt in a manner that prevents true healing. Couples who focus on the suffering that comes from the blame game instead of the real reasons for their overspending and money habits often find themselves going in circles and building up a ton of anger and bitterness that can be extremely difficult to overcome.

No matter where you are in your current relationship with regard to money drama, it's time to stop, take a deep breath, and start the conversation over with your partner. It's also time to get straight about your creditworthiness as a couple and understand what it means to take on a financial responsibility for someone else.

Couples, Credit Reports, and Credit Scores

Pop quiz: If you and your partner share a credit-card account and own a house together, do you also share a credit score?

Answer: No.

People routinely confuse the legal benefits—and consequences—of credit and couplehood. There is no such thing as a "couple's credit score." Each individual has his or her own credit report and credit score, regardless of shared accounts, debts, and assets. Even people who are legally married do not share a score, nor do they average scores together. This makes it critical for each person to have a high credit rating, because here's the catch: Conventional lenders will charge a couple applying for credit together based on the person with the *lowest* score. So if your credit score is 800 and your husband's is only 530, your loan officer is going to process your application for a home mortgage based on your husband's score. You'll probably also pay more for shared insurance policies and have to accept higher interest rates on joint credit-card accounts.

As we'll see in this chapter, mixing your financial life with that of another person can happen in two ways: (1) getting married, and (2) applying for joint credit, even if you're not married. Marriage and joint financial accounts add certain legal responsibilities to a relationship. Debts acquired, for instance, in the course of a marriage or as a couple with joint accounts are generally considered shared even if only one person created the debt. And if you split up, get divorced or legally separated, you don't automatically sever your financial ties to your ex. Even a divorce decree does not expunge your liability on what you and your ex still owe. You'll need to continue paying back that debt and then have that account marked as closed. It will remain part of your credit history and the negative information will still stay on your report for up to seven years.

Whether you're married or not, chances are you see your relationship with your significant other as a private bond. But in the eyes of the law, your relationship is not so private when you assume joint obligations over money. This is why it pays to know more about your partner than how well he treats you on Valentine's Day and your birthday.

Opposites Attract

In life, differences in values and attitudes are inevitable with couples. Perhaps it's the intrigue of those differences that provides the allure for opposites to be attracted to each other. For example, good girls are often drawn to bad boys. In the financial arena it's no exception—savers often match up with spenders. But that's not necessarily a bad thing. As a matter of fact, it can make for a mutually beneficial relationship, because individuals with extreme money behaviors can find middle ground or balance when they learn to compromise with partners at the other end of the spectrum. If one partner, for instance, is a frivolous spender and the other is a hoarder of money, finding a healthy medium can balance out the excessive behavior on one end and the deprived behavior on the other.

Know Thyself First

If you know yourself first, it will be easier to work out compromises as a couple—both before and after marriage. What are your personal goals, attitudes, values, assets, and liabilities? How do you currently use credit cards? Monthly or emergency use only? How do you pay on your credit cards? Minimum payment or balance in full? Do you understand your credit reports and credit scores? Are you satisfied with them or hoping to improve them? What is your preference of how bills will be paid after marriage? What percentage of each person's income should be contributed to household expenses? Have a sense of what works for you before coming to the table to meet with your partner.

Know How Your Partner's Financial Habits Compare to Yours

Once you have a clear sense of *your* money values and habits, you can then compare them to his. Are you the spender or is he? Does he buy impulsively and need to have the latest gadget and gizmo, or is that you? Do you have a savings account that continues to build, or do you assume

My sister, Ann, shared great relationship advice with her granddaughter: "Always listen to what the other is saying. If your spouse is complaining about something, maybe you don't think it's a big deal. But to him it's probably very important, so take it seriously and act on it."

he'll worry about saving for your future? Getting in sync with your partner about money's comings and goings in each of your hands is perhaps the most nourishing and important thing you can do for your relationship—whether it's new or set in its ways years later. Financial intimacy fosters a solid relationship.

Be open to making changes to your money habits if you know you're the weaker link in your partnership about money. Similarly, encourage your partner to learn how to make better choices about money if he's got issues. Consider speaking with a financial planner so you both are on the same page about your goals and can openly discuss your patterns and behaviors. Have an open mind with your open heart.

Honesty Is the Best Policy

In May 2005, I received the following letter in the mail along with a check for a two-hour financial-counseling session:

> *Dear Glinda,*
> *My name is Chanelle. I have contacted you by phone on several occasions but never taken the step to actually seek help. Now that I've lost everything I feel I have no choice. Please help me. I am a woman on the edge. You can reach me at [phone number].*
> *Sincerely,*
> *Chanelle*

This twenty-seven-year-old wife and mother of two was desperate. In our first conversation, Chanelle told me that she had been forced to sell her house on account of her financial situation. Now another nail was being driven into the coffin—her car was being repossessed because she couldn't make the payment. Chanelle had mourned the loss of her home, and now she had to endure the loss of mobility and independence. To make matters worse, she had no idea how she'd even begin to deal with her $20,000 student loan or the $15,000 debt she had in old credit cards, medical bills, and bank overdrafts. Chanelle and her husband, Delvin, constantly argued about money. Working together in a landscaping business, they had an unstable income that often fluctuated with the weather.

I was delighted to hear that Delvin was willing to take part in our initial meeting. Sometimes it can be hard to get both people to participate if one doesn't want to completely admit to the severity of the problem and seek help. But unlike some couples, Chanelle and Delvin shared the same goals: getting basic household bills paid by the due date, saving for emergencies and slow-income months, and improving their poor credit. I realized that since they ran a business together, they probably were tuned in to each other's money habits. But then Delvin made a startling revelation. He admitted to spending money to buy marijuana on a regular basis.

This was news to me, but not to Chanelle. Of course, to Delvin it was not a big deal. "Smoking marijuana is something I do to relax in the evening after a hard day's work," he said. So I asked him to do some calculations—$40 every other day for one year. The result was $7,300! Shocked at the amount, he then asked me to factor in the six packs of cigarettes he bought weekly at $3.69 per pack. That came to $1,151.28 annually. In total, he was spending over $8,400 each year on these habits! With annual revenues of only $40,000 from his business, it's no wonder his family's finances were in constant chaos.

Regardless of the moral and health considerations, anyone can see that this is an excessive amount to spend on a habit in the best of financial circumstances, let alone when your family is struggling to make ends meet. It doesn't matter if you habitually spend money on drugs, alcohol, gambling, food, clothes, or dependent adult children and grandchildren. Excess is excess. Don't think a substantial expense like Delvin's $20-per-day marijuana habit is the only type of expense that needs monitoring. Any seemingly insignificant daily expense for non-necessity items—even a $4 daily smoothie or blended coffee drink—over time can deplete cash flow, sabotage savings, inhibit debt reduction, and perhaps increase credit-card usage as a result.

If you're in a relationship, you must get honest, not only with yourself but also with your partner, about every issue related to money. Only then can you come to the table and have an open discussion, especially if things are getting serious and marriage is on the horizon.

The Discussion

One of the big pitfalls I see in couples is that they don't start talking about money issues early enough in the relationship. As soon as your relationship gets serious, you have to open up the dialog about money. If your partner is not willing to do that, just know you could be headed for a lifetime of frustration and disappointment. Because love is such a powerful emotion, we often forge ahead with these relationships thinking we can overcome any challenge. But if your partner is unwilling to take an active part in the discussions, consider that a major red flag that should not be taken lightly. His resistance may result from shame or embarrassment about his current circumstances, or it may be that he really does have something to hide. And don't be deceived by a potential partner's successful image. A big house or big car could simply mean big debts he is carrying. It doesn't mean you terminate the relationship, but you need to be aware of this before making a lifetime commitment and understand that the two of you must design a plan for how you are going to deal with his debt.

If you're in a serious relationship, be prepared to do some financial disclosure. It's important to review each other's bank accounts, credit reports, and credit scores together *before* getting married. Failing to do this could mean being forced to qualify for your first home alone if your partner's credit is poor; adding his name to the application for a mortgage might prevent you from obtaining *any* mortgage. And if there is outstanding debt on either side, determine how you're going to view each person's existing debt. For example, do you view it as "what's yours is yours" and "what's mine is mine"? Or do you say, "It's all ours, so let's work to pay it off and clear the slate"?

Being proactive in this way can help you avoid surprises like the one Monica received. She and her husband Marvin were solidly established in careers, with each making at or near a six-figure income when they met on a blind date. Several months later they married, but not without discussing finances first. Marvin admitted to having had some financial problems in his past, but Monica didn't actually *see* his credit report until after the honeymoon. That's when she hit the roof! His report was full of negative marks for late payments and mismanaged credit-card accounts. Despite his high income, his high-pressure job kept him from paying enough attention to where his money was going and whether or not he was managing it well. Unlike Monica, he wasn't very structured when it came to money. Now Monica had to rein in that structure for him. She knew it would be a long road ahead toward mending his credit and getting him up to her speed in creditworthiness.

Cohabitation

Just because you're not married or don't intend to marry doesn't mean you get a free pass and can skip out on acting responsibly with regard to jointly shared money issues. Lots of sisters cohabitate as if they are married yet don't take money matters as seriously as they should. Granted, without a wedding ring, your rights and responsibilities in a relationship are far different from those of your married friends. In the eyes of the law, you and your partner are legal strangers with no more rights to or responsibility for each other's assets and liabilities than two strangers on the street.

Your financial ties to your partner, however, do get legally intertwined the moment you open any joint accounts, such as a bank account, credit card, or home loan. This includes adding your partner to an exist-

Premarital To-Do's Before "I-Do's"

1. Review each other's credit reports and credit scores.
2. Disclose any and all debts, as well as assets—including all bank accounts.
3. Discuss plans for taking care of those debts.
4. If one (or both) person's debt and credit is suffering, map out a plan to get back on track. Make it a team effort, even if you don't "share" the debt.

ing card. On any joint accounts, you will be penalized for your partner's poor credit rating. And if he abuses your joint account, your credit rating will take a dive, too. In other words, as soon as you merge accounts and blend your creditworthiness, you each become legally liable for the entire amount of the total debt—regardless of who amassed it. At the same time, however, you won't be eligible for any benefits that married couples get, such as rights of survivorship under inheritance laws.

You should definitely keep all of your assets and debts separate except for any shared household bills, like rent and utilities. Some sisters fall into the trap of bailing out their boyfriends who do nothing but accumulate debt after debt and pay no attention to their credit. And I don't, by the way, recommend buying any large assets together, such as a house, car, or expensive household goods, unless you are married. Even items like expensive electronic and entertainment equipment, furniture, and computers can be difficult to split up if the relationship doesn't last. If you had the apartment first and he moves in, be wary about adding his name to the lease agreement and any accounts related to your living expenses, such as utilities, cable, and gas. As soon as you add his name, you both become liable for the bills. And if you then presume that he's taking care of the bills, and he fails to do so, you can wind up taking a loss in your creditworthiness. Bottom line: Stay as financially independent as possible regardless of the relationship. Stay on top of the bills that include your name, even if he doesn't hold up his end of the bargain.

Cohabitation Rules
Here are some basic rules I recommend following if you and your significant other share a home but don't share a marriage license:

- Share household expenses fairly, as any married couple would.

- Avoid joint credit cards.

- Avoid joint bank accounts; it's okay to keep one joint checking account for paying household bills if you can both manage it responsibly.

- Beware that if you put both of your names on your lease agreement, and on accounts for services like gas, utilities, cable, and phone, you are both liable for those bills no matter who pays them.

- Avoid purchasing major goods and services together, like a car, house, or plasma television screen.

Before You Jump the Broom

I'm not saying the relationship can't work if you avoid the money topic for a long time, but it's not ideal whether you're married or not. If discussing finances is uncomfortable for you, be open to marital and pre-marital financial counseling or coaching. This is a great way to learn the skills necessary to be clear about finances, and an opportunity to see how willing your mate is to communicate and compromise in a healthy way. It can also help you to better plan a financially realistic wedding, allowing you to make wise decisions about your spending plan. Planning a wedding is an extremely anxiety-ridden experience no matter what kind of budget you have. It's easy to get carried away with expenses. Unfortunately, plans have a tendency to take on a life of their own; every time you discover a fun, fresh idea to add to your celebration, you make the bottom line grow exponentially.

The wedding industry is a monster in its own right, and it conspires against a couple's wishes to keep costs down to a reasonable, rational level. Just getting through the day becomes the goal, and money issues are last on the agenda. Far too many couples will dump $20,000 in wedding expenses onto credit cards, banking on future income. Financing a wedding on high-interest credit cards is one of the worst things you can do. You'll likely find that debt haunting you many years down the road, when you need money for more important items like a home, or to support a baby on the way. Some people mistakenly think cash wedding gifts will ultimately pay for the event *and* put money in your pocket to boot. Not necessarily so! When Jackie and Trevon had the wedding of their dreams thanks to Visa and MasterCard, they weren't happy when the party was over and they were left with a huge bill to pay. Money collected from gifts didn't amount to anywhere close to the $19,000 they spent on their day. While they didn't necessarily regret the expense, because they enjoyed their day tremendously, they do regret not having thought through some of their costs along the way. Four years after the wedding, Jackie and Trevon are still paying it back—with new debts on the way because of children. I've heard that some parents now offer a home down payment to their children in lieu of a big wedding. I think that's a great idea!

Prenuptial Agreements

Prenuptial agreements: To have or to have not? Usually people who are sophisticated about money are more understanding about this subject and do not get offended by it. There are some very good reasons to consider a prenup. And they are no longer documents for just the rich and famous. In cases where children exist from a previous marriage, one may want to ensure that provisions are in place for those children in case of a breakup. Assets accumulated prior to the marriage can be designated to remain with the individual so they don't become subject to state laws like community property distribution.

Although prenups correlate to the risk of divorce, they should not be viewed as negative, and they can save you a lot of pain, anguish, time, and yes—money!—later on should your relationship not work out. Think of it this way: When you buy a house, you don't plan on burning it down, yet you buy fire insurance. When you buy a car, you buy insurance to cover a loss if you get into an accident or injure someone else, even though you hope that never happens. Well, the same holds true for two people who come together in a relationship and have some assets to protect. (By the way, you have about a 1-in-1,200 chance that your house will burn down; you've got a 1-in-2 chance of landing in divorce court!)

A prenuptial agreement typically lists assets and liabilities (i.e., debts) and details how each person wants those assets and debts divided in the event the marriage ends in divorce, separation, or death. The agreement can also address future earnings. State laws govern prenups, and the validity of any single contract depends on the state where you live.

When to Consider a Prenup
Based on the most common reasons people choose to have a prenup, you should think about getting one if

- You've acquired some considerable wealth, including a business, by the time you contemplate marriage.

- You have children from a previous marriage and you want to make sure they get some of (or all of) your assets at your death without them having to endure any legal contests and hassles.

- You've already experienced an awful divorce that cost you more than you were willing to part with, and you don't want that to happen again.

If you're interested in a prenup, ask family members and friends for leads on an attorney who specializes in these documents. However, you don't necessarily have to employ the services of an attorney to obtain this document. Reputable legal-document companies throughout the country can assist you in the process of creating one, which doesn't have to be filed with any court. You do have to make sure it meets your state's requirements so it can be upheld in court, but it then becomes something you keep in a safe, private place with other legal documents and records. (Hopefully, you don't ever have to pull it out!) If you're already married and wish you had drafted a prenup prior to walking down the aisle, post-nuptial agreements do exist, but they are much less common.

Checklist for the Engaged or Newlywed
The following is a checklist of issues that all couples should consider prior to marriage. If, on the other hand, you already are married but haven't had these discussions yet, it's never too late! These are often top-

ics that a pre- or postnuptial document will address, but you don't necessarily have to make such a formal arrangement.

- Will there be children? How many? When?

- Who will be the breadwinner? Who, if anyone, will sacrifice a career for taking care of the children?

- If one person gives up a career to support the other's career or be a stay-at-home parent, how will that parent be compensated—especially in the event of divorce?

- What kind of debt is acceptable?

- How should separate assets brought into the marriage be treated?

- How will marital assets get divided at divorce?

- Who will keep the home or other major assets acquired during the marriage?

- How will debts be shared at divorce?

- How will you buy property together? Will you share titles?

- How much will each of you financially contribute to the marriage? How will you share each person's income?

- How will you allocate money among accounts, such as the "mine," "yours," and "ours" accounts?

- How will you share household responsibilities, including paying bills, managing money, and maintaining the home?

- How will you plan for retirement together?

- How will you address money issues related to other people, such as siblings, aging parents, or friends who come asking for a loan?

- How will you share future decision-making, especially when it's serious?

- Where will you live, or where are you willing to move to—or not move to?

- How will you deal with issues related to children of previous marriages?

- How will you save for your children's education, potentially including their college education?

- How do you want to handle inheritance issues?

- How will you solve major debt problems that one person—or both—has brought into the marriage?

- Are there any assets that you'd like to address specifically in an agreement, such as a business or a piece of separate property one person brings into the marriage?

These are just a few items to consider. You can even include provisions for how you will handle serious disputes in your marriage, if counseling will be mandatory before contemplating divorce, and how you will split major holidays between two families. Your age and your wealth will determine where this conversation goes. Older couples typically have more to protect; younger couples, however, may not have as many weighty issues to discuss, but it doesn't hurt to lay out some expectations with regard to children, basic living issues, and how shared assets and debts will be managed.

The Children Discussion

The topic of children can be an extremely sensitive one to broach with respect to finances, but it's an important one to have as early as possible. According to a recent study by the U.S. Department of Agriculture, it costs a middle-income family $250,000 to raise a child from birth to age seventeen. That figure, by the way, does not include the cost of a college education. Private school costs an average of $4,500 to $7,500 per year at grade school level. High school costs average $7,500 per year and higher. And these are costs per child—before reaching university level!

In the first year alone, a single baby can cost you between $9,000 and $11,000 in expenses, many of which are not considered prior to pregnancy. The credit cards can quickly roll out at the birth of a baby to pay for unexpectedly large charges, which start with medical expenses and diapers and continue on to child care and hip baby clothes. Sooner than you could ever have imagined, you're in deep debt and your credit is taking a huge hit. Having a clear understanding of your financial goals with your partner and in consideration of children is essential.

Take Camille and Howard, for example. They both agreed before marriage that when the time came to start a family, Camille would be a stay-at-home mom and care for the children's needs. Howard made a decent living and was a frugal, wise money manager. What he hadn't counted on, however, was Camille being a compulsive spender.

Today, with children ages eight and eleven, Camille is a college student with plans to become a teacher and help supplement the family income. Her choice to be a stay-at-home mom certainly benefited the family by eliminating child-care expenses that could have easily cost $10,000 per year. But her habit of overspending impulsively on high-interest-rate credit cards with each trip to Target and Wal-Mart has countered a portion of the financial gains.

If this is an issue for your family, use your detailed spending plan to determine costs that can be eliminated, like health club monthly fees and hair and nail appointments. Don't forget to balance your spending habits against the loss of income you may endure while you stay at home to raise your children. Being a stay-at-home parent has tremendous emotional benefits for your family that may entail an emotional adjustment, too. A seemingly one-sided stream of income does not mean a couple must approach money management as a one-sided project. Each person must share equal duties in a couple's finance department.

'Til Death Do Us Part

Numerous things come together at the union of two people—other than just two people now sharing one roof with promises of raising a family together. Age and life experience affect each individual's basket of goodies and baggage brought into the marriage, but in general questions about money and assets, taxes, and insurance arise as soon as two financial lives merge legally. Let's look at these issues one by one, and how each of your credit ratings come into play.

Money and Assets

It used to be that two people who came together were likely to have roughly the same amount of assets—because they married when they were young and hadn't yet built up their wealth. But nowadays, people wait longer to get married and can accumulate a considerable amount of wealth during those years, as well as debt and credit problems. They also become set in their ways about money. Also, second and even third marriages can make the balance between two people's "assets and liabilities basket" skewed. A thirty-year-old sister who marries a forty-year-old man might find that she doesn't have nearly as much to contribute to the marriage in terms of assets, but she does carry a lot of credit problems. Likewise, two thirty-eight-year-old individuals who marry might each be bringing boatloads of assets—and debts—to the union. Every situation is different. And every relationship should be evaluated on an individual basis. The golden key in this department is, not surprisingly, conversation. Having an open conversation about money that continues to evolve will save you and your partner lots of anguish, frustration, and disappointment in the long run. Achieving financial compatibility does not happen automatically. It entails work, compromise, and a staunch commitment. It's a marriage, for heaven's sake!

I don't advise any couple to join all of their incomes together and share the same account. Yes, it's natural to want to merge your accounts and money with love. But neither of you should risk losing your individual financial identity. It's always a better idea to have "yours," "mine," and "ours" accounts—even if you're a stay-at-home mom who relies solely on your husband for income. The "ours" account can be the one that covers all the household bills, while you each maintain separate accounts for your own personal preferences. The "yours" and "mine" accounts are for each partner to maintain complete autonomy and manage on his and her own without reporting to the other. Contributions to these accounts can be determined from the individual needs detailed in the overall spending plan, or by a specific amount of allowance agreed upon by each partner. The point is to establish a set amount that can be spent without getting your partner's agreement or permission. If you insist on having your hair done at least once a week and your partner insists on watching football in a bar with friends on Sundays over beer and burgers, you can each agree to cover those costs out of your own accounts so there's no argument.

You can also maintain a savings account labeled "ours," for combining your efforts to save up for larger, big-ticket purchases, such as a college education for your children, a home, or renovations to your current house.

Managing the "Ours" Account Fairly

Options for contributing to this account include depositing all monies into one pot; having a 50/50 split where each person adds half of his or her paycheck to the account; or each person contributes a percentage of his or her salary based on the discrepancies in salary amounts. For example, the split could be 60/40 or 70/30, depending on how each person's salary compares to the other. If he earns $75K and she earns $50K, she shouldn't have to cover 50 percent of the living expenses, since she's making only two-thirds his salary. That wouldn't be fair, because she'd have to pony up a greater chunk of her total income each month and be left

How to Determine Individual Contributions to Household Expenses

1. Determine total, combined household income (his + hers net or take-home pay):

   His ($3,800) + Hers ($2,300) = $6,100

2. Determine each portion of total income:

   His (3,800/6,100) = 63%

   Hers (2,300/6,100) = 37%

3. Determine total living (overhead) expenses:

   $3,500

4. Multiply each individual's portion of the total income (his 63% and her 37%) by the total expenses in order to determine each individual's share of expenses:

   His = $3,500 X 63% = $2,205

   Hers = $3,500 X 37% = $1,295

with very little. Instead, each person would contribute his or her share of total household income to total expenses. This method works well for couples who have very different incomes.

Let's work through an example and take this couple's total overhead costs into consideration. In this scenario, let's say their total monthly, shared overhead equals $3,500. This includes mortgage, utilities, groceries, insurance, entertainment, plus 10 percent added on for incidentals. And let's say his take-home pay is $3,800 a month and hers is $2,300. You can see what would happen if they each contributed half of the total $3,500 overhead—or $1,750—to the pot. He would have $2,050, and she would have only $550 left over. Because she earns less than what he earns, to make this fair they would determine what percentage of their combined household income is his and what percentage is hers. Then they'd each apply those respective percentages to their total living expenses.

You should also determine whether you want overdraft protection, and if so, whether it should be tied to a savings account or credit card. Schedule regular financial meetings weekly or biweekly to discuss your needs for the upcoming week, assess your spending plan, and keep track of where the money goes and whether or not you're within your overall plan. Consider it like your regular day for workouts at the gym or your standing hair or nail appointment. Except this is much more important to your long-term financial well-being—and long-term relationship!

A similar scenario can exist with respect to credit cards. Keep one or two accounts in your name alone—with no other authorized users—and the other cards can be held jointly. It's critical that you maintain your own credit identity. This protects you in the event your relationship ends in divorce or separation and you want to go out and apply for credit or a loan in your own name.

Credit Cards and Credit Scores in Holy Matrimony
The following is a list of questions that I typically get from married sisters. The answers cover a lot of territory:

Q. I just found out that my husband has had a "secret" credit card for years that I never knew about. He's late on payments and the balance is close to $6,000. Could I be responsible for this debt even if the card is in his name and I knew nothing about it?

A. If your husband accumulated this debt during your marriage, the creditor may view the debt as a "marital debt" and try to come after you even though your name is not on the card (and if it is, then yes you are responsible). But in the event of bankruptcy, death, or divorce, you are not responsible if you are not named on the account—even though you are married and may have joint checking, savings, or other accounts.

Q. My husband and I have two joint credit cards. How do they affect each of our credit scores?

A. How each of you uses your joint cards affects both of your credit scores. So if your husband is irresponsible with money, both of your scores will be affected. Similarly, if both of you use the joint credit responsibly, each of your scores will get a boost. While there are no "joint credit scores," how you each handle money on a shared credit account will have both positive and negative effects on your individual credit profiles.

Q. I have very low credit limits and high rates on my cards, but my husband has premium bank cards with low rates. Is this a good thing or a bad thing? He wants me to close my accounts and move over to his.

A. Don't close your accounts. If you do this, you'll lose your credit identity and history. Instead, keep one or two cards in your name alone, but do not carry a balance on them. If you need to carry a balance, focus on paying down that debt to zero. Ask that your husband add your name to some of his accounts as an "authorized user." From a credit perspective, this means you each will have your credit histories updated with the information from these accounts. You'll soon get a better interest rate and build future credit without having to give up your own cards.

Q. I got divorced last year, but I still have a joint credit card account with my ex. Am I responsible for the debts he is now accumulating?

A. Yes. As long as you are named on the account, you are jointly responsible. During your divorce, you may have agreed to accept the house debt while he promised to pay the credit-card debt. But that divorce agreement doesn't matter to the creditors. This is why it's better to cancel that joint card and apply for new ones in each of your names. (Either person may close a credit card account or other unsecured consumer line of credit on which both people are contractually liable. All one has to do is give written notice to the creditor.) To take charge of this situation and prevent further damage, call the credit-card company and close the account to new purchases. Send a certified letter to the company as well, so it's in writing. Although the account can't be closed until it's paid off, you can limit your responsibility for any additional purchases made after the credit-card company has received your letter and can act on it.

Managing the Debts—Yours, Mine, and Ours

There are two kinds of debt in a marriage—*individual* debts, or those that predate the walk down the aisle, and *marital* debts, or those that you accumulate together as a husband and wife. You and your partner have to determine how you'll approach all of your debts. My advice is to treat all individual debts separately but design a plan as a team for working in harmony to get either or both partners out of their respective debts. This establishes a strong financial foundation for the new relationship to build upon. It's rare that a couple that comes together with individual debts that are similar in both type and size, so you'll both need your own strategy.

What you can merge, however, are your marital debts. Of course, you'll want to formulate a spending plan that meets both of your needs, addresses your shared debts, and can be agreed upon without any huge sacrifices for one person. Again, you can use the seven steps outlined in Chapter 3 to reduce your collective debts together, then create a spending plan using the instructions in Chapter 4 to address your bills responsibly.

Couples who need to cut back on their daily spending to reduce overall monthly expenses can also benefit enormously by going on the cash-only envelope system, a method you're already familiar with from Chapter 4. As I detailed in that chapter, the cash-only system is an extremely effective strategy for reducing expenses, especially those frivolous, on-the-spot impulse purchases. For couples, using this system helps prevent one person from exceeding the spending plan unfairly while the other feels deprived. Here's how it works in a nutshell (refer back to Chapter 4 for more instructions):

→Set a daily allowance for spending on items you pay for in person and for which you'd normally use a credit card or debit card (e.g., lunches, afternoon coffee break). Base your allowance on the spending plan you and your partner created.

→Split that daily allowance between you. Say it's $40, so he gets $20 and you get $20.

→You and your partner avoid using any credit cards or other sources of money to get through your days. You each use the cash-only from your own designated envelope. When the money is gone, you can no longer buy anything. You have to wait for your next allowance.

Going on a cash-only basis is an extremely effective tool for keeping you and your partner honest about daily spending. You'll each reduce excess spending that together can amount to a lot of extra money and go toward debt repayment.

Sharing the Task of Bill Paying

You and your partner should share the responsibilities of checkbook management, planning, spending, and tracking expenses. It helps to cut down on resentment if each person plays a role and ensures that the burden is not too heavy on either person. Again, even if you're the stay-at-home mom and he's the sole breadwinner, you should approach bill paying and financial planning as a team. This means equal access, equal say, and equal shares. When you're both on board for paying the bills and eyeing your spending plan once a month, there can't be a blame game. You both also stay tuned in to where your money goes and any debt you might have. If, when you do your monthly bills, you come up short, you can both talk about how you're going to get through this fix and avoid problems the following month. Similarly, if you wind up with excess cash, you can decide how you're going to either spend or save the money. That way, no one person is hiding either accumulating debt or income on a monthly basis.

Since most people's deadlines for paying bills are staggered throughout the month, some of them coming in right at the start while others trickle in three weeks later, pick two days each month when you and your partner sit down and handle the bills. Mark those two days down on your calendar and do what you need to do to make it as fun and relaxing as possible. This can mean having a glass of wine or planning to cook dinner together and watch a movie right after it's done. Avoid doing any bills just before bedtime or after one of you has had a very bad day.

If sitting down together to do your bills once or twice a month doesn't work for whatever reason, you need to talk about how you'll approach bill paying, saving, and investing so that they are equally shared tasks. Because each of you probably has your own set of skills and values when it comes to money, understanding your differences and finding the compromise that allows you to both contribute equally to your financial life is important. And if children from previous marriages are part of the mix, you know how complicating that can be. Discuss how you'll each contribute to the welfare of those children, and whether one or both of you will equally share the parenting duties—including the financial responsibilities. For some blended families, the biological parent will assume a greater responsibility for supporting, for example, a child's educational costs.

Every family's situation will be different, however. Don't assume anything when you begin a relationship with someone who has children or if you've got children yourself. Be clear and specific about your intentions and expectations—from the very beginning. Try writing down your wishes in your GIRL journal and sharing them with your partner. Just as you and your partner probably spend money on yourselves differently, you each likely allocate money differently to your kids, too. He might give in to the kids' demand for money all the time, whereas you don't acquiesce so easily. Setting some guidelines can stave off a variety of problems later on. It can also send a clear message to your children about what they can expect and what their boundaries are. If you receive child-support

Money Rule of Thumb. Save for your own retirement before you save for your kids' college education. A kid can finance his or her education through low-interest loans, grants, and scholarships. You can't finance your retirement in the same manner!

payments from your ex, be sure that the money continues to support the health and well-being of the child for whom that support is designated.

Keeping Credit in Your Name Only

I can't reiterate this enough: No matter how much you love and trust your partner, keep at least one or two credit cards in your name only. This protects your credit identity and history. If you were to become separated, divorced, or widowed, it would be more difficult to obtain credit without having maintained your own credit history. Keep in mind that 74 percent of women will manage finances on their own at some point in their lives. You can have some joint credit accounts with your partner, but never let go of your own accounts—and don't have any other authorized users on those accounts, either. As with the checking and savings accounts, have "yours," "mine," and "ours" credit cards.

Taxes

Speaking with a tax advisor will help you determine how you and your husband should file your taxes so that you keep more money in your pocket. Generally speaking, you might pay more in taxes if you and your spouse each file separately ("Married Filing Separately") than as a married couple that file jointly ("Married Filing Jointly"); additionally, the greater the difference in your incomes, the more benefit you potentially get from filing a joint tax return. Calculate your return both ways and see which is the most advantageous for you. You want to have as much extra money as possible to help reduce debts.

Whether or not you should itemize or take the standard deductions will also depend on your particular situation. For example, if you run a home-based business as a sole proprietor while your husband works for a company and cannot claim any self-employed income, you will probably want to itemize your deductions so you can claim the maximum expenses related to your business. Again, however, you'll want to run the numbers both ways—using the standard deduction and the itemized deductions—to see which is more advantageous. In 2005, the standard deduction for married couples filing jointly increased to $10,000, from

$9,700 in 2004. The 15 percent tax bracket for filers who are married and filing jointly was also expanded in 2005 to twice the income range of that of a single filer, thus reducing the marriage penalty.

Watch that Wedding Date!

The IRS considers you legally married for tax purposes if you get hitched as of the last day of the tax year, or December 31.

Insurance
Auto Insurance

Deciding whether or not to combine your policies is a numbers game. Will it be more expensive or cheaper to combine policies?

Start by calling your insurance company or agent and ask how much it would cost to add your husband to your policy. Your husband should do the same. Then see what the difference is. For some, maintaining separate policies is the cheaper way to go. A lot of factors go into the formula that insurance companies use to price premiums, including age, driving record, driving experience, credit history (in some cases), type of car (make, model, mileage), commuting distance, average mileage per year, and so on. These factors can be radically different for one person than the other. If your husband's credit score is dismal compared to yours, and it means accepting a higher premium, you may want to keep your policy separate— and use any extra cash to help pay down your debts as a couple.

That said, sometimes it is better to combine. Certain discounts can be applied to policies that have more than one insured. And if you maintain your auto and homeowner's or renter's policy with the same company, you can reap ever bigger discounts. So it's just a matter of pricing it out and going with the cheaper route. You are not required by law to combine policies just because you're married! If you do decide to combine, revisit the terms of your policy, too. Speak with your partner about which kind of deductible you want and what liability limits you'd like. Changing these amounts can quickly change premium amounts.

When in doubt about your auto insurance, call an insurance broker who deals with multiple insurance companies and get some advice tailored to your circumstances. If you don't know any brokers, ask family and friends for leads. (Try looking up "Insurance" in your Yellow Pages, where you can find a listing of independent insurance agents and brokers. Also, refer to Chapter 8 for more resources.) Keep in mind that some insurance brokers deal only with certain insurance companies. If your heart is set on staying with GEICO or Mercury because you've been a happy customer over the past ten years, you'll have to find a broker who deals with these companies.

Health Insurance

Making sure you've got adequate health insurance is important whether you're married or not (more on this topic in general in Chapter 8). Health insurance is one item you don't want to mess with if you've got good coverage. Medical bills can easily—and very quickly—set you back financially if you don't have the right coverage to protect you. The goal is to find the best plan for the best price, regardless of your marital status. Unlike other forms of insurance, such as auto and homeowner's/renter's, it may not be cheaper to share the same plan. There isn't necessarily a discount for the both of you having the same plan. Your age and medical history will be greater determinants in what you'll pay, as will the type of plan you have.

Generally speaking, if you can enter into a group plan you can access the best coverage for the right price. So if your husband has a great plan through his job but you don't, ask that he add you to his plan. Likewise, if you're the one on a group plan through work and he doesn't have as good a plan, call your plan provider and fill out the paperwork that adds him to your plan.

If each of you has an individual policy, you'll have to price it out and compare whether you should combine under one or maintain separate policies. Simply call your insurance provider and ask a representative what it will cost you to combine policies—or to add a spouse to the existing policy. If you do not have the same provider, one of you might have to apply for a new policy with the provider that you choose to go with, then combine your two policies at a later date. With individual policies, it's not as easy to add individuals to an existing policy. The insurer will want to underwrite (insure separately) that individual first before adding him or her.

A health insurance broker can also help you determine what your options are, given your particular circumstances. You'll want to find someone who can evaluate your situation objectively and not push you into buying one type of policy because he happens to work for that company. Again, this is where referrals through family members and friends can be of help. Ask your sisterfriends how they handled health insurance when they got married.

Life Insurance

As soon as you've got other people dependent on you, whether it's a spouse, kids, or an aging parent, you need life insurance. It's also a good idea to buy at least enough coverage for burial services should something happen to you prematurely—even if you don't have dependents. Life insurance creates a safety net for loved ones if you die and don't have enough assets or wealth to help support them, or cover burial expenses. In general, term life insurance is the most popular and is often touted as the best kind of insurance for most people. But other types do exist, such as universal life, whole life, and variable life, one of which may suit you better depending on your circumstances.

Term insurance, as its name implies, covers you for a set period of time—say, five, ten, twenty, or thirty years. You decide how long you want that term to be, considering how long you expect your dependents to need you. For example, if you're buying insurance to protect your kids, you'll want to buy a policy that lasts until your youngest reaches the age of about twenty-three. If you can accumulate enough wealth on your own to cover them in the event of your death prior to your youngest turning twenty-three, you may not need such a long-term policy. How much coverage should you get? This figure varies from person to person. Some experts suggest ten times your current salary, but that might be too high or low for you. Your insurance broker will be able to guide you in this decision. (I'll discuss more on the insurance topic in Chapter 8.)

For Richer, for Poorer

Everybody has a financial life story. Our money autobiographies are full of colorful and varied history of good and bad, dumb and dumber experiences. When we bring a life partner into the equation, it's always a good idea to disclose our financial history and start the relationship on a clean slate. Don't continuously beat yourself up or hide your misspent financial past. And don't blame your partner or allow yourself to be blamed for past financial indiscretions—whether he was there with you or not. Judgment and never-ending criticism builds resentments that eat away at a relationship.

No matter at what stage in the relationship you are, or how much money you and your partner make, you're bound to run into money issues that can bruise your ego and relationship. It's just a part of life. Working through those problems as a team will help bolster your relationship and keep your financial goals in check. You don't have to have all of your money issues resolved and preplanned at the start of your relationship. Take things in stride. Have a time line and agree when you and your partner will meet to discuss certain issues. Set appointments up with your financial or tax advisor if you need to, and be sure that both of you can attend. Remember, this is a relationship that requires two people to tango, so it also requires two people to make money matters work out successfully. Each of you plays an equally important role—regardless of who's the breadwinner or who's good at math.

Exercise One: Get Your Priorities and Goals Straight with Your Partner

Sit down with your partner and write out each of your top three goals in order of priority. Compare your lists. Are they the same goals? Do you share the same order of priority? Different?

> Ex: Save, get out of debt, buy a house
> Buy a house, save, get out of debt
> Get out of debt, buy a house, save

Share why you chose your priorities and what they mean to you. Be open to what your partner says and try not to criticize or judge his choices. This is an exercise to open up the dialogue—not incite confrontation and instigate an argument.

Exercise Two: Get Real with Your Partner

Make a checklist with benchmarks for stages in your financial dialog, and then discuss them with your partner so you're both on the same page and can pursue your dreams together. If you are . . .

Dating:

> determine if you like being around the person
> examine how he handles money (e.g., is he frivolous or cheap?)
> see who pays for what if you invite him out for an evening

A Serious Couple:

> discuss values, attitudes, and beliefs about money
> share experiences—past problems or successes or patterns
> discuss goals as a couple

Engaged:

> full financial disclosure
> view credit reports
> discuss how to view and handle prior savings and debts (i.e., are they "yours" or "ours")
> who handles what part of the finances?
> discuss how to determine percentage of household contributions
> share feelings on prenuptial agreement

Newlywed:

> update beneficiaries
> review and update insurance policies
> if you're changing your name, be sure you contact your creditors, DMV (Department of Motor Vehicles), Social Security office, Passport Agency, insurance companies, and so on
> if you're sharing any joint accounts (household checking account, investment account, insurance policies, etc.), be sure to notify the corresponding financial institution or company

In a Seasoned Marriage:

> revisit short-term and long-term financial goals
> discuss any existing debt and credit problems
> evaluate retirement plans
> if you haven't already, consider new financial-planning tools, like a living revocable trust that includes a living will, incapacity clause, and durable power of attorney document

Exercise Three: Get Your Allowances Figured Out

Once you and your partner figure out a proper spending plan, figure out how much of an allowance you should give yourselves on a daily basis for personal needs. Then go on a cash-only system for a month to see if you can stay within your parameters.

Getting Straight Do's and Don'ts for Financial Harmony

DO be open and direct with your partner about money issues.

DON'T avoid understanding each other's money values, including strengths and weaknesses.

DO agree to a practical, concrete plan for managing money routinely, including debts and assets.

DON'T forget to set short-term and long-term financial goals with your partner.

DO schedule regular financial planning sessions with your partner to review, revise, and revamp goals; consider a financial advisor or coach for help.

DON'T cosign a loan or agreement with anyone who can't live up to the agreement's obligations, even if it's your beloved boyfriend. Avoid joint obligations with people who don't have good spending habits or credit.

Part Three

On Level Ground: Forward-Thinking Strategies to Prevent Debt, Preserve Credit, and Keep Your Spirit in Check

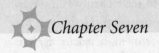

Chapter Seven

Increase Your Income: 101 Ideas to Raise Extra Revenue

Susan L. Taylor, editorial director of *Essence* magazine, is among the most admirable women I know. First, I have been a fan of the magazine for as long as I can remember—even before having the honor to write several feature articles dating back to 1994. But I was incredibly moved by Susan's revelation in her *In the Spirit* column of May 2005 titled "State of Readiness." In the piece, she described how she moved into a tiny apartment in Manhattan when her daughter was five years old. The luxury place had sweeping city views, and at the time the $450 monthly rent was a stretch for her budget. Her daughter took the tiny bedroom and Susan herself slept in the living room. The building was built for wealthy people who at first didn't want to live in a somewhat seedy area of New York, but later, gentrification of the neighborhood led to the units' conversion to condos. Susan's unit was now worth $199,000. But because she had no money saved, spotty credit, and couldn't qualify for a mortgage, she could not afford to buy and continued to rent. Then wealthy New Yorkers had a change of heart and started buying up the units in her building. By the time Susan left her tiny apartment, her daughter was married with a daughter of her own. And the apartment was valued at $650,000.

Clearly, if we're not able to pay off debts, straighten out our credit, and generate extra cash from which to prepare ourselves for serious opportunities like the one Susan had at one point, we'll stay in a cycle of earning and spending. Most of us ask God for favor and abundance, but if we don't take action to modify our finances, we're not ready when the opportunities present themselves. In hindsight, Susan describes how she could have readied herself for the $450,000 appreciation. She admits she could have gotten herself out of the "work and spend" mode and planned a strategy for the acquisition. If it happened to Susan, it could happen to any of us. To be prepared for opportunities, we sisters must maximize our current resources. After you've reduced expenses as much as possible, you need to decide how you can increase your income. And I don't necessarily mean looking for two or three part-time jobs! I'm talking about tapping into your creativity and hidden talents, and using resources that you already have.

A lot of sisters make the mistake of thinking the best way to improve credit scores is to focus on one's current financial status and pay down debt with current income. But it's much easier to achieve better credit if you simultaneously focus on raising your income, which then automatically allows you to pay down debt faster, mend poor credit, and boost your credit score. Don't know how to raise your income? I'm going to give you some ideas—no, actually *a lot of* ideas. By the end of this chapter, you'll have gotten at least 101 ideas for generating extra cash. One of these suggestions may even spark an interest in changing careers or testing out a whole new business area.

This chapter may seem like a complete departure from the tactical ideas already presented in the book that focus solely on fixing credit. But I don't want you to stay focused only on your current financial status and just keep looking back upon your mistakes. It's time to do some forward thinking and get ready for your future, which will protect your credit time and time again. As we move into Part III of the book here, you'll notice that the material includes bigger goals that you should be thinking about now, even though you may not be able to use the information in these next two chapters right away. I predict, however, that the day will come very soon when you'll want to consider new ways to make more money and ultimately keep debt and credit troubles forever in your past. When you reach the last chapter, you'll learn some healing, self-affirming rituals that you can use to stay on an even financial track for the rest of your life.

Start with What You've Got

The easiest way to make more money today is, not surprisingly, to ask for a raise or work overtime at your current job. Too many sisters don't remember to stay on top of their job status, keep their résumés up to date, and remind their employers when it's time to get a raise. If you work for a large company, you may already have annual reviews scheduled, at which point you may also be rewarded with a raise. But don't just assume that's going to happen automatically. Be proactive and make sure you schedule those reviews at least annually. Go into your reviews knowing:

- the value you bring to the organization

- what you've contributed to your organization in the past year

- ways to demonstrate and show your efficiency, accomplishments, or performance

- what you plan to contribute to your organization in the coming year

- why you love your job and want to maintain your job

- what problems or weaknesses you see in the organization that you can help address

- how you plan to build upon your skills and add more value to the organization

- what challenges you want to take on in the coming year

- what other people in your same position are getting paid at *other* organizations

- how much you want in terms of a raise

Be as specific as you can with the above items. Highlight specific accomplishments and results in the past and what you plan to achieve in the future. Inquire about putting in more hours or joining special teams designed to manage special projects. Make suggestions that reflect a win-win strategy where both the company and you will benefit from the agreement.

Another mistake sisters make is assuming that what their employer offers in terms of a raise is the end-all and be-all. Did you know that most employers actually respect those who negotiate better pay? It shows that you're strong-willed, focused, and business-oriented. You're not going to just sit back and accept what's given to you. Instead, you're going to take charge, be assertive, and do what's in your best interests. This kind of attitude translates to the kind of attitude a company needs in its employees. It says you're going to do what's in the best interests of the company *so long as* the company treats you in your best interest. This is a mutually beneficial relationship.

If your employer can't meet your salary expectations, don't just walk away disappointed and call on your sisterfriend to complain. Consider other forms of compensation besides money. Ask about annual bonuses, more flex time, more vacation days, freelance opportunities, or a bigger

Rule #1 at the Negotiating Table with the Boss

Never assume your boss will give you what you're worth right off the bat. Why would he want to pay you more when he can get you for less? You have to think like a businessperson, just like him. Why would you let him pay you less when you're really worth $5,000 or even $10,000 more a year? Be assertive, positive, and confident about what you bring to the table. And if he can't pay you in dollars, he can make it up with other forms of compensation.

title. You can also request that your next review happen in six months instead of a year, so you can discuss a possible salary boost contingent on your performance.

One sister, Megan, loved her job but wasn't happy about the pay, especially since she'd been devoted to the company for more than five years. She also was frustrated that her job contract prohibited her from doing any freelance work outside her publicity position at a major New York firm. When she got another job offer at a competing firm for more money, she was tempted to move but hesitated because she loved the people she worked with and didn't think she'd be happy at the other firm. What did she do? She used the job offer as leverage to renegotiate her contract with her current employer. Although she didn't get as much of a raise as she had wanted due to the company's financials, she landed a huge promotion in terms of her title, opportunities to earn more money in the future, and greater flex time so she could pursue projects outside the firm.

Ask yourself: Is your employer paying you under market? Is he undervaluing you? Is he out of touch with what you're worth and what you bring to the organization? These are questions you must continue to ask yourself. Don't base your salary expectations solely on your current earnings, either. Have you been in the position for several years and are you already earning what the market "suggests" you're worth? Know your market, but keep in mind that salary ranges provide for a broad spectrum of candidates and your experience or relevant skill set may not be considered to be at the top—or bottom—of that range. Don't make the mis-

Four Quick Tips to Increasing Your Income ASAP

1. **Ask your employer for a raise.** Schedule a meeting with your boss, perhaps over lunch or coffee. Prepare for this meeting by writing down why and how you are an asset to the company. Be specific. Include examples of accomplishments. Then explain to your boss why you deserve a raise and how much you think you're worth.

2. **Increase your fees.** Send a letter to clients detailing your new set-fee schedule. Explain that you haven't increased your rates in five years and this reflects new costs you have to bear in the market. Specify the percentage increase and when it's effective. For example: "Effective May 1, 2007, all current fees will be increased by 10 percent."

3. **Seek opportunities** to take on projects outside your current job on a freelance basis or, if you're self-employed, spend at least five hours a week or one hour a day focusing on reaching out to potentially new clients.

4. **Get a second job.** Eight and a half million Americans have already done so to meet regular household expenses or pay off debt, according to the Bureau of Labor Statistics. A second job doesn't have to be permanent. But it can give you the cushion you need now in preparation for a more financially secure future.

take of assuming too little or too much. Also, be sure to keep your boss apprised of your accomplishments and triumphs at work. How else will he know what you contribute to his bottom line?

Know Your Market

Before you schedule a meeting with your boss so you can inquire about a raise or promotion, you must have a keen sense of your market and your particular position's financial potential. Luckily, the Internet provides a multitude of resources for you to gather all the information you need. Of course, you can also start by talking with colleagues and others our same business. But even with the advice from friends and fellow es, it's worth jumping online to check out sites that specialize in nation. At SalaryExpert.com you can search by job title and alary.com is another one. If you're good at using search engines, you can sometimes find results by using keywords like "salary information" and "salary guides." Try and narrow your search by job type or profession, as in "graphic artist salaries" or "publicist salary guides."

Another resource is the Bureau of Labor Statistics (BLS), which provides comprehensive occupation information for specific jobs. Go to www.bls.gov and pick your industry and then your job title. The site will give you median earnings for a range of roles per job description. Keep in mind that this information is based on national figures, though, and probably won't reflect median earnings in your geographic location. A graphic artist working in Chicago will make more than one working in Tulsa, Oklahoma.

There is no set percentage on raises. Generally speaking, the percentage raise you can get will depend on a variety of factors other than just your individual value and performance. Average salary increases often reflect not only a company's financials but the general state of the economy. In good years, people see fatter paychecks. During economic downturns, those raises become harder to get.

Finally, don't forget about trade publications and professional associations related to your field. They can offer a wealth of information about your salary and job prospects. Association sites for a particular profession might be the most reliable sources of salary information. If you can't find salary surveys listed among their menus, call or e-mail the site administrator and ask about how you can obtain more information. Trade publications often run their own salary surveys, so search their Web sites. Likewise, Web sites geared toward a particular industry are also a great source of information. Mediabistro.com, for instance, is a site devoted to anyone in the media industry—from fledgling freelance writers to established PR sophisticates and television producers. The site offers job postings, community support, advice, event listings, plus an enormous library of tools and materials for both the amateur and experienced media professional. One downside to many of these trade and industry sites, however, is that you may need a subscription to access all the information. So you must weigh that cost against what you're seeking, and whether or not you can obtain that information elsewhere for free.

Web Resources

Use the following Web sites for finding and investigating new jobs . . . and potentially new careers! Also, go to your local newspaper's Web site and link up to your city's job listings. If your town doesn't have an online newspaper, pick up a copy or log on to the nearest metropolitan area's main paper. Major city papers typically have entire sections devoted to job and career building at least one day of the week.

www.monster.com
www.careerbuilder.com
http://hotjobs.yahoo.com
http://job.aol.com
http://careers.beyond.com
www.craigslist.com
www.snagajob.com
www.summerjobs.com
www.fedworld.gov/jobs
www.careerjournal.com
www.salary.com
www.salaryexpert.com
www.bls.gov

Know Your Limitations Today *and* Your Greatest Potential Tomorrow

It's important to realize that no jobs last forever, even the good ones that pay extremely well and are associated with a certain level of high esteem. Be open to new job opportunities both at your current place of employment and elsewhere. Look for ways to add more meat to your résumé; seek any short-term opportunities at work that can earn you more money and add great experiences to your résumé. This might require coming in earlier, staying a little later, or giving up some Saturdays. The sacrifice will be worth it. Always keep your résumé updated and ready to go at the drop of any new opportunity that comes your way. Your résumé should be clear, visually inviting, and succinct.

As happens to many sisters, you may reach your fullest potential at your job and need to find a new one in order to grow and face new challenges. Think of it this way: The bones in your body can't continue to regenerate, maintain their strength, and support you forever unless you put pressure on them and force them to renew themselves. This is why exercising and resistance or weight training is so important for women if they want to avoid bone loss and osteoporosis. Stressing the bones increases their mass. Well, the same holds true when it comes to the health and wellness of your job and, in reality, *you*.

I know, it's not necessarily fun to think about changing jobs or even shifting careers. It requires work, time, effort, and perhaps a push in a direction that can make you uncomfortable at first. Change is hard. But change is good. It's okay to feel a rush of many feelings upon contemplating such a move: fear, apprehension, anxiety, stress, and a vague excitability. You can alleviate some of that building pressure by taking time to learn all that you can from the resources you've got available. The Web sites CareerBuilder.com and Monster.com are a great place to start. Those two sites alone will overwhelm you with information and inspiration. They offer cover letter and résumé services, career assessments, information about opportunities to work from home, information on continuing education through avenues like online training and obtaining online degrees, plus tips and advice on finding the most in-demand jobs, relocating, starting your own business, and how to perfect the handshake before you arrive for your interview.

Interviewing Tip. Always pose questions when you interview for a job. This is your chance to learn more about the job and how you can contribute to the organization. For bonus points, disguise attributes about yourself in those questions by sharing ideas you might have and that can benefit the company. For example, "Your company maintains an excellent and useful Web site, but I've been looking around at other sites and have some ideas I think will work for you and that can really enhance what you currently have. If I come work for your company, will I have the opportunity to share my creative ideas as well as explore new ones?" This question covers lots of ground. It compliments the company, it shows you've done your homework and can bring fresh, new ideas to the table, and it also shows your particular interest in that company.

Expose Yourself

Career fairs are another great way to expose yourself to new opportunities and get some ideas. CareerBuilder.com posts a listing of all career fairs throughout the United States. Over at Monster.com, you can find contacts by skill, occupation, company, and even school to enter a network and start communicating with others. Never underestimate the power of a network. You know what they say about real estate: location, location, location. Well, I say that when it comes to getting ahead in this world and achieving your greatest potential, it's about networking, networking, networking! It's simply a mathematical equation. The more people you know, the more chances you have at landing the job of your dreams and then some.

Don't like to network? Don't think you can do it?

These days, you don't necessarily have to have a solid network of friends, colleagues, and family members in your inner circle to get ahead; the Internet has opened a whole new doorway to networking, building bridges, and establishing large forums and communities where opportunities flourish. Start online and then move out into the real world and meet people. Face-to-face personal relationships still count for a lot.

Even if you're comfortable and happy with your current job, make it a goal to take the temperature of your job prospects and your market now and in the future by **setting aside two hours once every six months to investigate opportunities.** You can do the bulk of this research online at any of the above-mentioned sites. See where one site takes you.

And don't ever be afraid to take on a second job when money gets tight or your emergency fund gets used up. According to the Bureau of Labor Statistics, four out of ten people have taken second jobs to meet regular household expenses or pay off debt.

Open Your Mind to the Possibilities

Opportunities abound once we open our minds to the possibilities. I often find that there's a bundle of money in people's lives that's being

The Power of a Network

You don't have to have personal connections anymore. Expand your offline connections by adding a few online ones. Try these networking sites and get into one today.

www.linkedin.com

www.ryze.com

www.friendster.com

www.spoke.com

www.entremate.com

www.tribe.net

Don't know what kind of a job you want? Don't know where or how to apply your skills? Go to http://a.livecareer.com, where you can get your own personalized career report by simply answering a series of questions.

overlooked. Once you identify ignored sources of money and take action, you'll feel more self-reliant and resourceful. You'll amplify your self-esteem. You'll also find that you're much happier when you pinpoint a passion and build a new career around it. And like magic, you'll naturally get rid of debt and straighten up your credit.

Negotiating, by the way, doesn't start and end with annual reviews. Negotiation starts at the very beginning of a job. Just as I said above, how sisters fall prey to thinking they're only going to get what *someone else* thinks they're worth at an annual review, they also can fall into the trap of thinking that an offer for a new job is written in stone. Not so! You have to be negotiating from day one. You have to know what you're worth no matter what someone else says, and be willing to stick by that figure. Or go find a better job.

According to a survey done by CareerBuilder.com, 58 percent of hiring managers say they leave some negotiating room when extending initial offers. The survey also found that most hiring managers are accommodating when a candidate asks for a better offer. Nearly six in ten say they will extend a new offer once, and one in ten will extend a new offer *twice or more* if they really want you. Only 30 percent of hiring managers say the first offer is final.

When you begin to negotiate your potential new job contract, have a clear idea of what you want. Determine your needs based on your living costs and how you want to live. The salary conversation with a potential employer can be tricky. You don't want to ask for too much and then get shown the door. Neither do you want to easily accept too little when your employer had a higher threshold in mind. Escaping from this awkward place entails doing your homework first. Find out exactly what the position you're vying for earns in the industry you're seeking. Have facts to back up what you propose. Then add any supporting evidence to why you're valuable by sharing your personal attributes and describing why you stand out from the rest.

Top Five Things to Consider When Seeking a New Job

Money alone can't be all that you think about when contemplating a new job. You have to be happy at your job, too. Job satisfaction, after all, is made up of many elements that all coalesce. Here's my list of what I think every sister needs to consider before saying yes and beginning a new commute:

Relationships. How will you relate with your new colleagues? Do you like your new boss? What kind of environment do you see at the company? Is it diverse and welcoming of all people from different backgrounds? Do you see yourself communicating and integrating well in this environment? Does the environment elicit warm and friendly feelings, or is it cold and uninviting?

Company policies. Do you agree with the way this company runs its business? Are there any company policies that make you uncomfortable? Do you believe in its mission?

Job description and compensation package. Are you happy with what you've been offered? Have you considered the entire package, from benefits and actual pay to your title and your specific duties? Will you resent any aspect of your package at some point? Do you know what is expected of you? How much room do you have to grow—professionally and personally? Will you be able to work in the way you want; for instance, if you're used to working independently, will your new job allow for that? If you're not a team player but your new job requires you to be, can you make the necessary accommodations and self-improvements to become one?

Balancing work and home life. How long is your commute? What does your family think about this job? How will your home life change as a result? Will you have to travel a lot?

Inner truths. Why are you taking this job—for more money, greater opportunities, and/or better benefits? What will this job do for you and your future? Is this a step forward or a step back? What does your gut say?

Work Smart, Not Hard

If you focus too much on the money and not enough on all the elements that come together in finding the perfect job, you won't ever be happy and you'll likely continue living paycheck to paycheck. Working smart means finding ways to capitalize on your passions and talents and shifting away from having a JOB—just over broke—and instead fostering what you really want to do. At this point, if you've already checked out some of those Web sites I listed, you know that a lot of opportunities exist out there. All you have to do is be willing to take the challenge. In the beginning, you may have to do double duty—maintaining your current job while you investigate other opportunities or build up your own business. Be patient with yourself and realistic about your goals—personal, professional, and financial.

In the next section, I'm going to list 101 ideas for supplementing your income or discovering new career paths. I'll start with those jobs that require very little talent or knowledge base. As you move down the list, the jobs begin to call for certain sets of skills, some of which can be mastered with the proper instruction.

Evaluating Costs, Learning Curves, and Short-term vs. Long-term Payoffs

Before getting to the list, I want to share a few words about what it might take to make this shift in your life in pursuit of greater income and overall satisfaction. Some of the jobs listed will require up-front costs, like obtaining certification or a license after taking courses and passing tests. Becoming a personal trainer for a gym or mediator for a divorce court entails this kind of commitment. Such jobs will require longer learning curves, during which you may not make a lot of extra money, if any. Likewise, some jobs will provide you with short-term cash but no real long-term benefits, while others will reward in the long term but not so much in the short term. Getting a real estate license, for example, takes time, and then you need to build up your skills through practice. But getting a commission on every home you sell can add up to megabucks down the road.

The more licenses you have, the more options and flexibility you'll have for making money. Imagine having a real estate license and a cosmetology license. If the real estate market is slow in the winter where you live, you can work more hours cutting and styling hair during those months. When spring comes around, you can switch to spending more time working the real estate market and closing deals. How exciting would it be to have two very different jobs that you actually love and that pay well. You'd never get bored and you'd expose yourself to people from all walks of life!

As you read through the list, consider both your short-term goals and your long-term ones. Get a pen out and circle any job that sounds like a good idea for either (1) helping to take care of your bills today, or (2) helping to take care of *you* in the future. I want you to approach this with an eye for paying down your existing debt . . . and an eye for building up your future wealth. Be a mystery shopper to erase that $5,000 on your Visa, but consider becoming an Avon or Warm Spirit representative and start selling products from home for a commission. Or take your most passionate hobby and think of ways to turn it into a money-generating machine. That said, I encourage those with serious debt problems to avoid spending a lot of extra money until they've gotten some of their debt down and under control. If you deem it necessary to spend money now in pursuit of one of these ideas, just be sure to modify your spending plan accordingly so you can free up the cash you need to cover any expenses.

Have fun with the list. Dream a little, sister. And don't let any idea intimidate you!

Obviously, I say "keep one eye on the short term and the other on the longer term" figuratively. I suggest that you go through this list at least twice. Then put it down, let your ideas run around your head, and go back to the list. Take your time with this exercise. And remember that goal in the back of your mind: boosting income, *booting* debt, and boosting credit.

Six Quick Rules to Reading the List

1. Get a pen or highlighter. Get ready to mark up these pages!

2. Focus one eye on ideas that appeal to you on a short-term basis.

3. Focus the other eye on ideas that appeal to you on a longer-term basis.

4. If any of your circled ideas entail schooling, a license, an up-front cost, or a longer learning curve, get out a piece of paper (use your journal) and write that idea down at the top. Then go do some investigative work to see what kind of costs there are, how long of a learning curve, potential rewards down the line, and so on. Take notes. Find out, given your geographic location, how difficult it will be to achieve your goal. (I'll give you your launchpad here with a few pointers in the right direction. Much of the investigative work involved is just a mouse click away.)

5. As you reflect on your circled choices, consider why they appeal to you. Will you be good at this job? Will you enjoy this job? For example, if you pick something that requires lots of people skills and acquiring clients, you should already be a good talker and enjoy making connections with other people. It can be difficult to become a savvy sales person overnight. For some sisters, selling goods or services to strangers and badgering people for referrals isn't their idea of fun. Hence, rule number six . . .

6. Be honest with yourself. Don't shoot past the moon, but don't undercut your hidden talents, either.

101 Ideas to Increase Income and "Fund" Your Creditworthiness

The Top Two Ways to Increase Your Income at No Cost to You

1. **Get a raise or look for a better-paying job.** Okay, so I've already gone over this one, which is by far the most important idea on the list. It needs to be reiterated. Even if you love your job, it may be time to consider other alternatives—especially if you've reached an income ceiling that you can't break through. Finding a better-paying job in tune with your lifestyle will relieve the stress that weighs you down. Take skills assessments to identify other types of work you might be suited for and enjoy. Do the research. Conduct information interviews. Consult experts who can assist you.
→ Go to www.CareerBuilder.com and www.Monster.com.

2. **Get a roommate.** Take in a roommate for a year or two. If your mortgage payment is $800 and the roommate pays half, that would increase your income by $4,800 a year. Some sisters have major resistance or too much pride to share their space and end up denying themselves a long-term gain that would come from a short-term inconvenience. You might also consider renting out space when big events, such as the Super Bowl or All-Star Games, come to your area.
→ Go to www.Craigslist.com and post a "Roommate Needed" advertisement today. You can also get referrals from friends and relatives. Keep the relationship professional.

Eight Ways to Increase Your Income Using Whacha Got

3. **Organize neighborhood garage sales.** This is a great opportunity to get better acquainted with your neighbors (and start a network!). Cross-selling one another's items increases the sphere of purchasers. Also, you can share the advertising

expenses and e-mail addresses. Create flyers and spread the news to people outside your immediate community. If you can't get your neighbors rallied, have your own garage sale. Earn $250–$1,000 in one weekend.

4. **Sell on eBay.** Carefully select the items you want to sell and make a profit. If you're not sure what items are best, do a little research on the Web. Due to the popularity of this option, some community centers are offering related workshops. (One hint: Don't sell off family heirlooms, but do sell your extra televisions and gadgets you don't use.) Earn $85–$150 per week.
→ Go to www.eBay.com.

5. **Sell used books.** Get some of the clutter off your bookshelves. Instead of selling books on eBay, take them to general bookstores or a specialty store that focuses on selling used books. Antique and hard-to-find popular books will earn you more money. Some stores also buy old comic books and magazines that might earn much more than you paid for them if they are special issues or collector's editions.
→ Go to www.abebooks.com and www.alibris.com

6. **Sell antiques/collectibles.** Similar to the books, check your home for antiques or collectibles that might have more monetary than sentimental value. This might include old jewelry or furniture. Have items appraised and sell them to a dealer or independently. You can also shop these items on eBay.

7. **Do quarterly closet raids.** Purge your closets of items you no longer wear or use. Sell them on consignment, on eBay.com, or at a garage sale. Don't let sentimental attachment hold you back. If you haven't worn an item in more than a year, it's time to say good-bye; chances are you wouldn't step out on the town in it again anyway.

8. **Collect your change and visit a Coinstar.** Whether you have a piggy bank or a money jar, you can see how the change adds up. No one likes to roll coins up anymore, which is why Coinstars are so popular. For a small percentage of your sum, Coinstars count your change quickly and give you a receipt that you can then deposit into a bank account. You can probably find a Coinstar at your local supermarket. If you collect all of your change for one month, chances are you'll have about $30 to $40! If you cash your receipt at the market, be sure to then transfer it to your bank. In other words, don't spend it. (If you can find a bank or credit union that will do this change sorting for free, avoid the Coinstars and get *all* of your coins converted to cash!)

9. **Modify your withholding exemptions.** You can automatically increase your take-home pay by changing your tax withholding so you keep more money instead of Uncle Sam throughout the year. Be careful, however, as this will reduce your annual tax refund and may result in your *owing* money to the government come April 15. You can't avoid paying taxes, even though you get to keep more in your pocket at every paycheck.

10. **Collect on loans.** Call friends and family or anyone who owes you money and collect. You might be surprised at the responses. Sometimes people just need a reminder about the debt or loan. Make sure you are clear about the original agreement and amount due.

Two Ways to Increase Your Income via Owning a Machine

11. **Own a vending machine.** Lots of people throughout the world like to purchase tasty snacks and drinks from vending machines. You can have one strategically placed in a high-traffic area earning money for you. Check with warehouse

stores, such as Costco and Sam's Club, for more information. Warning: This does entail the up-front cost of purchasing the machine, which can run from $300 to $3,000+, depending on the size and style of the machine.

→ Go to www.costco.com or www.samsclub.com

12. **Own an ATM.** In a fast-paced world, some people view ATMs as a necessity for their busy lives. You can help people access their funds on the run. Check out the profitable opportunities for a much-appreciated service. You can buy or lease an ATM, place it strategically where people typically need cash on the spot, such as at a box-office window or movie theater, and collect a fee for every time someone withdraws money. Warning: This does entail the up-front cost of purchasing or leasing the machine, plus negotiating placement. (These machines cost about $3,400 to buy, or you can apply for a lease-to-own program for about $125 a month.)

→ Google "owning an ATM" and start researching opportunities in your area.

Seven Ways to Use What You (Probably) Already Know How to Do

13. **Be a mystery shopper.** Become a person hired by retailers to evaluate customer service. You might be asked to visit different retail-store settings and complete reports about your observations. Other times, you might complete assignments by visiting banks or apartment complexes, or by making telephone calls to selected businesses. Remember to closely follow guidelines when assisting with this significant research process. Your feedback will help companies decide how to conduct business in the future.

→ According to the Better Business Bureau, the top ten mystery-shopper directories and services are Paid Mystery Shopper, Shopping Jobs Here, Mystery Shopper Service, Shopping Jobs Directory, Money & Shopping, Dollar Frog, Shop Til You

Drop, Surveys Paid, Paid for Free, and Get Paid 2. The BBB also says that Shopping Jobs may be the most useful in terms of finding mystery-shopping jobs in your area. For more information, and to read reviews, go to www.betterbusinessbureau.com/shopping. Because scams do exist out there, always do your homework first!

14. **Be a house sitter.** World travelers take comfort in knowing someone is watching over the home front. Some well-organized house sitters have a regular schedule of venues. It is important for you to be detail-focused when meeting with the residents. You will need to get specific instructions about what they would like to be handled in their absence. You may even be able to charge a premium fee for taking care of the mail, as well as bills. It is also important to discuss what to do if emergencies occur and whom to contact about them. Post an ad for this service in a listing such as Craigslist or post flyers in your community.

15. **Operate a pet-sitting/walking service.** Like pets? Love to walk dogs? Plan on spending quality time with cats and dogs. Their owners will appreciate knowing their furry friends are well taken care of during their absence. A bonus is that you get to enjoy companionship and have a buddy along with you while going on exercise walks. Simply post an ad on Craigslist in your area or post flyers in your neighborhood to find people who need such services.

16. **Be a focus-group participant.** By attending these sessions, you can share your views and get paid to do so. You can give your opinions about products, services, or marketing ideas. Fees vary depending on budgets, but some range from $75 per hour to $800 per day. There are opportunities for kids, too. They can sample new and improved cereals, sip juice, and try out toys. If you or your family wants to assist with

other research projects, watch out for announcements requesting individuals to participate in studies conducted by students and companies. Earn $250+ per month. Examples of paid survey membership sites include Survey Absolute, Survey Scout, Expre$$ Paid Surveys, Survey Platinum, and My Shopping Jobs. As with the mystery-shopping sites, be watchful of scams and double-check with the Better Business Bureau any membership site you decide to join. Another great site to check out that reviews online businesses that can be vulnerable to fraud is www.topsitereviews.info.

17. **Run an errand service.** Do you love to shop and check off a list of Things To Do? You can be a generalist by running all kinds of errands for others who don't have the time or would jump at the chance to pay someone else to do it for them. Consider limiting the type of services you provide, such as by geographic location or by what type of errands you're willing to do. Either way, don't forget that your clients are counting on you to be dependable. Post an ad for your services on a site like Craigslist, send an e-mail out to your contacts in your address book offering your services, and/or create flyers to post in your community.

18. **Be a personal shopper.** Similar to running an errand service, being a personal shopper for a choice few clients can be a fun way to spend other people's money for a change. Clients could include busy executives who want you to pick up designer gifts for their customers. Career women might need assistance in selecting items for their wardrobe or accessories. Knowing about fashion trends and how to track down bargains is an advantage. Earn up to $3,000 per month.

19. **Tutor.** Students of all ages need assistance with their educational pursuits. You can decide to focus on certain subjects/age groups based on what you already know. For example: Tutor el-

ementary school math, high school algebra, or college calculus. Start with what you're already good at, and then build from that. Consider opportunities to teach skills, too. These can include test-taking skills, preparing for a standardized test, writing an essay or thesis statement, and so on. Earn $20+ per hour.

→ Contact your local schools to inquire about advertising for your tutoring services in their publications or PTAs. Post an ad for your services on a site like Craigslist or as a flyer in your community.

Thirty-Seven Ways to Put God-Given Talent to Work for Money

20. **Be a singer.** Even if you never had aspirations to be a soul singer or a rock star, it can be rewarding to just sing a song. Entertainers are needed for weddings, receptions, and parties. You could earn from $50 to $1,000 per gig. Spend some of the profits on recording a CD and you can sell it after your performances. Or put your kids to work if they are the family songbirds. You can act as their agent/manager.

21. **Be a writer.** If you have some great story ideas, submit them for $1 to $2 per word. When an editor assigns you to write a story, expect to earn more for feature articles or those with higher word counts. A 2,000-word story makes for a nice chunk of change. There are lots of opportunities to write for publications throughout the world and share insights about a variety of subjects. Flip through *Writer's Market* (Writers Digest Books) or other resource directories for publications to contact. Look beyond just major newspapers and magazines to expand your opportunities. Some community and niche magazines hire regular contributors for articles or columns published in each issue. You can earn steady checks from them.

22. **Be an interior designer or redesigner.** Brighten up other people's homes with your creative ideas. You can help new-home purchasers make sure the environment reflects their personal

taste. Learn more about art and fabrics. Study the use of color and lighting. Your work will reflect these insights. You can help clients redecorate with new furnishings, or simply help them "redesign" their homes using what they've already got.

23. **Be a public speaker.** Conference organizers are always looking for speakers and workshop presenters. If necessary, start by offering your services for free to get practice and build a reputation. Get on a national tour with a sponsoring company. One sister charged $2,500 per event to share expertise learned on her job and created a sizable second income.

24. **Be a sports coach/referee.** Athletes need guidance about how to really play the game. Share your insights about what it takes to be a winner in the game and life. If you know about the rules and enjoy attending sports games, consider being a referee. This job also affords you the opportunity to become a mentor to other sisters and encourage their own personal development through teaching leadership, sportsmanship, and the value of teamwork (and physical activity!). They'll gain self-esteem, self-respect, and certainly reward you with feelings of pride and accomplishment.

→ Contact your local schools, sports clubs, and community centers that offer after-school activities for kids.

25. **Sew or do tailoring.** You can sew and mend clothes in the convenience of your own home. Some people might hire you to hem clothes for them because they never learned to sew. Others know how but are too busy to spend the time doing it. You might decide to specialize in a certain type of sewing/tailoring—for example, men's clothing or women's high fashion and gowns.

26. **Be a fashion designer.** You can create distinctive or original one-of-a-kind fashions that are the talk of the town. Some

designers specialize in certain types of clothes—for example, business attire, children's clothing, or wedding dresses. If your clothes are showcased at retail outlets or in fashion shows, be prepared to handle more orders efficiently.

27. **Personalize clothing** (embroidery machine). People like to wear distinctive outfits that family and friends will admire. You might want to attend classes at craft stores to learn more about fabrics and tools to use for making your work more impressive and easier to complete.

28. **Teach a class.** People of all ages need to obtain more knowledge. In addition to traditional schools, consider contacting other sites offering educational opportunities. Think about community centers and churches in your community. Businesses might be willing to sponsor your class if you can enlighten people about specialized areas or topics.

29. **Be a dance instructor.** Teaching people how to step in time with the music is a fun opportunity. You can work in a variety of settings, such as homes, community centers, or apartment complexes. Start with your favorite type of dance, but don't limit yourself. Even if you have to take some classes, it might become clear that there are other great options for teaching dance, too. An affinity for hip-hop or jazz might lead to exploring ballet or ballroom.

30. **Be a photographer.** If you enjoy taking photos, consider earning money for capturing special moments. You might decide to focus on a special type of photography—for example, children, pets, or weddings. Make sure you have good equipment to get the job done right. Taking classes or assisting professional photographers may help you to learn techniques and build a resume. Earn up to $2,000 per month.

31. Be a videographer. This is a later generation of the family slide show. You can help people tell their stories on video. Sometimes this involves attending events and filming them. You might also work with creating presentations that feature family photos and music. Earn $300–$500 per booking. Check into opportunities to own low-investment franchises of video businesses.

32. Be a caterer. If you enjoy cooking delicious meals, this might be right for you. Plan your menus or offerings around the special recipes people rave about. You can set up your business so that the food is delivered or made available for pickup. Some caterers specialize in certain types of food, such as soul food or sweet-potato delicacies.

33. Be a personal chef. If you are an experienced chef (or just a really good cook!), this is an ideal opportunity for you. Busy families or professionals get to enjoy your delicious prepared meals. All they have to do is heat them up and dig in. Some people also order from personal chefs because they have special dietary needs. As you work with your clients, a comfort level will be established that makes it seem like you're cooking for your family.

34. Decorate cakes. Customized cakes always add to the excitement at celebrations for anniversaries, birthdays, graduations, and weddings. Bake eye-catching, mouthwatering desserts and positive word-of-mouth advertising can help your business grow. If you are creative and enjoy baking, more practice time might be all you need. Cake-decorating courses can help you refine your skills. Cake decorators can stay busy all year long, especially those who live in areas without bakeries and those who network with other celebration professionals, including wedding consultants.

35. Bake. If you enjoy baking, plan on creating some tasty sensations for others. Some people order batches of brownies or dozens of cookies for meetings or public events. Others, with special diet considerations, may hire you to bake special recipes for them that they can't purchase elsewhere.

36. Computer installation/repair. Busy or befuddled people will appreciate your helping them get and keep their computer equipment up and running for the best level of service. Some high-tech experts working in this area are on call offering to assist clients on an emergency basis so they have minimal downtime. Depending on your expertise, you can charge an hourly rate and offer a premium for "in-home" services.

37. Be a computer trainer. It takes patience and technical expertise to be an effective computer trainer, but if you've already got the technical skills and you love sharing them with others, this could be a great way to make money. You can teach general skills or focus on a specific type of software and/or hardware. Both individuals and classes will value the opportunity to learn proven tips. In addition to making house calls or visiting office sites, computer trainers work at schools, community centers, and many other places.

38. Be a Quicken specialist. Speaking of software specialties, many small-business owners don't take the time to balance their checkbooks—or even stay up to speed with how a program like Quicken works most efficiently. Offer a service to update banking records and ensure checkbooks are reconciled monthly. You may even be able to turn this task into a full-time small business of your own.

39. Do data entry. Hiring a typist can save a lot of time for small-business owners. Build up your typing speed and you will be able to take on large jobs and complete them efficiently. The resulting word of mouth could lead to high demand for your services. Keep in mind that students need to have their papers typed, so you might want to advertise your services in places near colleges or universities. Earn $9–$15 per hour.

40. **Start a translating service.** Do you speak more than one language? In this global economy, clients and competitors might not speak the same language. Your bilingual or multilanguage skills can help everyone communicate better. You might decide to focus on translating for businesses or governments. Companies offering marketing services also need translators.

41. **Do calligraphy.** This beautiful penmanship adds to invitations, programs, and signs. Calligraphers are also frequently asked to copy poems and quotations. Let other service providers know that you are available for hire. Take classes if you want to learn more about this form of expression. Then practice what you've learned to perfect your writing style.

→ Contact stationery stores in your area to advertise for your services. Also post your services online at a site like Craigslist, as well as in your community with flyers.

42. **Be a celebration poet.** If you're a gifted writer and enjoy composing humorous or sentimental poems, commemorative poems presented at anniversary, birthday, graduation, retirement, and wedding celebrations, you can eloquently express the significance of the occasion. You might have to interview the poem subjects or review background materials about them. Again, you can post an ad for your services online as well as in the community with flyers.

43. **Do carpentry.** Carpenters use wood to build things for a variety of settings. You might assist people with home-improvement projects. Businesses also need carpenters for expansion or ren-

ovation projects. Some carpenters focus on specific types of products, such as building bookcases.

44. **Do painting.** The constant need to periodically freshen up exteriors and interiors means painters will always provide valued services. Some painters focus on creating distinctive murals. If you are talented when it comes to painting portraits, commissions can be profitable for you. Talk to art galleries about allowing you to sell paintings there. Consider participating in art fairs and shows.

45. **Do Web site design.** Web site designers create masterpieces that attract visitors. Just spend some time looking at sites and you can see which ones have distinctive home pages. If you can create dynamic sites that are easy to navigate, your work will earn rave reviews. Talented Web designers can command up to $10,000 for a professional site.

46. **Be an actor/actress.** On the screen or on stage, actors and actresses keep us entertained. You will need to speak clearly and present yourself well. Be prepared to memorize your lines and recite them in character. Your kids might want to get in on the act, too. Cable TV or community and regional theaters are good places to start.

47. **Write plays.** Playwrights enlighten others while sharing their knowledge and opinions. Both large and small communities often have playhouses, or you could start your own. Study scripts to learn the correct formats and stage directions to use. Join a local playhouse or watch for classes in your area where you can hone skills.

48. **Direct plays.** Directors have the ability to bring everything together before opening night. In addition to being familiar with the script, you should be knowledgeable about various

aspects related to theater. You might be asked to assist with casting, production staff, and music selection. While you can dream big about directing in large playhouses or on Broadway, start small in your local community.

49. Be an illustrator. These artists share their talents in a variety of ways. You might work with advertising firms. Publishers keep illustrators busy working on children's books. Sometimes business owners collaborate with illustrators to create art for product manuals or newsletters.

50. Be a comic strip artist. Draw a great cast of characters and you will earn more than peanuts. Try smaller, local publications to break in. Eventually, you might want to work with publications creating special comic strips for their readers. If any of your comic strips become syndicated, there is good income potential. Awareness of your work might result in merchandising spin-offs. Earn $10–$50 per strip.

51. Be a book reviewer. If you are an avid reader, sharing critical comments about books might be at the top of your list. You can be the first in your circle of friends to read new editions. This can be done on a freelance basis, or you might be a regular contributor for a newspaper or magazine. Some book reviewers specialize in specific genres, such as business or children's books.

→ Start by contacting your local newspaper or magazine publication that has book reviews. You can get practice writing book reviews at Amazon.com.

52. Be a children's party character. If you enjoy making children happy and being the center of attention, this could be a fun thing to do. You can get dressed up in a costume for a popular book, movie, or TV character, or make up one of your own. Clowns who make people of all ages laugh are still party favorites.

53. **Be a gallery/museum assistant.** Love art? Your creative assistance can help gallery and museum owners reach out to their visitors. You might assist them with putting up displays or exhibits. You could also plan and coordinate programs that support the exhibits.

54. **Braid hair.** Braiding hair is a possibility for people of all ages. If your children are good at braiding hair, encourage them to consider working with you. At the least, they can help spread the word. Their friends and classmates might be good clients for you. In fact, Susan L. Taylor's loyal braider started as a teenager and now keeps a celebrity client list. Her success has allowed her to launch a whole line of hair products and even land a reality TV show.

55. **Style hair.** Some people start to do this or braiding hair independently, then progress into working for a beauty shop. Either way, you can develop a diverse customer base eager for you to assist them.

56. **Do nails.** Many beauty shops offer nail care services, too. You can also work for a nail salon or independently. It helps to have an awareness of effective color combinations and fashion trends.

→ If all of the last three ideas grabbed you, consider being a *stylist* and perform all three jobs. Don't live near Hollywood to cater to the stars? Stylists are in demand everywhere, and can typically ask for premium fees climbing toward $100 an hour with set minimums. Think about the needs of brides, bridesmaids, and those attending formals, proms, and other fancy events. If you're really good with styling a sister's head of hair, and word spreads quickly, you could be setting up shop in no time. Note that you'll have to get a cosmetology license to make it official.

Forty-three Ways to Become an Entrepreneur

Have you ever thought of yourself as an entrepreneur? An entrepreneur is someone who simply turns a passion into a money-generating career. Some of the ideas in the list above can lead to the founding of an entire business, so you're going to find some similarities in the types of jobs listed below and those I've already mentioned. Just as before, when reviewing the following list, find what piques your curiosity and keep building on that curiosity through a little investigative work. Maybe one particular idea will jump out at you. See if you can transition from your current job into a lifetime profession that makes you feel rich from the inside out every day. It's easier than you think. The world will open up to you and your ideas if you just let those ideas come to life.

Recall what I said earlier: JOB stands for "just over broke." A career, on the other hand, can last a lifetime and can take care of you as long as you nourish it well. That's right: Instead of expecting a job to nourish your bank account week after week, I want you to try shifting your mind so that you view what you do as an act of nourishing your career—which then automatically returns riches to you. This mind-set can get you out of living paycheck to paycheck and into living beyond your wildest dreams!

Establishing a small business isn't necessarily easy, so I won't sugarcoat it. It requires research, some instruction, time to generate a loyal client or customer base, time and experience to generate a reputation and reliable contacts, continual investigative research into maintaining a leading-edge business that's up to speed with technology and industry trends, and maybe some certification or a particular type of degree. Don't let any requirement intimidate you. Just start by understanding what interests you most, pinpoint what you're truly passionate about, and then take baby steps. Step one is educating yourself on what you have to do logistically speaking, such as writing a business plan, taking courses, or entering through the back door by working with someone already established. Step two is getting the word out

Entrepreneurial Starting Points

No matter what kind of business you want to start, there are lots of resources to help you get going both in books and online. For instance, for general information on starting a business, as well as leads for buying a franchise or business, finding business brokers, and obtaining business planning tools, an excellent place to visit is the *Wall Street Journal*'s Center for Entrepreneurs at www.startupjournal.com. You can always Google keywords related to the type of business you want to operate, and visit a library to peruse books dedicated to guiding you through the initial phases with insider tips to dealing with all the odds and ends. If I didn't list any direct launch point via a Web site or contact recommendation beside a given idea, all you have to do is use any online search engine—like Google, Yahoo, AOL, or MSN—to start learning about the road ahead of you by plugging in keywords. Or try any of the sites already listed in this chapter. Other Web sites to check out are:

  *www.entrepreneur.com,
  *http://entrepreneurs.about.com (also check out simply
    http://about.com and do a search in your chosen field), and
  *www.inc.com.

  www.iVillage.com—the popular site aimed at women—is also a great source for sisters who want to start their own businesses but don't know where to begin or how to balance their home and work life. And for information about obtaining degrees and certificates, many of which you can do online, try Kaplan University (www.kaplan.edu) and the University of Phoenix (www.universityofphoenix.com). For other schools and a comprehensive list of online degrees, courses, and programs, go to www.directoryofschools.com.

about you and your services so that you can begin to acquire customers and clients. This usually entails marketing yourself and posting the services you offer on job boards that potential clients use routinely. It's never been easier to self-promote: Today there are relatively cheap methods, such as sites like Craigslist and affordable printing shops like FedEx Kinko's.

Remember the power of a network; if you don't have one started, get one going! Once you find what you're interested in pursuing, start on a journey and make it your goal to land and establish as many referrals and contacts as you can. You don't have to become best friends with everyone you meet for purposes of making connections and gathering information; even loose acquaintances come in handy when you need advice or ideas. This means making connections with other people, joining associations and networking groups in your line of business—or establishing one on your own in your geographic area. Ask for referrals. Think of all the people you know who know lots of other people that could use your services. Reach out to them. Be bold. Land one client, then multiply that by as many as possible. And keep going.

I've left these ideas for last because they are not necessarily jobs you can do overnight and quickly transition into establishing your reputation (and hence, moneymaking contracts) in a brief time period. If you find something that gets your blood running, however, the time, effort, and any up-front costs will be worth it in the long run.

Keep in mind, of course, that you're reading this book because you want to get your credit straight. For some of these career paths, **getting your credit straight must precede taking serious financial risks with starting a business.** Be careful about abusing your credit cards for the purpose of obtaining extra degrees and utilizing expensive resources to establish yourself in a profession you don't ultimately want or that won't work out for you. As I said before, be realistic about your goals and your wishes for your future. My advice to you is to consider this last batch of ideas as long-term goals that you can certainly start working toward today step-by-step while **focusing on paying down debt and mending your credit in preparation for that future achievement.** These ideas should inspire you to work as fast, as smart, and as diligently as you can toward getting your credit straight so that you can genuinely tap into your greatest potential. Then you can really finance your wildest dreams.

57. **Be a consultant.** Management-consulting business generates $100 billion in worldwide revenues. These professionals help clients manage *their* clients within their industry. Specialties include accounting, finance, human resources, logistics manufacturing, marketing, purchasing, research, and technology. Marketing consultants work across industries, including domestic and international, with a strong focus on ethics and strategic planning. You may even be able to create a wonderful niche for yourself by targeting African-American women in business. It's possible to become a consultant entirely based on what you currently know and the services you provide in your current job. You simply transition from working for a company to providing the same services working for yourself in a self-employed consulting capacity.

58. **Be an executive coach.** You can help professionals achieve their personal best. There might be opportunities for you to assist with leadership and communication training or retraining employees. You might be called upon to assist with or handle employee evaluations. Keep detailed records and be prepared to discuss the suggestions you offer to employees. Being an executive coach can entail having a graduate degree.

59. **Own a carpet-cleaning service.** There are various options with this business idea. You can go commercial and focus on apartment buildings and small office buildings. Or you can go residential and do individual homes. A great opportunity awaits if you contract with an apartment building to clean lobbies and hallways, but you can also market to apartment residents and build a solid revenue stream. (Note that this business entails an investment in the equipment.)

60. **Do relocation consulting.** Provide assistance to executives in the midst of transferring to your area. They might need help

finding temporary housing or finding out where the hot spots are located in big cities. Some related specialists also assist professionals considering relocating to other areas by conducting research for them. Chamber of commerce and tourist bureaus are great resources. Earn $15,000–$25,000 part-time.

61. **Do PR consulting.** Public relations consultants try to get their clients in the news. They prepare and distribute news releases to the media. Their creative ideas and contacts help to get newsworthy information in the news without spending a lot of advertising dollars.

62. **Do landscaping service/snow-removal service.** Do you have an eye for arranging beautiful gardens and turning a dull front yard into a winning model home? Keeping people's homes "aesthetically managed" with both landscaping and seasonal snow-removal services can be an in-demand job, especially in certain communities. You can decide to work during certain seasons by limiting service options, or all year long by expanding service options. It is important to own or rent dependable equipment so you can get the job done in an efficient manner.

63. **Plan reunions.** There is a lot more involved in hosting a reunion than just calling classmates or family members. Many people turn to reunion planners who set up/maintain databases, coordinate communication efforts, send out invitations, take reservations, book sites, and hire entertainment. As with all of the other event-related opportunities in this list, plan on being available to be an event-day on-site resource. And you don't have to plan reunions for your own class or even your own alma mater. You can establish a reunion-planning business, open to any type of school or family, that can support you year-round!

64. **Be a massage therapist.** Help others relax by working as a massage therapist. Some people work in parlors or for other businesses. Others pack up a kit with essential oils and other supplies, then visit their customers at their homes or business sites. In a high-stress world, the related services are often praised and much appreciated. You'll want to get certified to command top dollar. Earn $60–$70 per hour.

→ For a complete list of massage schools in your area, plus other similar schools, such as acupuncture, herbal, naturopathic medicine, and homeopathy, go to www.naturalhealers.com.

65. **Provide business-plan-writing services.** By writing business plans, you can help new or experienced entrepreneurs get off to a good start. The contents must be researched, selected, and formatted to reflect specific industry and company focuses. Good business-plan writers are definitely considered to have earned their fees. The plans they write help companies attract new investors, obtain business loans, and stand out among competitors. Earn $30,000–$50,000 per year.

66. **Be a grant writer.** Grant writers earn money for themselves and others. They research opportunities and tap into resources and connections to determine the best grants for consideration. Nonprofits depend on them to generate funds necessary to operate their programs and services. Some grant writers charge flat fees, while others earn a percentage of the acquired grant money. The earning potential in this field is enormous if you become an indispensable asset to a company, university, or organization that needs constant grant proposals—especially in the technical arena.

67. **Be a speechwriter.** Speechwriters help others say a lot in a few words. They review mountains of research and stacks of data to determine what information is the most significant to

share. In addition to writing-related tasks, speechwriters might also be asked to coach their clients in the correct way to deliver the speech. They may accompany their client when speeches are given and offer critical commentary afterward.

→ Contact a speakers bureau or go to the National Speakers Association at www.nsaspeaker.org for more information.

68. Operate a tax service. People value the benefits offered by tax-service providers—especially during tax season. These experts stay up to date on tax-code changes. They are capable of offering related advice for future planning and efficiently handling tax-form preparation. Some tax-service providers work with business clients throughout the year.

→ Google "income tax training school" and your city to find where you can learn how to prepare tax forms in your state. If one particular business dominates your geographic location, such as H&R Block, visit an office and ask about how you, too, can become a tax consultant.

69. Operate an accounting and bookkeeping service. Small-business owners depend on accountants and bookkeepers to help determine whether they are in the red or black. They might audit books or set them up and maintain records. A lot of these professionals work with databases and financial-software programs such as Quicken. If you can acquire a solid network of clients, you can establish a lucrative small business of your own providing these services. If you become a certified public accountant, you can even command higher fees.

→ Google "CPA schools" to start looking for schools that provide the education you need. Stick to accredited schools.

70. Be a mediator. These professionals facilitate conflict resolution. Diverse people call on mediators to act as an objective third party. Take a class, pass a test, and become a certified mediator for unions or circuit courts. The starting rate can be $150/hour. Some mediators make up to $1,000 per session.

→ Go to www.mediate.com/careers for more information.

71. **Organize parties.** Party planning is great for creative people who enjoy entertaining others. It gives you the opportunity to plan elegant dinners on somebody else's budget. By pulling all of the details together, you become a valued asset to your clients. Earn $1,200–$1,500 per month.

72. **Be a special-event or wedding planner.** Events take place every day; there are lots of opportunities for special-event planners to help clients create unforgettable celebrations and fund-raisers. These events sometimes have guest lists with hundreds of people and require an enormous amount of organization and coordination among vendors. They are held in a wide array of settings, including some of the most popular venues in town or major tourist attractions. Some event planners command fees of $100 an hour (plus expenses like driving time and incidental costs), with minimums of $2,500. If you decide to work with nonprofits, it may be rewarding to know that your efforts will enhance awareness of and generate revenue for important causes.

73. **Be a festival coordinator/assistant.** You can work only on event day or assume a larger role. Major festivals require staff to work on planning processes, confirming arrangements, recruiting/ signing up participants, and site coordination all year long. Some staff members fulfill specific tasks—for example, contacting schools and community groups.

74. **Be a professional organizer.** Help people get their act together in the home or office setting. You can bring an objective approach to handling clutter and challenges related to organiza-

tion. Your tips can have a substantial impact on how people handle things in the future. Keep up to date on organizational tools, products, and resources. In major metropolitan areas, organizational services can run into the hundreds of dollars—per "room" or focus. You can choose to specialize in a particular area, such as the kitchen, the closets, the office paperwork, and so on. A professional organizer typically charges between $50 and $200 an hour.

75. **Be a professional car detailer.** How about establishing a mobile car-wash business? Make an arrangement with a company to provide services in a specified area of their parking lot to clean cars for executives and office workers. It's one less stop they'll have to make on the way home. You can take this type of service to the limit and offer extensive services such as paint repair/touch-ups, superior interior and exterior cleaning, upholstery treatments, and so on. You can earn $30 to $60 an hour, or, if you happen to live in a place where the market can call for more money, you may be able to charge upward of $200 per vehicle, depending on the extent of your services and the size of the vehicle.

76. **Start a specialty-gift-basket business.** Think about creative ways to showcase items fitting in with holidays or themes every day of the year. For example, you might put together baskets for Christmas or new-baby arrivals. Plan ahead for upcoming seasons and stay tuned in to special interests or opportunities in your area. For example: there might be a lot of pet lovers in your area or a big rival sports game coming to your town. You can work independently or collaborate with gift outlets. Some people also like to set up booths at craft fairs. Just watch how much you spend on items for the baskets so there is a good return on your investment. Consider buying in bulk from discount resources. Established

gift-basket companies can easily command at least 100 percent markups on the price they put on their baskets relative to what it cost to create them! Earn $10,000+ per year.

77. **Create wedding favors.** By creating beautiful or functional keepsakes, you can make the big day even more unforgettable. If you are creative and can make nice items for economical prices, happy couples and their guests will refer others to you. Shop at dollar stores for discount items to use in your creations. Again, the markup potential on expertly created designs and gift bags can be well over 100 percent of the cost you have to bear.

78. **Market handicrafts.** You just might enjoy making craft items for your family and friends. There are, however, many ways you can earn money from crafts. Sell them independently by special order or at craft events. Talk to boutiques or gift stores about allowing you to sell the items on a consignment basis. You can have a limited amount of available items or a catalog of possibilities.

79. **Start a scrapbook business.** Encourage people to get those old photos and postcards out of the storage boxes. You can show them how to create beautiful books spotlighting their keepsakes, or take on the responsibility of putting together their scrapbooks. Scrapbook materials are sold in craft and specialty stores. Consider taking a scrapbook class to get even more creative ideas. You can then *teach* do-it-yourself classes for a fee at your community center, and establish private clients who want you to take on the entire job of putting together their scrapbook. Earn $50–$150 per hour.

80. **Do direct sales/operate a home-based business.** Consider direct-sales businesses that allow you to sell established and/or innovative product brands. Investigate working with proven

industry leaders such as Avon and Mary Kay. Others with a healthy lifestyle focus include Melaleuca and Warm Spirit (an African American–owned company). Some people involved in direct sales choose to partner with others or host events showcasing their products.

→ Learn about home-based businesses at sites like Inc.com and Startupjournal.com.

81. **Be an in-home personal trainer.** Help people get in shape in a comfortable environment. You can create customized exercise routines based on your client's individual needs. Many people like the one-on-one approach that enables them to work at their own pace and build a rapport with their personal trainer. To command higher rates, such as $200 an hour in major metropolitan areas, get certified by an accredited professional organization—e.g., ACSM (American College of Sports Medicine) or ACE (American Counsel on Exercise)—and keep your community CPR certification and first-aid training up to date, too. The fitness world has never been so hot, and consider how much you can also benefit healthwise by becoming a trainer in tip-top shape!

82. **Be a virtual office assistant.** You don't have to work on site in order to be considered an important part of the office team. There are a variety of things you can do to help clients reach their goals. They might include taking messages, data entry, following up on inquiries, and assisting with client presentations/pitches. If you've been a traditional secretary in the past, chances are you can transform your skills into being a virtual office assistant today just by learning how to be efficient remotely—via the computer, Internet, phones, faxes, and personal digital assistant (PDA). Earn $40,000 per year.

→ Google "virtual office assistant" and investigate companies that provide virtual office assistants. You'll want to know how to provide those same services, which you can then advertise for on a site like Craigslist to get a few clients and your business going.

83. **Be a notary public.** A notary public is a public servant authorized by the state or local government. The process of becoming a notary public varies from state to state, but in general it's relatively easy and cheap to do. As a notary public, you would be appointed to witness the signing of documents and administer oaths. Your expertise with notarizing documents would help deter fraud and ensure that parties entering into agreements are knowledgeable about them so the terms can be properly executed. Fees for a notary public can be anywhere from $2 to tens of dollars, depending on what notarial act is performed (sometimes several notarial acts are performed at the same time, thus accumulating fees).
   → Google "notary public" to start researching how to become a notary public in your area, or go to www.becomeanotary.us, or visit the National Notary Association at www.national-notary.org. Because states can limit what fees you can charge for notarizing documents, being a notary public is a good backup to another career pursuit (recall the power of multiple licenses).

84. **Buy items wholesale and sell them retail.** Find stores/resources in your community, via direct-mail catalogs or on the Internet. Let others know what types of items you are looking for so they can help you find bargains. When you buy in bulk, your profit opportunities will be increased. You may even be able to find a niche market from which you can then found an entire business.

85. **Operate a grocery-delivery service.** Busy professionals hate spending time shopping for groceries, waiting in long lines, and then lugging bags from door to door. Offer a service to

complete this task on demand. This is similar to operating an errand service or being a personal shopper.

86. **Master desktop publishing.** With the right software, you will be able to design impressive materials for all kinds of businesses. Consider also the abundance of opportunities for you to create newsletters and other publications. By networking with advertising agencies and marketing service providers, you can dramatically increase your customer base.

87. **Operate a résumé business.** By creating target résumés for clients, you can help people put their best foot forward when applying for their dream job. You might have to conduct interviews, review and consolidate records, and conduct industry research in order to create the desired product. Expand your business focus by also writing cover letters and working with clients making midcareer changes. Run promotions encouraging everyone to have an up-to-date résumé available. Earn $150 for entry-to-mid-management job seekers. Earn $250 for senior management to executive job seekers.

88. **Edit.** As an editor, you can make valuable suggestions for writers and publishers to consider. There are many different kinds of editors who work on a variety of projects. It helps to be knowledgeable about proper grammar and punctuation usage. Some publications require that editors reference certain style guides, such as *The Chicago Manual of Style* or the *MLA* (Modern Language Association) handbook. Never pretend to be familiar with certain styles of editing if you don't know about them. Style manuals are available in bookstores and libraries. Some have online "cribsheets" for download.

89. **Proofread.** If you are a good speller or typically spot errors when you are reading, proofreading might be of interest. You can assist writers, editors, and printers. Be prepared to han-

dle requests for reading material quickly and returning it efficiently to meet deadlines. There may be opportunities for you to assist college students by proofreading their major papers for degree projects or theses. Proofreaders for businesses can charge at least $50 an hour.

90. **Be a database-management specialist.** Assist small-business owners with establishing and maintaining their databases. While they are busy working with new clients, you can help them keep track of what is happening with their entire customer base. If you have an affinity for computer technology but don't have experience in this area, take a few classes.

91. **Research.** Assist with acquiring valuable data. You can do this on a freelance basis, work with research firms, or even start your own business. This may require you to conduct interviews via the telephone or in person for survey projects. If you like conducting searches and learning new things via the Internet, assignments collecting research data might suit you well. Keep in mind that general-service and specialized libraries still offer a lot of resources, too.

92. **Operate a distribution/delivery service.** You can deliver newspapers, magazines, or flyers to homes or businesses. Another option is to deliver telephone directories. Dependable transportation is required for efficiently handling deliveries.

93. **Child care.** Preschool children may come to your house or the center where you work and stay all day. Older kids might spend a limited number of hours with you before or after school. Create more demand for your services by assisting special-needs children. Check on licensing guidelines if you want to establish any care center. You can also provide specialty child-care services, many of which command high rates, such as on-site or near-site babysitting services offered

during "adult-only" events, like weddings and other large parties or celebrations. These can cost clients upward of $400 or more for a mere five hours!

94. **Elder care.** This is very similar to child care except you will be working with seniors. They might require you to come to their home or a nursing center. You can also relieve other caregivers when they need a time-out. Earn $13.50–$17.50 per hour.

95. **Operate a moving service.** Help others pack and move their precious possessions. Some services also buy moving supplies in bulk and sell them.

96. **Operate a transportation service.** If you have dependable transportation, there are short- and long-term opportunities to assist others. You might want to transport people on a limited basis to a select number of locations. Or you could set up arrangements with clients to take them wherever they want to go.

97. **Be a relocation resource specialist.** Provide a service to individuals new to your city. Help them locate the best hair salon, dry cleaner, or handyman in the area. Offer a specialty service for welcoming new sisters into your community who may be eager to meet other sisters already established. This can afford you a great opportunity to start a network with a variety of sisters from different professions and backgrounds.

98. **Be an archivist.** Collectors, groups, or nonprofits with large inventories may need assistance with documenting the items they own. It is important for them to have records/catalogs reflecting contents before loaning them to others. Attention to detail is essential.

99. **Be a human-resource specialist.** Small-business owners count on human-resource specialists to assist them with employee recruiting and training. You might be called upon to create and place ads, screen candidates, and make recommendations. Some human-resource specialists also assist with employee evaluations. Due to corporate downsizing, there are more opportunities for independent human-resource specialists to work with large corporations.

The Last Two Ways to Apply What You've Learned or Experienced

100. **Publish a workbook or pamphlet.** This is a way to share some of the professional insights and wisdom gained during your lifetime. You can sell your publication in a variety of different ways. They include networking with others, via a Web site, and after public appearances. Keep down production costs so you can price the publication competitively and economically but still make money selling it. If you will be mailing the publication, consider the costs for postage or shipping and handling when setting your price.

101. **Be an executive director/board member.** When you have the opportunity to serve in this capacity, ask if any compensation is provided for some or all of the services you will be providing to the business or organization. Keep in mind that these positions are prestigious but can be time-consuming, too.

I Don't Have Time for Another Job, So What Do I Do?

If my list of job and career ideas overwhelmed you, stop and take a deep breath. *All good jobs come to an end, yet all great careers don't happen overnight.* It might take you working several "jobs" at once or in a series as you build toward a career. We all have our personal limitations to consider, such as balancing the act of managing the home front, caring for small children, being the family CEO while our husbands go missing because they work so much outside the home, and lacking the time to devote to thinking, researching, and planning for new income streams. Moms are among the most overscheduled and overstressed people on the planet, and sisters in particular have a tendency to put everyone else first before they say "Me." Now it's time to give yourself permission to engage in routine income strategizing regardless of your current responsibilities. As I tell many clients, "You don't find time, you *make* time." And you can make time in a variety of different ways.

Here are some last bits of advice for those who still feel intimidated and who can't fathom changing anything in their life to accommodate any of the suggestions I've presented in this chapter:

1. Reconsider your priorities and aim for better time management.

   a. Turn mindless activities into mindful ones by avoiding pointless Internet surfing and e-mailing, chatting on the phone with girlfriends, watching TV, window shopping, catalog flipping, and participating in happy hour on a regular basis. If you were to add up all those minutes a day spent doing "nothing in particular" and that may even be costing you money, you'd be amazed at how much extra time you can build into your day for income sleuthing.

   b. If your kids are old enough, give them more chores to do so you can omit at least twenty minutes of housework a day from your personal schedule. Reward them with their favorite meal on the weekend, or simply up their household responsibilities without a reward. Limit their activities if you can't keep up with their demanding schedules, or seek help from other parents who can take over duties like carpooling. If they are in their later teens, encourage them to get part-time work or summer jobs so they can pay for some of their own expenses—especially the ones you shouldn't be bearing, like excessive entertainment, personal splurges, and dating costs.

c. Speak with your husband about your goals and how he can help you achieve them. Ask if he can find at least thirty minutes a day to either join in your efforts or at least take care of your young children who must be supervised while you devote time to income sleuthing. If he cannot afford the time, find a local babysitter or neighbor who can watch your kids for a mere thirty minutes. Even if you have to pay a small babysitting fee, it's an investment in your family's future.

2. Make a specific commitment and stick to it no matter what.

a. Find and box out a specific time period on your calendar for income sleuthing and career research. It can be daily, biweekly, or weekly. The key is to be consistent and don't miss a day. Be as specific as possible, whether it's every other day for thirty minutes or a total of at least two hours a week.

b. If your schedule is so varied day by day and week by week, then cut out time every Sunday to prepare for the upcoming week by mapping out your income-sleuthing time-outs based on your rough schedule. Do your best to predict scheduling conflicts or have a backup plan for days when you don't know, for instance, if those thirty minutes will happen right at 3:30 P.M.

I-STOP stands for "income-sleuthing time-out periods." Schedule as many I-STOPs into your week as possible, and guard those periods well. Balancing family and work—even if you're a stay-at-home mom—doesn't mean you can't set aside time for yourself and I-STOPs. Communicate your goals and wishes with your family. They will likely rally behind you and be more accepting of any challenges that arise as a result of your pursuits. As you proceed, check in with them once in a while and ask for feedback. Be accountable to them, as they are to you. Their input may surprise you!

Exercise One: Take Inventory of Your Interests and Potential and Map Out a Future

1. If you didn't get out that paper and take notes or circle ideas from the previous pages, as I suggested in the "Six Quick Rules to Reading the List" box, now it's time to do so. Make a notation of your interest next to each income opportunity, indicating yes, no, or maybe. Separate your "yes" list into two categories: "skills I already have" and "skills I need to learn." Now, using your GIRL journal, list all of the opportunities you are interested in and have the necessary skills for. If any other types of ideas came to mind that I didn't list, by all means add them to your list!

2. Next, analyze your calendar and determine the time you have available to generate extra income—for example, weekday evenings from 7 P.M. to 10 P.M. and Saturdays from 11 A.M. to 5 P.M. Get out your calendar and see if you can chart all of your I-STOPs over the next month. Make these separate from your bill-paying sessions and your "focus sessions" during which you review your credit-boosting strategies.

3. Start doing research on what is necessary to begin generating income with the opportunities you have selected—for example, updating your résumé, training, licenses, supplies, creating a network, asking for a promotion, and so on.

4. Create a time line for completing the preparation, research, and analysis that will help you start your new job or business. Map it out using your calendar.

I would love to hear your ideas and stories of how you increased your income. Let me know what happens. Contact me through my Web site, www.bridgforth financial.com.

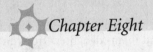

Chapter Eight

Protecting Your New Financial Health and Financing Your Wildest Dreams

Bravo for getting to this chapter of the book! You've learned more than you ever thought possible about credit, and the previous chapter hopefully inspired you to think about new income opportunities that can accelerate your financial healing. While at times debt and credit problems can make life seem hopeless, it's not a lifetime sentence. You can work your way out of debt, mending your credit in the meanwhile, and begin to think more seriously about the bigger picture—the dreams you've had since you were a little girl. Maybe it's owning a beachside home, or traveling the globe and taking a safari to Africa. Maybe it's being able to fund your children's and even grandchildren's education. Anything is possible if you set your goals high and prepare yourself to work on reaching them day after day.

One sister, June, recalls how her life changed after getting a shocking telephone call. The caller reported that her husband of ten years, an attorney named Troy, had been killed in a car accident. The young widow soon realized that she would be forced to make some sacrifices in order to raise their eight-year-old son and infant daughter, Troy Jr. and Angelyne.

"My children's necessities always came first," June explained. "There were many, many times when I saw things it would have been nice to have but left them in the store." Still, throughout the years, as her career as an educator evolved and the children grew up, June continued to be conservative in her discretionary purchases. "My daddy always told me to never spend what you don't have," June recalled. "And I repeated those words over and over to myself every time I felt tempted." Even though she remained single, she took pride in never having to seek public assistance for her family. "That's why I'm like I am today and was able to save up money to buy the house for us to live in," June said. She always kept her priorities and credit straight.

Quite often we don't reduce our expenses until we are forced to do so by our circumstances. Other than tragic instances like June's, we might experience unexpected health costs or the loss of a job. June's daughter, Angelyne, while a young woman in her early thirties, suddenly received an indefinite layoff notice from the advertising agency where she had enjoyed working for five years. She wasn't the only one surprised by the news; many of her colleagues were surprised that Angelyne was let go. She was a hard worker who had received high scores on performance reviews.

Although Angelyne surely wasn't alone in her layoff experience at that company—others included a recently relocated graphic artist who had just signed an apartment lease and a senior copywriter who was within months of retirement—it didn't help her feel much better about the situation. She spent the first evening after the big announcement overwhelmed by a torrent of emotions. She was hurt that her employer had cast her aside despite all the energy she'd expended for the company's benefit. What would she tell her family and friends now that her great job was gone? How could this have happened to her? Eventually, she exhausted herself and cried herself to sleep.

The next morning, Angelyne sidelined her emotions and decided to take stock of her life. First she sat down and made a list of how she could cut expenses. This meant less money spent on restaurant meals, theater tickets, and Christmas presents. She also canceled reservations for a business-conference trip. Then she quickly realized there were some moneymaking opportunities to follow up on. She had done freelance projects on the side in the past, and some of those clients had mentioned they might want more work done. As soon as Angelyne began making those calls and reconnecting with old clients, she was back in action. She eventually launched her own communications firm, which still thrives today—fifteen years later.

"Being laid off was ultimately one of the best things that ever happened to me," Angelyne acknowledges. "Even after growing up with my mother, June, and watching her exemplary money-management style and unselfish tendency to make sacrifices, I had to learn some things the hard way. Although I was never extravagant, it was important to make some adjustments for living well within my means."

We all have to learn the hard way once in a while. It's what makes us human. But there are plenty of lessons you can learn ahead of time to help cushion any unexpected event or experience. This chapter further helps you clear the path ahead of you by sharing some of the tricks savvy financial planners know and that you might not pick up on your own in everyday life. Or, if you do, it's because you've had to learn the lessons the hard way.

In this chapter you'll learn how to bank cheaply, how to use your good credit score to snag the best interest rates, and how to avoid the perils that can wipe you out financially. You'll also learn more about avoiding identity theft, the fastest-growing crime in America. By the end of the chapter, you'll have so many things straight in your mind that you'll be ready to take on just about anything. The important thing to remember is that you are not alone in your journey, whether it's climbing out of the debt and poor-credit hole, or moving forward with a renewed sense of self and financial strength. Once you've bolstered your creditworthiness, the world will open up to you.

Prevent Debt and Protect Credit

When I hear stories from people who find themselves deeply in debt and unable to apply for good credit terms, it's amazing how many of those people got that way through one event in their life that set them back financially. For some, it's one medical bill or a judgment handed down to them from a lawsuit. For others, it's a divorce or a lost job. With 30 million Americans living on minimum wage and about 70 percent of people living from paycheck to paycheck, it's no surprise that the subject of debt and credit is constantly in our faces.

According to a study by ACNielsen, the marketing arm of TV ratings giant Nielsen Media Research, about one in every four Americans admits that they don't have any spare cash. If you can count yourself among these people, make it a goal today to stand up for yourself and put the advice of this book into action. You're going to become a member of the 40 Percent Club—those who pay off their credit cards every month. And you're going to become a role model for other sisters in your community. That's right: Once you implement my strategies and financial ideas, you'll find the changes in your life to be too good to keep to yourself. You'll want to share your secrets with other sisters and encourage them to follow your example.

Let's assume you get back on solid financial footing and are enjoying the merits of a good credit score. Life is great. But then another crisis strikes that requires lots of money to settle. Will you plunge back into debt and suffer another blow to your credit? Is this possible? Of course it is. That's why this book can't be just about reducing debt and boosting credit. You have to know about ways to protect and preserve your credit and avoid future debt. This is when several key things come into play, which I'll outline below.

Plan on Establishing a Savings Cushion

I mentioned the merits of having an emergency fund, which I prefer to call a savings cushion, many times throughout this book. If you feel too far in the hole right now to worry about stocking up on savings while you've got creditors at your back, it's okay to focus on taking care of your debt and credit problems first and then concentrate on building your fund. While you pay down your debt you may be utilizing potential savings, but consider this: The faster you eliminate burdensome debt, the faster you'll establish financial security. Soon enough, you'll find yourself accruing massive savings that translate to big financial rewards that can last a lifetime.

Ideally, you should aim to keep enough aside to cover living expenses for at least six months in case you lose your job, become ill and can't work, or something happens in your family that forces you to stop everything, including a steady flow of income. But six months sounds daunting, and it is. Start with smaller goals, such as by saving $500. Then make a goal of saving $1,000, then $2,000, or the total of your average monthly expenses. As you likely know from past experience, an unexpected, unplanned emergency that requires substantial dollars can happen at any moment. All too often, we have a knee-jerk reaction and become vulnerable to using expensive sources of money, such as a high-interest credit card or convenience checks. We then get sucked into the bottomless pit of anxiety and despair. Of course, we resolve to do what's necessary to get our heads back above water as soon as possible. But too often that decision made in panic ends up throwing us overboard with rocks in our pockets. To complicate matters, many of us feel shame as well as stress.

Cash crises are a fact of life, but we need to know ahead of time what steps to take so that when a cash crunch hits, we can catch our breath, calmly assess the situation, find the help we need, and make our way back to a safer financial state. By evaluating and weighing your options, then making an informed decision, you will not only reduce the stress and alleviate the shame associated with your crisis, but you will gain a greater sense of confidence and financial peace of mind. Your finances will become stabilized, and you will continue to improve your credit score and position yourself to accomplish your financial goals in the future. Over the years, many of my clients have done just that.

Preparing yourself for those cash crunches—instead of trying to treat them on the spot when they strike—is the best medicine. Prevention means establishing a fund of money that you can tap when you need your personal payday in advance. It's much cheaper to borrow from yourself than from a creditor!

Saving for Unplanned Emergencies Pays Off

Six months of living expenses in a savings account = "No Problem" for these commonplace scenarios:

My car broke down and it requires a new transmission.

I got into a fender bender and owe my deductible.

I lost my job and need time to find a new one.

I needed emergency surgery and the medical bills are significant.

My mom is ill and I have to take unpaid time off to be with my family.

It may take time to build up a cash fund that can cover your living expenses for up to six months or more, but that should be your goal. Take your monthly overhead, multiply that by six, and open up a savings account dedicated to building that fund via monthly deposits. That number may seem impossible to reach, but stashing away a little bit each month eventually adds up to a lot! Even if it's only the change in your purse at the end of the day, it could add up to $30 per month, or $360 per year. But start with saving one month. When that's accomplished, go for two. That's progress and something you should feel good about!

Continue Talking to Creditors and Lenders

I've given you a lot of advice in this book about how to call and talk to your creditors. As you gain more experience negotiating payments and money matters, you'll soon be a whiz at taking future money pinches in stride and not have those knee-jerk reactions. You're likely to encounter many more cash crunches in the future as a fact of life, but you'll be much more prepared to think clearly through any problem and map out a plan of action.

That's exactly what Claudia did when she accidentally ran up a tremendous cell-phone bill when she forgot to contact her cell-phone company and switch to an international calling plan prior to her trip to Mexico. (You may have read Claudia's story in an *Essence* magazine article I wrote. It bears repeating.) Weeks later, she nearly collapsed when she received a bill for almost $1,000! From past experience, she knew that anything could be done if you approached it correctly. "It's all about how you speak to people," Claudia says. "Black women tend to get an attitude," she explains. "You have to ask for help as opposed to demanding it. You have to ask, 'Can you please help me?' Not 'This is bulls——t!' "

Claudia knew how to speak to creditors with respect and deference. "They are already in a position of power," she says. "They can flex by helping or they can flex by giving you a hard time." Claudia's deference paid off when she got an $870 reduction and only had to pay $130!

When we're hit with a huge bill, we're tempted to grasp at any immediate solution to address the problem. However, contrary to conventional wisdom, desperate times do not call for desperate measures. Desperate times call for a cool head and a clear plan.

When Deena, from Chapter 1, faced the prospect of a $4,000 repair bill on her 2001 Ford Focus (it was valued at $3,000), leasing a new vehicle seemed to be the best option. But she refused to accept the high-rate dealer financing offered to her because of past credit problems. Instead she calmed herself with prayer and positive affirmations, then she got busy. Her research led to a plan: Although her upcoming final semester in college was paid for by scholarships, Deena took out a student loan (at an interest rate of just 2.77 percent) for $5,000. Prohibited from using a student loan for anything other than school-related expenses, Deena then deposited the funds into a credit-union savings account and obtained a secured bank loan for the same amount. Deena used the funds from the secured loan to prepay a two-year lease on a 2005 Pontiac G6. The prepay option ensured that the $199-per-month lease payment wouldn't come out of pocket, which would have resulted in a hardship for her and her kids. Meanwhile, payments on the secured loan would be deducted monthly from the prefunded credit-union savings account.

This smart move on Deena's part positioned her to really accelerate forward in her life and establish her creditworthiness. Today, she pays her credit cards off monthly, her car lease is paid on time, and her credit score has climbed from 594 to 715. She eventually earned her college degree, got a real estate license, and found a mentor to help her become established in the industry. She said good-bye to credit and debt problems, she is extremely happy now, and continues to improve her credit.

Even her children have savings accounts and they get excited when they go to the bank and make deposits. I'm confident that one day she'll buy the home of her dreams and continue to teach her children valuable lessons about money.

Protection from Perils

Having a savings cushion and being a savvy negotiator with your creditors won't always protect you from the bigger mishaps that can occur. I'm talking about a serious health crisis, a fire in your home or apartment, or a lawsuit from an unscrupulous neighbor, stranger, or friend who wants to blame you for something bad that happened to them.

An example: You host a Super Bowl party. You invite your friends and your friends' friends, who also bring along friends. You can't even remember meeting Henry, but two weeks later you get slapped with a lawsuit pegging you as liable for his injuries when he left your place and got into a car after having been served several cocktails. On his way home, he veered off the road and hit a tree. Now he wants you to pay for his medical bills, car repairs, driving citation and court fees, and lost time from work. When you call a lawyer to find out how much it could cost you to defend yourself, that's when you learn about "social host liability," which means you can be held liable for his irresponsibility, much as a bartender or restaurateur can be in some circumstances (and depending on state law). And that cost exceeds anything you've got in your savings.

The above example is why we've got insurance. There are hundreds of ways that you can be found responsible for some terrible situation, but there are only a few ways to protect yourself—legally and financially—from the consequences of bad luck. Of course, all the insurance in the world won't protect you from every single loss. Why not? Because there are simply more claims than there are types and breadths of coverage. But it's better to have some coverage than nothing at all; every sister should carry some form of insurance to protect herself from the what-ifs.

Personal liability, in particular, is something few of us think about on a daily basis (unless we're lawyers!). But it's the price we pay for living in our capitalistic, money-conscious society. It's also the price we pay for being part of a thriving economy. You might not think you've got enough in assets and personal wealth to worry about personal liability, but let me tell you, sister, you don't have to be rich by any means to find yourself in a lawsuit with the finger pointed at you. In a worst-case scenario, a judgment can result in *future* earnings being taken away from you, in addition to your car, house, and any means of maintaining acceptable living standards. No sister likes to plan for misfortune and disaster, because no one likes to consider the bad things that can happen and take precautions. But the more you insulate yourself from the possibility of sudden, bad things happening, the better you can cushion that potential fall and protect not only your life and health, but also your means of comfort—your assets, income, and credit.

Below I'm going to outline the types of insurance you should have, or plan to have as soon as possible. They will protect you from the perils of everyday living. If you've never carried insurance before, the most important ones to consider are:

- auto

- homeowner's or renter's

- health and (maybe) life

You can't absolutely protect yourself from every bad thing that can happen, but you can absolutely use insurance to minimize the risk you live with every day.

Auto Insurance

Chances are, if you have a car, you already have this coverage. It's required by law. But do you have enough? With good credit you qualify for better rates (lower premiums), so you can then afford more coverage. Driving a car is probably the most risky thing you do on a regular, if not daily, basis. Most states have set minimums for basic coverage, but driving can easily result in personal liabilities that basic coverage just won't take care of. As soon as your credit score goes up, call your auto insurance carrier or broker and request a new quote. Inquire about boosting your limits; you can often up your limits by a lot without its costing you that much more. And since your new credit score works in your favor, you may be able to decrease how much you pay in premiums while increasing what your policy covers!

When you price out insurance policies, be sure to ask about the following:

Safety discounts. Some companies offer discounts if your car has special safety features, like automatic seat belts, airbags, antilock brakes, daytime running lights, side-impact protection, and head restraints.

Low-mileage discounts. If you drive less than a certain amount a year—say, 15,000 miles—you may qualify for a discount.

Other available discounts. These can include discounts for any of the following:

- insuring multiple cars with them

- electronic payments directly from your checking account

- keeping a clean driving record for the past three years (no accidents, no tickets)

- having a long driving history

- taking driver's training courses

- being over fifty years old

- having a good grade point average if you are a student

- keeping your car in a secure, locked garage at night

- living in a neighborhood with low crime rates, specifically with regard to stolen vehicles

- being a long-term customer with the company

Homeowner's and Renter's Insurance

The second-largest source of personal liability is residence-related liability. Accidents and disasters that happen in relation to your home or place of residence can create financial crises. You probably have a homeowner's policy if you own a home. Lenders typically require you to carry a policy before closing the deal for the mortgage. But do you have enough? With the cost of home repairs rising at 7 percent annually, it's best to buy a Homeowner-3 (HO-3) policy with a "replacement clause." These policies pay for the cost of rebuilding your home at its full value in today's market. To help lower your average HO-3 costs, consider installing a home security system, including smoke and burglar alarms, and keep your home upgraded. If you replace old roofs, windows, plumbing, wiring, and heating and cooling systems, these improvements should augment the soundness of the structure, which reduces the chances of problems arising. Hence, your insurer will view your home as less of a risk to insure and pass a discount on to your premium. And if you don't file a claim for five years, you might also qualify for a reduced premium fee.

If you're a renter, you may be missing this important coverage. Few renters think about insurance to pay for sudden losses that result from fires, natural disasters, theft, or lawsuits against you for negligence. Your FedEx guy can sue you when he slips and falls on your doormat; your friendly neighbor can sue you claiming your perfume and hair products are toxic and affecting his health. Lots of sisters assume that their land-

What Is "Liability" Anyway?

Liability does not just mean *debt,* or an obligation to pay. The word also implies responsibility—the state of being responsible for someone or something. In terms of auto insurance, liability insurance pays for the bodily injury, property damage, and intangible losses suffered by others in a car wreck. Property damage, by the way, includes medical bills, lost wages, actual property damage (i.e., the other cars, the $5,000 CD player, the Waterford crystal vases in the trunk); intangible losses include pain and suffering.

lord's policy will cover them when a fire rages through the building and destroys all of its contents. Well, the landlord does have insurance, but it covers only the building—not your personal possessions inside it. You need to have your own insurance policy in place to recover any loss or damaged property of your own. Otherwise, you risk having to use your credit cards to pay for basic living expenses and recoup lost possessions. That can land you back in serious debt very quickly.

Also called an HO-4 policy, renter's insurance covers the cost of replacing personal property. If someone else injures himself while in your rented unit and needs medical care, the policy would help cover those costs. And if you are sued for negligence, the policy would defend you; if you are found liable, the policy would provide some coverage for what it takes to get you back to where you were before the problems arose.

Two other important items a renter's policy covers, which most people don't think about, are (1) the loss of property when it occurs away from your apartment, such as a camera or a bicycle stolen out of your car; and (2) temporary living expenses should you be displaced from your apartment while the building is being fixed, or aired out for smoke damage. Most policies offer limited coverage for temporary living expenses. This is also called the "loss of use" or "additional living expenses" clause.

Now, you're probably wondering how much a renter's policy would cost you. About the cost of a deluxe pizza once a month. The average cost of renter's insurance is $12 a month, or $144 a year, for about $30,000 of property coverage and $100,000 of liability coverage. Some policies cost less, some more. It all depends on how much you own and where you live. And even if you've got a lot of valuables to protect, live in Los Angeles, and your policy runs you $350 a year for $50,000 in property, the monthly cost to you is around $29—or the cost of a T-shirt from the Gap.

Life Insurance

As I covered briefly in Chapter 6 when I talked about couples, as soon as you've got people who depend on you and your income, you need life insurance—the most reasonably priced kind is usually term life insurance. If you're single with no dependents, ideally you should also consider a

Money Rule of Thumb: If you use the same insurance company for both your auto and home/renter's insurance, you'll likely get a discount. When you call your insurance company or broker about a renter's policy, be sure to get **replacement cost coverage** so it pays for what the items cost to replace in today's market. If you go for the cash-value policy, then it only covers the value (considering depreciation) of your possessions at the time of the loss, which can be considerably less than what it would cost you to replace them outright. You can lower your premium if you accept a higher deductible, the money you pay out-of-pocket before the policy kicks in. This means it's important to balance your ability to cover the deductible with the monthly premium savings.

small life insurance policy, such as one for $10,000, so burial expenses could be covered in the unlikely event of your death. Term policies cover a specified period of time, generally one to thirty years. If the policyholder dies during this period, the beneficiary gets the money without going through probate—the legal court system—and after this specified term, coverage ends. Whole-life insurance, on the other hand, is sometimes called "cash-value" insurance, because it combines death benefits with a savings component. As long as the individual continues to pay the premium, whole-life insurance continues through her lifetime, regardless of her age or health. And as the premiums are paid, a portion of each payment is set aside to create a cash-value vehicle that earns interest.

Some insurance brokers suggest buying a policy that bridges both term life and whole life—for example, having $200,000 in term and $25,000 to $50,000 in whole-life coverage. Once the term coverage ends, the policyholder still has some permanent coverage. Your individual circumstances and needs will dictate which kind of life insurance is best for you. I can't possibly tell you which kind of insurance is right for you. For example, whole-life insurance might be worth considering if you are starting a family later in life, if you fear your health could deteriorate, or if you're looking for a way to save some money that has some tax-saving advantages. On the other hand, term insurance might be the only one that suits you. This is why consulting with a professional well versed in all types of life insurance policies, and who can review your circumstances and financial goals objectively, is key.

Health Insurance

According to a report issued by the Federal Reserve in 2003, about 52 percent of all collection activities arise from unpaid medical bills. Health insurance is a lifesaver in more ways than one, but it is trickier to buy than a homeowner's, renter's, or auto policy. You can't make one phone call or double-click your way to a good health policy. With 47 million Americans with no health insurance, the task of getting affordable insurance might seem impossible. But do your best to get some coverage, and at the very least, so-called catastrophic coverage, which will protect you if you land in an emergency room following a very bad accident and subsequently rack up hundreds of thousands of dollars in medical bills. If enormous medical bills were what landed you in debt and poor-credit territory, you must do what you can to buy some health insurance.

If you cannot afford an individual policy or join a health maintenance organization, you can look into organizations or associations you can join that offer policies (think alumni organizations, guilds, unions, etc.); think about changing jobs to one that offers health coverage; and look into state-run programs that offer programs for your uninsured children. Health insurance may become a larger expense in your life than you feel you can afford, but it will protect you in the long run and should not be considered an excessive expense. Find a way to bring down another expense so you can fit health insurance into your monthly budget.

Let's say, for example, that you and your husband are both in your thirties without children. Your husband is named as an additional insured on the health plan you have through your current employer. But now you're worried about losing the policy because you're looking for a new job. You're also concerned because you've got diabetes and need to have daily insulin injections, which are not cheap. To make matters worse, you also find out that your husband is being laid off so you can't seek coverage under his employer's plan.

Fast-forward a few weeks. A good job offer comes your way that you accept and that includes health insurance. But your new policy won't cover your insulin injections for your diabetes, which is deemed a "preexisting condition." In many cases, preexisting conditions, defined as those for which the individual has received treatment in the last six months, do not qualify for benefits until after a stipulated period of time has passed, usually one or two years. What do you do now?

Instead of signing on to the new health plan immediately, you do some homework to find out which policy would cover your condition as quickly as possible. Meanwhile, you have your husband look into COBRA coverage, since he has to wait six months before your policy could include him. The Consolidated Omnibus Budget Reconciliation Act of 1985, better known as COBRA, is designed for people in between jobs or stuck in a waiting period before being eligible to enroll in a plan. Under COBRA, if you voluntarily resign from a job or are terminated for any reason other than "gross misconduct," you are guaranteed the right to continue your former employer's group plan for individual or family health insurance for up to eighteen months at your own expense. You can learn more about COBRA from www.insure.com or through the Department of Labor Web site at www.dol.gov/index.

When searching for health insurance, start by asking your friends and family members where they get their insurance. Call and speak with a professional health insurance broker who can guide you through exploring your options given your circumstances. If you use the Internet for research, watch out: Avoid any health insurer that has offers too good to be true. There are plenty of unscrupulous companies out there posing as legitimate health insurers; they will take your money and never help you out when you need them most—in the ER or at the doctor's office. Stick to health carriers you've heard of. Get some referrals. Make sure they are well respected. You can find consumer guides to health insurance options and laws by state online at www.healthinsuranceinfo.net. Another good Web site that provides information about low-cost health insurance for children is www.insurkidsnow.gov.

Shop for Insurance Like You Shop for Shoes
The insurance market is so competitive that you can shop for insurance like you shop for a car or cell-phone service. And the better credit you

have, the better rates you'll get. As I said, companies typically offer discounts for people who buy more than one policy, so if you use ABC company for your homeowner's insurance, you'll get a discount on your car insurance if you use the same company.

While some Web sites offer free quotes, it's a good idea to find a good agent or broker and discuss your particular needs. Referrals are always best, but another place to start is your state insurance department. You can get a list of insurance providers in your area. Remember that a policy is only as good as the company that's writing it. Stick with insurance companies that have good reputations. Compare prices, too. Quotes and coverages will vary from company to company. Get quotes from independent agents who can place business with many insurers, and get quotes from exclusive agents who sell for one insurance company only.

A good Web site for researching insurance companies is www.jd power.com. (J. D. Power and Associates is a private company that conducts research used by a variety of industries to improve product quality and customer satisfaction. It bases its research solely on responses from millions of consumers and business customers worldwide. J. D. Power gives consumers free access to its library of research online.) Other sites include:

> www.iii.org (Insurance Information Institute)
> www.ambest.com (A.M. Best)
> www.standardandpoors.com (Standard and Poor's)
> www.moodys.com (Moody's Investor Services)
> www.weissratings.com (Weiss Ratings, Inc.)

If you haven't called and gotten a recent quote for premiums on your policies, do so as soon as your credit score moves up. Chances are, you can obtain lower premiums once you've improved your credit.

Umbrella Policies

You may not be ready for a personal umbrella policy yet, but it's worth being aware of them now as you begin to get your financial life straightened out. At some point down the road, as you accumulate more assets and gain stellar credit, you'll want to look toward guarding yourself even more strongly. The more you have to protect, the more you stand to lose. An example: Let's say a court hands down a liability judgment against you that exhausts the limits of your homeowner's or auto policy. You are responsible for the balance, no matter what. This may entail your having to sell your home, max out your cash advances on your credit cards, cash out your retirement funds, or sell other assets in order to make the payment on the judgment. And if your assets are used up and the judgment is still not satisfied, you may even have to dip into your future earnings to pay the remainder of the outstanding judgment. A personal umbrella policy, however, kicks in once you reach the limits of your other policies. It's your safety net—the extra cushion you give your basic policies. Remember: One major liability case can wipe out the assets that took you a lifetime to create. So think about this type of insurance when you're ready. It's the golden seal on your insurance box.

Other Forms of Insurance

Depending on your needs and family circumstances, you may opt to obtain other types of insurance beyond the basics. They can include:

Disability Insurance. This replaces lost wages if you are ill and unable to work.

Mortgage Insurance. This pays off the balance of your home mortgage in the event of your death. Using term life insurance, however, can also meet this need.

Business Owner's Insurance. If you plan to start a home-based business or any type of business, look into a business owner's policy (called a BOP) or adding some business owner's liability coverage to your existing homeowner's policy.

Long-Term-Care Insurance. This provides an ever-changing array of services aimed at helping people with chronic conditions cope with limitations in their ability to live independently. The insurance covers a portion or all of the expenses incurred if you enter a nursing home and require intermediate medical attention, as opposed to isolated illness or problems. Long-term-care insurance (LTC insurance) is wise to consider when you're fifty years old. You will, however, have to qualify given the state of your overall health. The earlier you look into LTC, the better. Many baby boomers today are part of the sandwich generation— caring for aging parents and their own children at the same time—and they feel the pinch of paying for both sets of family members. This is why paying for your own LTC insurance and obtaining it early on can help ease the costs of caring for you later in life. If you have aging parents without an LTC policy, you may also want to consider paying the premium for them to have this coverage, or expenses could come up later that will cost you more in the long run than had you set up a policy for them now.

Other Forms of Protection

It's impossible to do justice in this book to all the ways in which you can buy protection, peace of mind, and independence. The main focus has been on building good credit, which is how you lay your foundation for accumulating wealth and living the way you want to live. But as you simultaneously mend your credit and literally boost your bottom line, you'll increase your assets and require sources of protection and financial planning beyond insurance and retirement accounts. Once you're at that point, I encourage you to seek guidance on the following: a will, a revocable living trust, as well as documents that designate a financial power of attorney and a durable power of attorney for health care. These are important documents that have the potential to safeguard you and your family in the long run.

Banking to Your Benefit

In previous chapters, you learned how fiercely competitive the credit-card industry has become, thus affording you the leverage to request better interest rates and terms of payment. Well, it's no surprise, then, that the banking industry in general has likewise gotten so competitive that you can insist on better service. Banks vie for your attention as much as credit-card companies do, so you get to choose how you want to do your banking.

Like credit-card companies, banks make money from the fees they charge customers. When you track your spending and watch the transactions that go through your bank on your monthly statement (or online), you might come across strange debits in your account thanks to bank fees and charges you never "authorized." Well, you did authorize those debits when you signed up for your account at your bank.

Every bank has a list of charges it can apply to your account. If you don't bother to read the fine print or remember the terms of your accounts when you set them up and begin banking, these charges and fees might surprise you. Examples include checking fees, minimum-balance fees, ATM fees, returned-item fees, debit fees, monthly service fees, NSF (nonsufficient funds) fees, ATM replacement-card fees, currency-conversion fees, and so on. One popular bank even charges an "excess activity" fee when you do too many transaction online involving a savings account instead of visiting a teller or ATM, or sending correspondence by snail mail. You want to avoid as many fees as possible, which entails understanding all the terms of your banking agreements and occasionally fighting fees that pop up and that you think are not necessary.

Find a No- or Low-Cost Bank

There are plenty of banks today that offer free checking with just as many services and perks as those premium banks that will cost you unnecessary money to bank with them. When you find your bank, ask about minimum balances, ATM fees, and how to avoid commonly charged transactions.

Bankrate.com estimates that Americans dropped more than $4.3 billion in ATM-withdrawal charges in 2005 for using ATMs not owned by their own banks. All those charges happen when we swipe our cards through dinky cash dispensers at the mall, a corner convenience store, or someone else's bank. If your bank charges you $2 for the transaction, and the machine that dispenses the cash charges another $1.50, you're wasting $3.50 every time you get that cash. If it happens three times a week, you waste $546 per year. How can you cut back on these fees? Limit your ATM visits to those machines in your bank's own network, and withdraw larger amounts each time to avoid limited-transaction fees. Or if you pay with your ATM card at "point of sale" locations, you can get cash back for free.

Open a High-Interest Savings Account

You'll want to stash your savings in a high-interest savings account—not under your mattress or in a closet. Figure out a reasonable dollar amount you can devote each month to this account and be religious about adding that money to it. You may be able to set up an automatic transfer from your checking account to this savings account so you don't have to think about it. But if your regular bank doesn't offer good interest rates on savings accounts, don't be afraid to go elsewhere. Online-only banks can sometimes offer the best rates, beating out your brick-and-mortar banks. ING Direct, for instance, offers some of the most competitive interest rates around for savings accounts. Go to http://home.ingdirect.com and check out their Orange Savings Account; at this writing, you can earn a 4.15 annual percentage yield on an FDIC-insured savings account.

Once you have that savings cushion set up, keep adding to the account and do your best not to use the money unless absolutely necessary. As your balance increases, you'll qualify for even better interest rates.

You may even want to set aside a fund devoted solely to car-related issues. It will pay for those incidentals along the way that can be big, such as maintenance, repair, and deductibles on insurance claims. Costs related to your car can be sudden and unexpected, so setting aside $500 to $1,000 for those circumstances will ease any troubling situations.

Beware of Fraud and Identity Theft

As I first mentioned in Chapter 2, identity theft is a troubling consequence to living in today's high-tech, fast-paced Information & Internet Age. ID theft happens when someone steals a piece of personal information about you and uses it to commit a fraud in your name. The thief might steal your Social Security number, name, date of birth, credit-card information, bank-account numbers, mother's maiden name, and so forth, and use any of these things to:

- open up new accounts;

- change the mailing address on your current credit cards;

- rent apartments;

- establish services for utility companies;

- write fraudulent checks;

- steal and transfer money from a bank account;

- file bankruptcy;

- obtain employment;

- establish a new identity; and/or

- apply for a mortgage, car loan, or cell phone.

Once someone assumes your identity to get credit in your name and steal from businesses, you probably won't realize it happened until months later. As an honest person recovering from debt and poor credit, the last thing you need is an identity-theft problem. Yet unfortunately, you're a more vulnerable target than, say, someone who's never had a problem with debt or credit. Identity thieves prey on people who they don't think are going to notice a problem with their finances due to enormous debt and credit troubles. Now that you're taking control of your finances and learning how to remain vigilant of your money, you're arming yourself with the shield you need to stay far away from potential thieves.

The two best ways to prevent ID theft are to guard your personal information—specifically, your Social Security number, checks, and credit cards—and be very careful in every transaction you make, whether it's over the Internet, a counter, a phone, or by mail.

Tips for Preventing ID Theft

- Control access to sensitive, personal information, and ask your employer to secure anything that cannot be destroyed.

- Limit the use of your Social Security number, including in the workplace.

- Buy a personal shredder and use it to shred bank and credit-card statements, canceled checks, and preapproved offers before throwing away.

- Secure your mailbox with a locking mechanism or use a door with a mail slot.

- Avoid leaving outgoing checks or paid bills in your residential mailbox if it's unsecured. Use a mailbox for dropping off mail.

- When you check your credit report, look for address changes and fraudulent accounts.

- Pick up reordered checks at your bank instead of having them mailed to you.

- Notify your credit-card company if your card has expired and you have not yet received a replacement.

- Clean your wallet of excess information. Make photocopies of your wallet's contents in case it gets stolen. You'll know what it contained.

- Do not carry your Social Security card.

- Check your bills carefully. Look for discrepancies between your receipts and statements.

- Open bills promptly and report anything suspicious quickly.

- Limit the amount of information about you on the Internet, including your home page or Web sites that detail family genealogy.

- Don't give out personal information over the phone unless you initiated the call and know whom you are calling.

- If you do business online, don't respond to e-mails to "verify" credit-card accounts. This could be a ploy by hackers to obtain personal information. These people are so technologically savvy that they've even victimized huge companies. Numerous major fraud cases have involved companies like DSW, Lexis-Nexis, General Motors Master Card, and ChoicePoint, to name a few.

If you become a victim of ID theft, follow my instructions on page 67. Contact the three credit bureaus to have them "flag your file," then contact the Federal Trade Commission for more information. Go to www.ftc.gov for detailed advice and instructions.

The FTC does more than help identity-theft victims. The federal agency is a great source of information to use as you work your way toward being a smarter, more financially sound consumer. In addition to identity theft happening right and left, scams and other frauds take place every day—over the phone, Internet, e-mail, pagers, in your mailbox, and at your front door. As you begin anew and practice good money management, you'll need to be extra cautious about protecting yourself and your money. Examples of commonplace scams are those involving telemarketers, investment opportunities, travel, home repair, funeral chasers, fake contests, and self-employment pitches. You've seen these ads before: "Earn up to $100,000 a year working from home!" and all you need to do is attend a seminar and/or purchase a kit that teaches you how to become a millionaire from the comforts of your home. Be very wary about any "opportunity" to become wealthy through three easy steps, or some other such claim. Promises of quick, easy money can be a powerful lure. But if you buy into a business opportunity at a seminar, you may find that the products and information you purchased are worthless and that your money is gone. Always remember: The greater the potential return, the greater the risk. Investments seldom exist without some risk involved. Never invest what you cannot afford to lose.

Investment Accounts

Stocks. Bonds. Mutual funds. What's your investment style? Or have you simply ignored the subject as you focus on getting out of debt and mending your credit? Not to worry, sister. Investing is typically last on people's minds when debt issues take center stage. But no sooner will you clear your debt and clean up your credit than you will want to get your money growing more aggressively through vehicles that let you tap the stock market.

Beyond the savings cushion you keep for unexpected expenses—or even to build a fund for purchasing a home—having a retirement account that you fund once a month with a minimum amount is important for your future. I encourage you to pick up my book *Girl, Make Your Money Grow!* and read about all the ins and outs of investing. No sister can afford not to invest for her future.

If your employer does not offer you a 401(k) or similar plan, open an IRA (individual retirement account) with a discount brokerage house and commit to putting a certain amount into that account every month. Personal-finance experts call this paying yourself first. There are different IRAs from which to choose, such as a traditional IRA, a Roth IRA, a rollover IRA, SEP-IRA, and so on. Each of these accounts has set minimums for annual contributions. In 2006, if you file your tax return as a single person, you can contribute to a Roth if your adjusted gross income is less than $95,000 annually; for couples filing jointly, the threshold is $150,000.

The Roth IRA is a convenient way to give yourself access to tax-free money when you retire. Unlike a traditional IRA, where annual contributions are often tax-deductible and earnings are taxed, contributions to a Roth are taxed—but the earnings are tax-free. In 2006, the maximum you can commit to a Roth IRA is $4,000. As long as you have earned income equal to the amount of your contribution and meet the income restrictions, you can open a Roth even if you have a traditional IRA and an employer-sponsored 401(k). Single filers whose adjusted gross income is $110,000 or above and couples whose joint return is $160,000 or above cannot open a Roth. If you convert a traditional IRA to a Roth, your adjusted gross income must be below $100,000 whether you're filing as an individual or as a couple filing jointly.

Just about any brokerage firm, bank, credit union, mutual fund company, investment firm, and even many insurance companies will help you open a Roth IRA. Once you open one, you can fund it with new money or convert assets from a traditional IRA. Be cautious, however, about any tax consequences you might face when you convert one type of account over to another, especially going from a traditional IRA to a Roth. Earnings from the traditional IRA will be taxed as ordinary income, so if you need to use the IRA itself to pay the tax, it may not be a smart idea to convert. If you leave a Roth to your children, the money continues to grow tax-free. They have to withdraw the money only as quickly as you did. If you didn't withdraw any money, your heirs can continue to let the money grow tax-free for many years to come.

Consult your bank or a financial advisor for help in choosing a retirement account, or combination of several retirement accounts, that fits your needs. Fidelity has an IRA evaluator on its Web site to help you decide which IRA is right for you (www.fidelity.com). You can also learn more about these kinds of accounts online at sites like www.fool.com, www.money.cnn.com, and www.moneycentral.msn.com. These sites are comprehensive and great starting points for learning more about money. Some have life-expectancy tools for figuring out how much money you need to make before you can retire comfortably. Don't let your assets retire before you do.

Financing Your Wildest Dreams

At the start of this book, I asked you what "abundance" meant to you. By now I hope you've gained some knowledge about money and credit to know how you want that word to reflect your life. You can do whatever you want in life as soon as you take charge of your debt and credit and pursue your dreams and goals one day at a time. Whether you have your sights set on someday owning a home, buying a bigger home, or owning your own thriving company, those large-scale goals start with small-scale changes. They happen over time as you lay your foundation today with good credit.

The next and last chapter is one for exhalation. You've taken in a wealth of information and inspiration. I now turn to techniques for keeping your soul nourished and peaceful no matter what financial foes you face now and in the future. Prayer, meditation, affirmation, and visualization have been my saving graces time and time again, and I want to share with you ideas that can assist your own healing process. As technical and impersonal as credit and debt issues might seem, there's always a way to approach the recovery process and lifelong financial journey with an open heart and personal touch.

Exercise One: Commit to Saving

You may not be quite ready to start packing away extra money month after month for savings. But here are the steps to take now that will prepare you for creating that savings cushion in the near future.

1. Given your spending plan and tracking experience, which really shows you whether or not your spending plan foots all the bills each month, identify what your one-month living expenses amount to. This figure is what you need to set as your first savings goal.

2. Second, determine how much you'd like to aim for setting aside each pay period based on the number you got in step 1. For example, if your one-month tally equals $2,000, break that number down into smaller amounts and decide upon how much you'd ideally like to contribute each month toward that cushion so you eventually arrive at $2,000. Let's assume you think $100 a month is reasonable, which means it will take you 20 months to accumulate that one-month cushion. If you contribute more each month, it will take you less time. (Chances are you'll make more money in the future as your income increases, but so will your costs of living. This is an exercise to do now, and then repeat again later on as your situation changes. You may reach a point, however, where you can increase your monthly contribution and start saving more money.)

3. Now get out your calendar and decide when you would like to start setting aside that extra money each month toward your savings cushion—unless you can start today. If, for example, you want to give yourself thirty days working with your current spending plan and reducing your debt down, mark the day on the calendar when you will sit down again and evaluate whether or not you're ready to start saving.

4. If you sit down at the future date and determine that you cannot, in fact, start to seriously save, ask yourself why not. What is preventing you from starting? What can you do differently in your monthly spending plan to allow for that contribution? Then set another date thirty days out when you will sit down and go through that evaluation process again.

5. Remember, this is about progress, not perfection. If you can only start with $10 per month, do that. Once you start your savings cushion, make it a monthly goal as important as paying your rent or mortgage. In other words, don't let it be last on your list of priorities. If you have to, you can find other ways to cut your expenses or increase income during the month to make room for that contribution no matter what.

Exercise Two: Evaluate Your Insurance Needs

The first step in seeing to it that you're appropriately insured is to take an inventory of your current insurance coverages and see if you need to consider more coverage or plan for buying a new policy in the future. Set aside at least an hour for this task, depending on how organized your policies currently are. If you feel overwhelmed at the thought of getting out all of that paperwork and assessing your needs, you may want to set aside a "Mind Your Own Business Day" instead, when you devote ample time to this endeavor and follow it up with a fun activity, such as spending a night with friends or going to a movie. You can also choose to schedule one "Mind Your Own Business Day" per policy.

When you're ready, use the following steps:

1. Go to your local office-supply store and buy an expandable file so you can keep copies of all policies and important documents in one place.

2. Locate all policies and label each section on the expandable file by category—for example, "homeowner's policy," "auto policy," "health insurance," "disability," and so on. Place each policy in its own separate compartment.

3. Take your GIRL journal and designate one page for each type of policy you own. Complete the "Insurance Audit Checklist" using the questions below. Address each question that is appropriate for that type of policy. Note: you won't have to answer any questions related to deductibles on life insurance.

   a. Whom is the policy with?
   b. What is the policy number?
   c. What is the company address and telephone number?
   d. What is the payment schedule and amount of payment?
   e. What type of policy is it? For example, if it's life insurance, is it term, whole life, universal?
   f. Who is the beneficiary?
   g. What is your coverage?
   h. Are others in your family, including dependents, covered?
   i. What are the deductibles?
   j. How well is this insurance company rated?

As you review each policy using these questions, don't feel bad if you're uncertain about something. You can always call and ask an agent questions using the contact information provided in your policy; or, if you use a broker, call him or her. Make sure that the policy covers you as much as possible given your circumstances and current needs. For example, if you have a renter's policy that covers only $10,000 in personal possessions but you know that you own closer to $30,000 in possessions (when you think of what it would cost you to replace all of your things should your apartment go up in flames), then you should consider upping the limits of your policy. Likewise, if your grandmother just gave you a family heirloom as a gift, you may want to ask about buying an endorsement or rider to your current policy so that heirloom is covered in the event of loss.

When you've completed this exercise, you'll have a newfound awareness and confidence that in the event of some unforeseen circumstances, you and your family will have the financial wherewithal you'll need to see the crisis through and maintain your growing assets in the process. This ultimately also preserves your credit and prevents you from falling back into debt.

Exercise Three: Get Straight about Your Goals and Dream a Big Dream

Use your GIRL journal and write down the list of things you want to accomplish in life. Create sections for short-term, long-term, and very-long-term goals.

Short-term goals include things you would like to do soon or within the next year or so. Examples: finish school, buy a car, take a vacation, run a marathon, find a better job, plan a wedding. Long-term goals include things you want to accomplish in five, ten, even twenty years. Examples: buy a home, start a business, start a family, fund accounts for retirement and children's education. Very-long-term goals include retiring, sending children to college, and having money to support your medical needs later in life.

Be as specific about your goals as possible. You can also prioritize your goals specifically in years, listing one-year goals, two-year goals, five-year goals, ten-year goals, and so on. Don't be afraid to dream BIG!

Exercise Four: Map Out Your Dreams

Now that you have a list of dreams to realize, figure out how you're going to get there. Think about all the ways in which you can prepare for these goals financially. Mentally map out which kind of a spending plan can facilitate the achievement of these goals. Write down your thoughts. For example, if you dream of owning a home someday, decide how much of a down payment you'd need and how you're going to save up for that. Put a date on your calendar when you'd like to have that down payment ready to go. Then you can work backward and determine how you can devote a portion of your income each month to that down-payment fund.

As long as you plan well and save accordingly, there is no limit to the goals you can reach and the rewards you can achieve. Plan to revisit these ideas at least once a month and add new ones to the list.

Dream Mapping

1. Write down the dream. Ex: Buy a home.

2. Write down the date at which you want that dream realized. Ex: Within five years, or by the year 2012.

3. Write down what you need to do to achieve that dream. Ex: Clean up credit for loan application; save up for a down payment.

4. Write down when you think you can accomplish the "prerequisites" to realizing your dream. Ex: Determine how much of a down payment you'd like to make and when you can realistically set aside money for that fund, keeping in mind that your savings cushion should come first. Assess how you can speed up that savings cushion given this goal.

5. Using your calendar, map the dates when you will sit down and assess where you are in pursuit of your goals. Ex: Have you started a down-payment fund? If not, why not? When will that happen? By checking in on your goals regularly, you will reinforce your intention and stay accountable for taking action steps.

6. Place a photo of your goal in your calendar and in a prominent place like on your refrigerator door or your bathroom mirror. Use it as inspiration to minimize new debt and maximize your hard-earned income.

Getting Straight Final Do's and Don'ts for Managing Money and Credit Wisely

DO take an inventory of your insurance needs and protections once a year to make sure you've got enough coverage.

DON'T forget about your retirement, even if you're decades from it.

DO be aware of fraud and identity theft, another reason to scrutinize your bills and financial paperwork every month.

DON'T let banks take away your money unnecessarily. Avoid unnecessary fees such as those from ATMs, check-writing fees, monthly service fees, and checking fees. Use a "cheap" bank.

DO set up automatic deposits into a savings and/or investment account that you don't touch.

DON'T forget about your spending plan, even when you've cleaned up your debt and credit issues. Act like a recovering debtor.

DO avoid banking on future income.

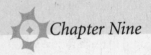

Chapter Nine

Healing Rituals for the Spirit: Prayer, Affirmation, Meditation, and Visualization

Debt upsets not only our financial balance but also our life balance and inner well-being. We lose our composure and become fearful, anxious, and insecure. Usually, we'll reach out to someone. How many times have you been hit with a crisis—financial or otherwise—and you immediately reached for the telephone to call a sisterfriend for support? It's almost automatic. We need to hear from someone else that things will be okay and that we'll be able to get over this hump. We also subconsciously think that by sharing our troubles, they might lessen or magically go away.

If you're like me, you've also had occasions when you call one friend . . . then another . . . and another. After leaving the third desperate voice mail, it finally dawns on you: "Maybe the Lord is trying to tell me something. Maybe I need to reach out to Him for divine guidance and direction instead of depending on mere humans to comfort me." When we are troubled, in pain, or in dire need, we don't always immediately call out, "Help me, Jesus!" (or Allah, Buddha, Jehovah, or whomever your religious beliefs follow), but it's in those moments that we most need to reach for the spiritual tools that are available to us 24/7.

I once heard a great analogy about the difference between treating a disease and treating a symptom. Think about what happens when you fall down and scrape your knee. You feel pain and immediately reach for a pain reliever like aspirin or ibuprofen. The pain reliever, however, is treating the symptom—the pain. It's not treating the *source* of the pain—the actual cut and its associated swelling and inflammation. When you catch a cold, you might opt to take cold medications, which treat the symptoms of your cold, such as the runny nose and cough, but don't do anything to attack the underlying virus. In the same way, I liken our financial behaviors—spending money we don't have and using credit that we shouldn't when we're emotionally upset and feel a sense of need—to treating a symptom. Instead, we should be targeting the source of our problems by using healing rituals that tap into our spirit for clarity. Once we achieve that clarity, we can then focus on curing our money disease. We can redirect our reasons for spending money and abusing credit. Attunement with our mind, body, and spirit alleviates dependency on sources outside of ourselves to heal the hurts in our souls.

I've treated the entire topic of debt reduction and credit mending with a holistic viewpoint, so by now you should feel confident in your plans for getting out of debt and paving a financially sound future. I've also given you lots of ideas for preserving your creditworthiness and preventing future debt. Now I'd like to devote this final chapter to briefly sharing with you my thoughts on how to use some spiritual strategies to pull yourself through any financial strife. I'm talking about the power of prayer, meditation, affirmation, and visualization. They can be just as practical as any of my step-by-step action plans for getting your credit straight, but what sets these strategies clearly above all else is that they can help you overcome *any* challenge—financial or not.

Whether these techniques are used individually or in conjunction with one another, they provide a sense of peace, confidence, and comfort that helps us get grounded and centered once again. These tools are important, valuable, and free! It's unfortunate we don't use them more often. The inconsistent usage makes it easy to get out of the habit of doing the things that work for us and make us feel good and feel better about our place in the world. And they can make the journey through financial struggles so much easier.

Prayer

Simply put, prayer changes things. It frees you to let go and let God go to work on your behalf. Prayer has been instrumental in my personal and professional life. Personally, I prayed God would send me a good man whom I would recognize as being the right person for me. I also prayed that the feeling would be mutual—he would *at the same time* recognize that I was the right woman for him. For years I had experiences where when I was ready the guy wasn't, and when he got ready, I was long gone! Timing is so critical. But not long after I started that prayer my childhood sweetheart, Edward, came back into my life. Today we are happily married and the rest is history!

Professionally, prayer is very important to me. It has a role in my day-to-day work with clients. In fact, I pray for all of my clients—past, present, and future. During financial-counseling sessions I have been known to silently pray, "God, help me with this one. This person's situation is so challenging I don't know where to go from here." Thankfully, within minutes an inspiration will come and we are able to move forward in resolving problems. In *Girl, Get Your Money Straight!* I spoke of staying "all prayed up." Prayer makes me feel much stronger and ready to take on new challenges. In fact, when I know I have a challenging couple to deal with—where resentment and hostility brew violently between the partners—I also don't take any chances. I pray up the room, inviting God to come join me, and will even add some aromatherapy as well.

Here's my advice: Pray daily and not just for yourself, but for your family, your friends, your clients, our government, and our world. Pray for all that brings you joy and happiness. In the words of Satchel Paige, "Don't pray when it rains if you don't pray when the sun shines." Pray for your health and the money that you do have. Pray for the creditors who extend credit to you and are willing to work with you in your journey back to financial health. And pray for your future and the exciting opportunities that await you. Pray for favor (God's special help) with everyone you come in contact with.

You never know when God is going to work in His mysterious ways and convey his guidance, support, and advice through other people. I believe God sends the right inspiration at the right time—sometimes directly to us and sometimes through other people. Years ago, I broke open a fortune cookie that read, "Just be yourself. You are wonderful." Years later, during a particularly stressful period when I felt confused and pulled in a direction that was extremely uncomfortable, my literary agent gave me some great advice. Her healing words immediately grounded me and helped me move forward with peace of mind. She simply said, "Just be your authentic self. Be the person you've always been. Be the person who got you this far." This instantly calmed me. Those words immediately brought me back to my center, nourished my spirit, and helped me recognize that I am enough—that I am good enough just as I am. My authentic self *is* my truth and my wellspring of success and achievement.

Meditations

It's been said that prayer is *talking* to God and meditation is *listening* to God. When we meditate, we think deeply and quietly. We ponder. We contemplate. I believe that in the quiet moments of reflection we enable ourselves to listen to our inner voice, our intuition—in other words, God's directions.

Joyce Meyer, a Bible teacher and prolific author, preached one day about our uncanny propensity to blame other people for causing stress or disconnects in our lives when in reality we are to blame. We are triggering that turmoil because we haven't taken care of ourselves. It made a great deal of sense to me. When we don't eat well, rest well, take care of the things we need to do to nurture our bodies and our spirit, we get anxious, irritable, and out of sorts. The slightest thing done by another person or even a loved one can set us off on a tangent where nothing is right and it's all that person's fault. She recalled taking a shower one morning, trying to get a few minutes' peace before starting a hectic day, and her husband came into the bathroom and questioned why she had put her bath towel on the toilet seat instead of on a particular towel rack. Because she was tired and irritable from not getting enough sleep and eating right in recent days, that set her off and began a huge argument that included why she felt her husband, an engineer, had picked such a poor place to install the towel rack in the first place!

The chaos and drama we create in our lives with our finances is often because we haven't taken care of ourselves. In one of my all-time-favorite books, *Lessons in Living* (Anchor Books, 1998), Susan L. Taylor describes it perfectly: "When we fail to nurture ourselves, our joy is depleted and our capacity to serve diminished. Giving from an empty vessel causes stress, anger and resentment, seeds that sow disorder and disease. Attempting to meet the demands of the world without first attending to our own needs is an act of self-betrayal that can cause us to lose respect for our value and worth. It is not enough to be kind: We must learn to be kind *and* wise." When we allow ourselves to get out of a peaceful rhythm in our day-to-day lives, we open the door to acting out with our spending—whether using cash or credit. Meditation can help us get back to a grounded and centered space, thereby allowing us to think clearly, do the things we need to do, and *not* do the things we don't need to do.

Some sisters choose to meditate by secluding themselves in the bathroom for twenty minutes and taking a candlelight bubble bath with beautifully scented essential oils. Some walk along the beach and listen to the rushing of the waves against the sandy shoreline. Some sisters use yoga, because it calms your nerves, tones your body, and relaxes you. Michele Berger, a yoga instructor in Chapel Hill, North Carolina, recognizes its benefits as a healing ritual for the mind and body: "Even the practice of yoga builds endurance and tones the system to not be reactive. It provides us with a set of tools to re-center ourselves." This practice allows us to not be impetuous, impulsive, and emotional, thereby enabling us to make better choices and informed decisions when it comes to our finances.

Ask yourself, What are the ways in which you choose to meditate?

Affirmations

Much like the age-old question "Which came first, the chicken or the egg?," I'm not sure where the process starts for us humans. My sense is that we think it, we speak it, we feel it, then we therefore manifest it. I have often heard folks say "Don't speak about that!" largely because they feel if you say it, that will make it so. Affirmations give us an opportunity to declare our positive hopes and ambitions to the universe out loud, and confirm our belief in ourselves and our personal strengths.

Throughout this book, I've stressed the importance of affirmations. They can prepare you for difficult tasks, like talking to your creditors on the phone, and they can keep you feeling strong and empowered. I have my own set of affirmations and mantras that I've come to rely on, and I'm certain that you'll find yours in your own journey.

I tell myself constantly that:

> *I approach credit with ease and confidence.*
> *I use my time just as wisely as I use my credit.*
> *God is my sounding board.*
> *As I trust God, I am filled with peace and strength. I know that everything is in divine order.*

The more confidence I gather from affirmations, the easier everything in my life becomes, whether it's related to credit and money or not.

One of my weaknesses is comparing myself to others, which sometimes results in diminished self-esteem. But my sister Yvonne gave me an affirmation that is extremely helpful when I start making those unhealthy comparisons: "I don't copy. I don't compare. I don't compete." Simple as that. Try that affirmation sometime when you feel like you're measuring yourself up against someone else in an unhealthy fashion or are tempted to spend to keep up with the Joneses. When someone shares an affirmation with you, or just compliments you in a way that sounds like an affirmation, write it down in your journal. Keep it on record and refer back to it often.

Visualizations

My client Ashley was challenged time after time, feeling her wardrobe wasn't good enough. We would systematically set a spending plan for clothes shopping and she would systematically exceed it. Each time she assured me that her closet was now complete, I knew that three or four months later she'd again express a need to buy more. Why was it never enough? Ironically, during a meditation exercise with her therapist, Ashley recalled an experience she had as a sixteen-year-old girl trying to fit in at a new high school. She worked and worked at her wardrobe and still went unnoticed. In a powerful moment, her therapist had her visualize the sixteen-year-old girl taking a shower. Not just a regular shower, but a shower where God's grace poured over her like running water. She was drenched in the power of God's grace and favor. Even as she described it to me, the image immediately gave me chills. Imagine being drenched in blessings of love, peace, comfort, and every good thing you can think of!

Now imagine a visualization of *you* being showered. Showered with an abundant life. See yourself surrounded by loving, supportive family and friends. What would you do—what could you do if you had no debt, no car note, no mortgage? When you allow yourself to be quiet, to get in touch with your inner self, you can tap into the things your heart really desires. What makes you feel relaxed and focused? What makes you exhale? What brings you peace?

Many years ago, San Francisco psychologist Dr. Brenda Wade shared with me the exercise of making a dream collage from photos in magazines. I cut out the pictures that expressed visual images of my desires—a classy, professionally dressed woman, a bride and groom joyously celebrating their wedding day, a beautifully decorated room with a spectacular view of crystal-blue water. Of particular interest and appeal was a six-page layout from *Architectural Digest* that featured a photo of an exquisitely designed Manhattan apartment with floor-to-ceiling windows, at dusk, just as lights from the surrounding skyscrapers began to illuminate. Whenever I looked at that photo a sense of calm and peace rushed over me. I studied every aspect of that photo intently, imagining that one day I'd have such a place. Eventually I placed the photo in a file. I didn't know when, where, or how, but I knew that one day I'd re-create that photo in real life. I wanted to have that serenity every day.

A few short years later, I made a decision to move from California back to Detroit and was blessed to purchase an apartment downtown with nearly floor-to-ceiling windows and a spectacular view of the beautiful Detroit River, the city skyline, and the lights of Windsor, Ontario, as a backdrop. My dream had become a reality, and it goes to show that visualizing is a powerful process, even when we don't specifically set out in search of the image. Visualize every day what you want and hope for, and know that it can be your dream come true .

The Power of Ritual

In life, there are no accidents. Every experience is a lesson to be learned for future use and to help us stretch and grow. Embrace where you are at. Had I not been challenged by my finances (and life) and gotten myself straight, I would not be in this business or have an opportunity to help others in this way. This is an extremely rewarding profession, but even with all I have accomplished, I must stay ever mindful and vigilant to keep my finances straight.

We all need rituals for use when we feel we're in over our head and when we are thankful that the Almighty has brought us through another challenging experience. I encourage you to pinpoint the healing rituals you routinely use to replenish your energy reserves and reflect more intently on your own inner being. A ritual doesn't necessarily have to refer to prayer or God, by the way. A ritual is whatever you make of it. I define a ritual as something you do on a routine basis that brings peace to your heart and soul, that revitalizes you, and that gets you thinking in ways that your everyday habits and activities don't let you. A ritual can be a daily walk in your neighborhood with your dog, an exercise routine, a time-out for prayer before bedtime, or just fifteen minutes you allocate every night after dinner to sit in your favorite chair and write in your journal.

Rituals are necessary and essential to our survival—like breathing. With success comes pressure, stress, and responsibility. So no matter how happy we are, no matter how successful we are, we still need these rituals. They keep us feeling at peace with ourselves and our world. They also help us deal with unexpected turns in life. Whether we encounter struggle or triumph, those rituals become our most trusted friends.

Final Words

I hope by now you've gained an appreciation for your credit and its role in your life. I hope I've given you the practical and spiritual tools you need to move forward and set a realistic plan for achieving all that you dream of for your future. Even when confronted with the most tactical, impersonal aspects of credit and money management, I hope that you don't forget to call upon the power of personal prayer, meditation, affirmation, and visualization rituals to help you stay spiritually grounded and physically healthy. After all, there's a strong connection between the strength of our spiritual selves and our physical beings. By taking care of yourself, adopting sound money skills, and getting your financial house in order, you will have an abundance of personal joy and satisfaction in life—I promise. And I promise you the foundations for living a happy, *healthy,* productive life for many years as well.

Exercise One: Establishing Your Own Rituals

What do you do on a routine basis that allows you to feel totally refreshed and spiritually renewed afterward? Is it going to church? Lacing up your running shoes for a morning run? Taking fifteen minutes in the evening to meditate or read a book without any distractions? Pinpoint what you'd love to do on a routine basis, if you don't already, and use your calendar to schedule more time slots doing this activity. Life can get so busy that our priorities can become skewed. Make it a priority to guard your special rituals and keep them part of your schedule no matter what's going on in your life. If you have to write them down on your calendar, do so! If time is tight, start with a five-minute ritual. Later, increase the time to ten minutes, then increase it incrementally until you sufficiently meet your needs. Remember: They are as much a part of your financial healing as any other strategy discussed in this book.

Exercise Two: Choose Your Daily Affirmations and/or Prayers

Pick five affirmations and/or meditations and two or three prayers that address issues you commonly deal with or need support around. Record those affirmations or meditations on an audiotape in your own voice. Replay that recording every night before going to sleep. For help in finding prayers indexed by topic, refer to *Prayers That Avail Much,* by Word Ministries, Inc. (Harrison House, 1995). Otherwise, you can find a multitude of affirmation and prayer ideas in spiritual books or by searching for them online. Ask your friends and family for their favorites. The sky's the limit in this department. Have fun with it.

In the words of Joel Osteen, pastor of Lakewood Church in Houston, Texas, and author of *Your Best Life Now*:

> *To live your best life now, you must look at life through the eyes of faith, seeing yourself rising to new levels. See your business taking off. See your marriage restored. See your family prospering. See your dreams coming to pass.*

And I'll add enthusiastically . . . See your debt dissolve and your credit score soar. Peace and blessings.

Let me hear from you!

If there's one thing I've learned after sixteen years as a financial coach it's that Black or White, rich or poor, male or female, everybody's got a story. Perhaps you read this book because you have a compelling financial challenge. Hopefully, in the process you used strategies and tools found in these pages to overcome some or all of those obstacles. Feel free to email me at glinda@bridgforthfinancial.com and share your experience. I'd love to hear about your progress and the creative ideas you used to approach your financial problems. I can't promise you we'll answer each one, but I can assure you we will read them all. Who knows? Maybe your success story could be told in the next GIRL book!

Much Love,
Glinda

P.S. Visit my web site at www.bridgforthfinancial.com, sign up for my e-newsletter, and be among the first to know the latest news with me and the GIRL series.

Index

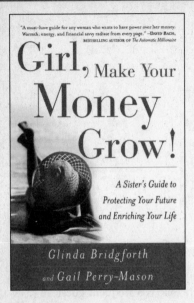
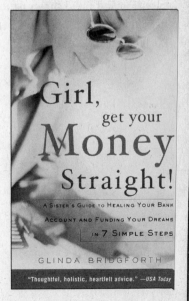

© Venti Valdez

Glinda Bridgforth is the founder of Bridgforth Financial Management Group, a financial management company that emphasizes holistic counseling. A regular contributor to *Essence*, she is a frequent guest on television and radio shows nationwide as well as a sought-after seminar speaker. She divides her time between Oakland, California, and Detroit, Michigan.